Lecture Notes in Economics and Mathematical Systems

459

Springer
Berlin
Heidelberg
New York
Barcelona
Budapest
Hong Kong
London
Milan
Paris
Santa Clara
Singapore
Tokyo

Hang K. Ryu Daniel J. Slottje

Measuring Trends in U.S. Income Inequality

Theory and Applications

Springer

Authors

Prof. Hang K. Ryu
Chung Ang University
Department of Economics
Seoul, Korea

Prof. Daniel J. Slottje
Southern Methodist University
Department of Economics
Dallas, TX 75272, USA

Library of Congress Cataloging-in-Publication Data

Ryu, Hang K. (Hang Keun), 1950-
Measuring trends in U.S. income inequality : theory and applications / Hang K. Ryu, Daniel J. Slottje.
p. cm. -- (Lecture notes in economics and mathematical systems ; 459)
Includes bibliographical references (p.).
ISBN 3-540-64229-3 (softcover : alk. paper)
1. Income distribution--United States--Econometric models.
I. Slottje, Daniel Jonathan, 1957- . II. Title. III. Series.
HC110.I5R96 1998
339.2'0973--dc21
98-3099
CIP

ISSN 0075-8442
ISBN 3-540-64229-3 Springer-Verlag Berlin Heidelberg New York

Typesetting: Camera ready by author
SPIN: 10649597 42/3143-543210 - Printed on acid-free paper

Foreword

This book is the culmination of roughly seven years of joint research between us. We have both been interested in income inequality measurement for a considerably longer period of time. One author (Ryu) has a background in physics. While he was working on his Ph.D. in Physics at M.I.T. he became acquainted with Robert Solow. Professor Solow introduced Ryu to economics. After finishing his Ph.D. in physics, Ryu went on to the University of Chicago where Arnold Zellner guided him to a dissertation on using orthonormal basis and maximum entropy as estimation methods in econometric applications. The precise definition and examples of orthonormal basis (ONB) and maximum entropy (ME) methods will be given in the book. As it turns out, a natural application of these methods is the study of income distribution. Professor Zellner suggested that Ryu look at some of my joint work with Robert Basmann on functional forms of Lorenz curves as one starting place to do his own research. Ryu requested some of our data and asked for several of our papers with the express purpose of introducing functional forms of Lorenz curves that Ryu felt would do a better job of approximating the empirical Lorenz curve. Thus, our first introduction was essentially one of Ryu trying to invent a better mousetrap. The interested reader can review the results given in Basmann et al. (1990) and Chapter Four of this book to see if Ryu succeeded.

In 1991, Ryu one day showed up at my office door in Dallas, Texas. We started talking and very soon thereafter we were collaborating. Hang Ryu lives and works in Seoul, South Korea. You may not think this is very unusual. Many of you have international collaborators. What is unusual is that Ryu flew over to Dallas roughly once a month for several years to get our research rolling. Our research output is due in no small part to Ryu's diligence and endurance in putting up with 19 hour plane trips so we could finish papers and begin new projects.

Several of the chapters in this book are based on our work that has been published, or will be published elsewhere. We thank the *Journal of Business and Economic Statistics*, the *Journal of Econometrics*, *Advances in Econometrics*, and Edward Elgar Publishing for permission to reprint portions of our work that appeared or will appear in those places. Most of that work has been revised and refined in the present book in order to make it even more current with respect to other work in the field and also to make the exposition a bit less technical. This is a very technical book. We have tried to write the book in a way that a reader primarily interested in inequality issues will find the book useful without getting too caught up on the technical aspects. It is important to keep in mind when you are working through this book, that the justification for our methodology is complex.The actual implementation is, in many cases, surprisingly simple. Thus, do not become reticent to keep going once you jump into the material.

The first chapter of the book introduces the reader to many of the issues that inequality specialists examine. This book does not take the traditional tact that previous research on income inequality measurement has taken. Rather, we are interested here in applying inequality indices to the detection and understanding of trends in U.S. inequality over time rather than the measurement of inequality per se. Focusing on inequality measurement per se has been the traditional tact and we say more on this below. A review of the relevant literature is presented here and some recent trends in inequality are explored. Chapter Two presents a guided tour on understanding and using the orthonormal basis and maximum entropy as estimation methods in econometric applications. Properties and characteristics of the orthonormal basis (ONB) and maximum entropy (ME) methods are discussed in this chapter. Chapter Three introduces a theoretical model to help motivate why the observed income distribution looks as it does. We introduce the notion of capability distributions in this chapter for reasons that will be explained in the chapter. Chapter Four presents the results of the search for a functional form of Lorenz curve that describes the observed data well and is not overly onerous to actually estimate. Lorenz curves have certain statistical properties which serve as a guide in how to approximate them parametrically. As will be seen in this chapter, the ONB method does a very good job of approximating the empirical Lorenz curve. Chapter Five demonstrates the usefulness of the ONB method in macroeconomic applications. Chapter Six compares so-called Index Space vs. Coordinate Space applications and evaluates the usefulness of both methods. Chapter Seven introduces the use of the ONB method when the variable at issue (here hunger) is latent. An econometric approach is introduced in this chapter to deal with this sort of problem.

Daniel Slottje
Dallas, Texas
1998.

Table of Contents

Chapter 1

INTRODUCTION

1.1 Introduction

In the middle of the 1980's, an interesting phenomenon occurred. Economists began writing about issues involving the size distribution of income. The fact that economists wrote about that particular topic was not novel or extraordinary. What was phenomenal was the magnitude of the writing. Suddenly, after years of benign neglect, income inequality became a much discussed and hotly debated topic. Literally hundreds of articles have appeared on the subject in the last ten years or so. New journals have been started dealing solely with income inequality. What sparked this renewed interest in questions of income distribution? One major factor has been the perceived increase in the level of income inequality. Bishop, Formby and Smith (1991) used statistical Lorenz curves to argue that inequality increased for most of the 1970s and 1980s and unambiguously did so from 1978 to 1982. The apparent trend towards increased income inequality has continued into the 1990s and the Gini coefficient for family income for 1993 as reported by the U.S. government is at the highest level in 25 years. Rising trends observed during the past two decades in income inequality are not unique to a particular income measure alone since wage inequality in the U. S. has also shown similar rising trends. Rising trends in wage inequality have also been observed in OECD countries. In a recent study, Raj and Slottje (1994) demonstrated that the rise in the trend behavior of inequality is in fact real. Even after adjusting for possible structural change in the time series properties of several well known measures of income inequality, they found that inequality had unambiguously increased (as measured by summary statistics). Furthermore, the increase began in the 1960's, not in the late 1970's or early 1980's as is commonly believed.

The purpose of this book is to explore some of the causes of the documented rise in inequality, and to do so utilizing econometric methods heretofore not relied on in doing analysis in the income distribution field. The primary focus of this book is to provide the reader with powerful new tools to explore issues of income distribution. The methods to be used in this book are based on the concepts of Orthonormal Basis (ONB) and Maximum Entropy (ME). These methodologies are introduced, defined and explained in Chapter Two. As was noted in the book's forward, the focus of this book is not on exploring characteristics of inequality measures per se, but rather on exploring and explaining trends in inequality in the U.S. over time. The reader interested in more traditional discussions of characterizing inequality measures can find excellent discussions in Charkravarty (1990), Lambert (1993), Eichhorn (1994) and Silber (1997), to name just a few. The rest of this chapter consists of a review of the literature in Section 1.2, an overview of recent trends in inequality in Section 1.3 and a discussion of the layout for the rest of the book in Section 1.4.

1.2 A Brief Review of the Literature

In order to put the contribution of our work in the proper context, it is necessary to first present a brief review of recent literature that has attempted to explain (or account for) the recent rise in income inequality. Research on the causal mechanism of income inequality change can be divided into micro research and macro research. The vast majority of the work in this field has been micro-oriented. Levy and Murnane (1992) present an excellent survey of this literature. One reason for this micro—orientation is of course the fact that earnings constitute a significant portion of total income (cf. Slottje, 1989). The significant rise in wage inequality has been the main motivation behind a whole set of papers in the February 1992 issue of the Quarterly Journal of Economics. These papers have attempted to explain the rising trends in inequality in term of changes in technology, due to changes in international trade and changes in the quality of education of the population. Levy (1987) and Bishop et al. (1991) have presented empirical evidence to substantiate the claim that there appears to have been an increase in the level of U.S. wage inequality. Juhn, Murphy, and Pierce (1992) argued that this increase in wage inequality is due to a change in the distribution of skills in the economy and a rise in the economic return to skills of highly skilled workers. Ryu and Slottje (1994b) focused on capabilities and found empirical evidence that corroborates these explanations. Chapter Three of this book presents their findings. Blackburn and Bloom (1987) argued that the increase in inequality has been primarily due top a shift in the age composition of males entering the labor force and the shift from manufacturing to an increase in service-oriented work. Slottje (1989) and Slottje et al. (1992) noted that changes in the labor force participation of women, the increase in service sector jobs and changes in retirement behavior of white male may all have impacted the income distribution. Bound and Freeman (1992), Card and Krueger (1992a, b), Juhn et al. (1993), Katz and Murphy (1992), Karoly (1995), Levy (1987) and Murphy and Welch (1992) have argued that the wage structure has changed due to education impacts (rates of returns vary across groups), differences in mobility, demographic changes which all have resulted in a change in the skill distribution an ultimately in a change in the earnings distribution. Cancian et al. (1993a, b) explored the role of family income changes (between husbands and wives) on the overall distribution. These and other studies in the labor economics tradition are reviewed in Levy and Murnane (1992). Slottje et al. (1995) find that education is not the dominant player generally believed in the rising inequality puzzle. In fact, they argue that the changing structure of the family has had much more impact than did the rise in educational attainment over the last decade, Karoly (1995) corroborates this finding.

There has been surprisingly little macroeconomic research done on the causal inequality issue. For exceptions, see the discussion in chapter six. Most early work was concerned with how various macroeconomic aggregates have impacted inequality (as measured by a given index) over time, cf. Blinder and Esaki (1978). These researchers examined the quantitative impacts of changes in unemployment (or employment), inflation, the money supply, and a host of other macrovariables on inequality. This body of work has concluded that employment has important redistributive effects; in addition changes in inflation and in the money supply appear to have played a redistributive role as well. The transmission mechanism concerning how macro variables affect income inequality, is not, however, very well understood, partly due to lack of a well-defined static or dynamic theory of income distribution to guide empirical studies. A recent conference at the University of Notre Dame led to an entire book published by North-Holland on how international trade factors, productivity and unemployment policies have impacted the level of income inequality in the U.S. Balke and Slottje (1993) were among the first to take a more general view and consider the possibility of feedback, i.e., they considered the impact of the level of income inequality on the macroeconomy. Johnson and Shipp (1995) have looked at the question by focusing on consumption instead of income. In Chapters 5 and 6 of this book we will introduce some new perspectives on analyzing the impact of the macroeconomy on the change in the income distribution. We now discuss measurement issues and recent trends in various measures of inequality in Section 1.3.

1.3 An Overview of Recent Trends in Income Inequality in the U.S.

Any discussion of change in the size distribution of income should immediately spark questions about how inequality is measured, about how income is quantified and about how we define the appropriate income receiving unit (iru). Kuznets (1976) pointed out that an ideal income-recipient unit must satisfy three criteria: identifiability, inclusiveness, and distinct independence. Since the income from family owned assets cannot always be identified as belonging to specific individuals within each family, considering the total number of persons as income-recipient units will not meet Kuznet's criteria. Families include both "economically active" and inactive members of the population, so limiting the analysis to only the "economically active" would eliminate a segment of population that is of great importance for analyzing long term economic trends, viz., the young. However, inclusion of the economically dependent deviates from Kuznets' criterion of independence. Therefore, "... in a meaningful distribution of income by size the recipient unit has to be a family or household and cannot be a person ..." (Kuznets, 1976, p. 1).

Another issue concerns the definition of income and time. As Cowell points out, what we really desire is a comprehensive concept of income... an index that will serve to represent generally a person's well-being in society, cf. Cowell (1977, p. 41). Obvious candidates are wealth, lifetime income, labor earnings in a given time period and Cowell's measure, the increase in a person's command over resources during a given time period (Cowell, 1977, p. 5). Theoretically, the latter would seem to be much preferred to the first three; however, practicability is another matter. Among the criteria that a definition of income should meet, measurability, comparability among individuals and accessibility for analytical purposes should all be considered. Wealth may include not only assets that are difficult to value in a market sense but also includes human capital attributes which may have important implications for future earnings that is impossible to measure. Lifetime earnings necessarily require a termination point and expectations about future earnings to be useful. Thus, the concept isn't very practical. Labor earnings are one aspect of an individual's ability to control resources but ignores other nonlabor income.

We have seen then, that two major issues are the appropriate specification of the income—recipient unit and a reasonable definition of income. In this book we focus on family income as the appropriate iru.

Once the choice of the iru is made, the problem still persists in how we are going to operationalize the concept of inequality. There are no a priori reasons for selecting one measure of income inequality over another, since any particular income inequality measure captures only one aspect of the observed distribution as we have continually emphasized. For this reason, several measures of inequality are employed in this study.

One approach to measuring inequality, without imposing a functional form of statistical distribution on the income graduation, is to use Lorenz-based inequality measures. We will do so in this book. As Kakwani noted, the Lorenz curve is defined as the relationship between the cumulative proportion of income unites and the cumulative proportion of income received when units are arranged in ascending order of their income.

Recall that the Lorenz Curve can be generated by defining the income earner units as (say) quintile shares where q_i, i=1, ⋯, 5 represents the ith income earner share and letting

$$0 \leqq q_1 \leqq q_2, \cdots, \leqq q_5 \leqq 1 \tag{1.1}$$

From this simple ordering many well-known inequality measures can be formulated. For instance, the Gini (1912) measure can be defined as,

$$G = 1 + \frac{1}{n} - \frac{2}{nN}[q_n + 2q_{n-1} + 3q_{n-2} + \cdots + nq_1] \qquad (1.2)$$

Here, n is the number of quantiles and N is mean income. The Gini measure is the average difference of all pairwise comparisons of income. It is most frequently criticized for putting more weight on a transfer between middle income earners than at the tails. This measure is bounded by 0 for perfect equality and one for perfect inequality. The relative mean deviation measure is defined as:

$$R = \frac{1}{2} \cdot \frac{n}{n-1}\left[\sum_{k=1}^{n}\left|q_k - \frac{1}{n}\right|\right] \qquad (1.3)$$

As Kakwani (1980) notes, "if the population is divided into two groups, (a) those who receive less than or equal to mean income and (b) those who receive more than mean income, the relative mean deviation represents the percentage of total income that should be transferred from the second group to the first so that both groups have exactly the same mean income." It also is a zero-one measure. The R measure doesn't satisfy transfer properties, but does have some economic intuition, which is why it is included here. Theil's normalized entropy measure is defined as:

$$T = 1 + \frac{1}{\ln(n)}\left[\sum_{k=1}^{n} q_k \ln q_k\right] \qquad (1.4)$$

Theil formulated his measure based on whether a given physical system was more or less orderly. He reinterpreted this "order" as income levels. The measure has a lower bound of zero and no upper bound.

Kakwani (1980) also introduced a measure. Kakwani's measure takes the form:

$$K = \frac{\overline{\ell} - \sqrt{2}}{2 - \sqrt{2}} \quad \text{with} \quad \overline{\ell} = \sum_{k=1}^{n} \overline{\ell_k} \quad \text{and} \quad \overline{\ell_k} = \sqrt{q_k^{\,2} + \frac{1}{n^2}} \qquad (1.5)$$

Where $\overline{\ell}$ is the length of the Lorenz curve. Kakwani's measure looks at inequality between the classes and the weighted sum of inequality within each class. This measure is not bounded by zero or one. This form is more sensitive to redistribution in the middle quintiles. Trends in these varialbes for normalized values are presented in Figure 1.1. below.

We also present the trends in some of Atkinson's social welfare-based inequality measures in this chapter. These measures give a different view of the level of inequality (inherent in a given distribution) than the statistical measures just discussed. In order to derive Atkinson's (1970) inequality index, again define the income earner units as quintile shares where q_i, $i = 1, \cdots, n$ represents the ith income earner share and letting

$$0 \leqq q_1 \leqq q_2, \cdots, \leqq q_n \leqq 1 \tag{1.6}$$

Each of the most commonly used inequality measures in the literature imposes a "weight" on the social importance of each quantile of income recipients in determining the overall level of income inequality. Atkinson's (1970) inequality index is explicit about the social welfare basis of the index itself for this reason we focus on his measure in this chapter. Following Cowell (1977) we define the index as,

$$A = 1 - \left[\frac{1}{n} \sum_{i=1}^{n} (nq_i)^{1-\epsilon} \right]^{1/1-\epsilon} \tag{1.7}$$

where n is the number of quantiles, q_i is the quantile and ε is the "inequality aversion parameter." Cowell (1977) gives a good example of how to interpret this inequality aversion parameter. He considers a rich man R with five times the income of poor man P. The degree to which we are inequality averse can be expressed as the amount of income we are willing to let R give up to give a dollar to P. In this case we will give $\$5\varepsilon$ by R to make a \$1.00 transfer to P. For example, if $\varepsilon = 0$, we will only take \$1.00 from R to give a dollar to P. If $\varepsilon = 1/2$, we will take \$2.24 from R to give \$1.00 to P. If $\varepsilon = 2$ we will let R give up \$25.00 to give a 1.00 to P. In other words, the higher the value of ε, the more averse to inequality we are and the more we are willing to let R give up to affect the desired transfer to P. Slottje (1989) calculate several Atkinson inequality measures by taking values of ε of .5, .75, .95, 1.5 and 2, to calculate A1, A2, A3, A4, and A5, respectively.

These alternative inequality measures are all frequently used in the literature. Each measures a different aspect of economic inequality. It is for completeness that we present the trend behavior of each of them in this chapter. The inequality measures above are estimated from consumer income data from the *Current Population Reports* for the period 1947—1992. The data are for families (defined as two or more related individuals *living* together). We use the CPR as it is available for the longest period of time in a consistent fashion. The definition of income in the survey is quite comprehensive in that it includes cash transfers; however, it does not include transfers in kind and taxes paid.

Figure 1.1 shows normalized values for these various inequality measures over time. This figure is from Raj and Slottje (1994). It is clear from this figure that inequality has a rising trend with a structural break in the mid 1960's. The results of this section are clear. Based on actual data, income inequality as measured by a number of summary measures of inequality has been on the rise since the late 1960's. Most of the rest of this book is concerned with exploring this increase. Section 1.4 presents an overview of the rest of book and lays out how we will go about analyzing this rising inequality phenomenon.

1.4 The Plan of the Book

The plan of this book is as follows. Chapter two will discuss the ME method, and it is based on Ryu (1990, 1993). Chapter three presents our attempt to explain in part how the observed income distribution is generated. We posit a latent distribution of capabilities and demonstrate how this unobserved capability distribution can be mapped into the observed size distribution of earnings. Chapter three was first presented in a book published by Edward Elgar and edited by John Creedy (1994). Chapter four presents a discussion of approximating Lorenz curves and is based on work of Ryu and Slottje (1997). In Chapters five and six of this book we will introduce some new perspectives on analyzing the impact of the macroeconomy on the change in the income distribution using the orthonormal Basis (ONB) method. Some of this work has appeared in Ryu and Slottje (1994a) and

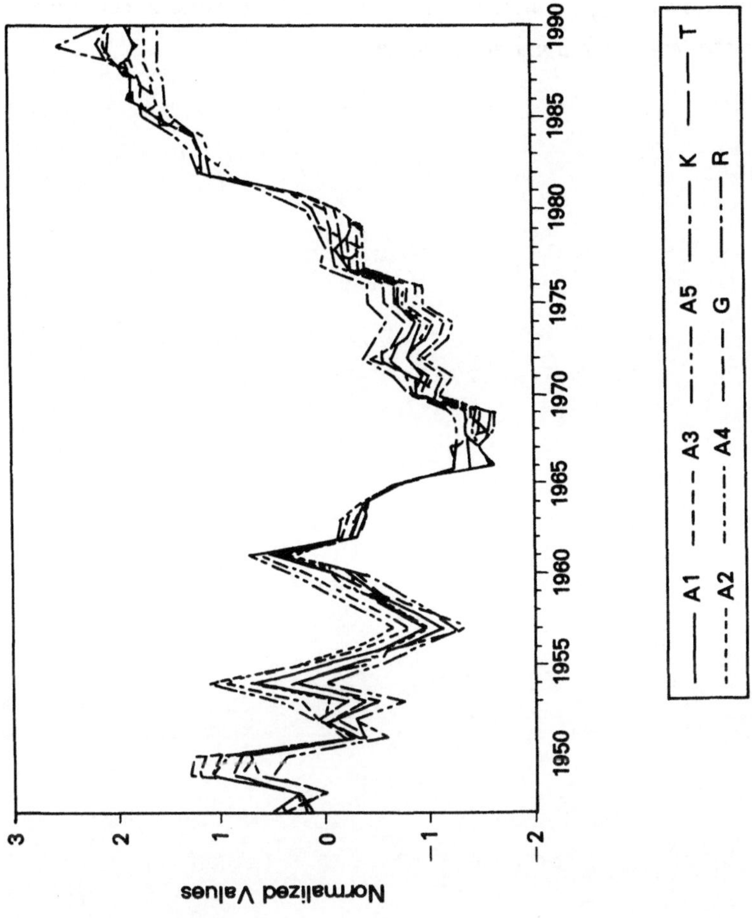

Fig. 1.1. Inequality Measures, = Normalized : 1947 − 1990

some of it in Ryu and Slottje (1996b). Chapter seven of the book deals with the analysis of hunger, a difficult concept to quantity and hence to analyze. The ONB and ME methods afford us a framework in which we can actually analyze how hunger varies in the U.S. and how various economic factors impact the level of hunger across states.

Chapter 2

Maximum Entropy Estimation Method[1]

Before using ONB and maximum entropy to analyze changes in inequality, this chapter develops the formal theory necessary to do so. That is, in this chapter, we develop mathematical and statistical properties of the maximum entropy (ME) method and then relate it to other well known flexible functional form approaches. First we shall explain what we mean by the ME principle and then review the Jaynes' (1979) concentration theorem to provide some justification of the ME method as a density estimation method. Since there has been little previous research on applying the ME principle to derive economic relationships,[2] we shall begin with the physicists' view of this principle. The ME principle means that the entropy of the physical universe increases constantly because there is a continuous and irrevocable degradation of order into chaos. As a simple example, we can consider a closed system filled with a large number of interacting particles and leave the system to interact freely for a long time. Then the system will reach a maximum entropy state. Statistical physicists find the ME density function for this equilibrium system which is described by a constant average energy per particle. See, for example, the Maxwell-Bolzmann distribution in Rao (1973).

To understand this interpretation of the notion of entropy, Jaynes (1979) indicates that we can define a kind of measure on the space of probability distributions such that the distributions of higher entropy represent greater "disorder," or that they are "smoother," or that they are "more probable," or that they "assume less". In contrast to the above intuitive explanations of entropy as a measure, Jaynes' (1979) entropy concentration theorem presents a quantitative demonstration which shows, in what sense, and how strongly, the distribution of maximum entropy is favored relative to

[1] This chapter follows Ryu (1990).

[2] An exception is the work done by Georgenscu-Roegen(1971).

alternative distributions of lower entropy.

2.1 Review of Jaynes' (1979) Concentration Theorem

A random experiment has n possible outcomes at each trial. Thus in T independent trials, we have an enumeration of T outcomes $x_1, \cdots, x_T$, where x_t is a realized outcome at t^{th} trial. We call this space Ω_T with containing the n^T conceivable outcomes. In T independent trials, if the first outcome was observed T_1 times, the second outcome was observed T_2 times, and the last n^{th} outcome was observed T_n times, then we can define an entropy,

$$H(f_1, \cdots, f_n) = -\sum_{i=1}^{n} f_i \log f_i \tag{2.1}$$

with frequencies $f_1 = T_1/T, \cdots, f_n = T_n/T$. The conceivable frequencies $f_1, \cdots, f_n$ may be regarded as cartesian coordinates of a point P in an n-dimensional space restricted to $\left\{S : 0 \leqq f_i, \sum_{i=1}^{n} f_i = 1\right\}$

Consider the subclass C of all possible outcomes that could be observed in T trials, compatible with N+1 linearly independent constraints,

$$\frac{1}{T}\sum_{t=1}^{T} x_t^j = \hat{\mu}_j, \qquad \text{for} \qquad j = 0, \cdots, N \tag{2.2}$$

Out of the n^T conceivable outcomes $x_1, \cdots, x_T$, the number which yield a particular set of frequencies f_i is[3]

$$W(f_1, \cdots, f_n) = \frac{T!}{(Tf_1)!\ldots(Tf_n)!} \tag{2.3}$$

[3] Suppose we interpret our problem as a multinomial distribution with cell probabilities $\pi_1, \cdots, \pi_n$. In T independent trials, we have a sequence of numbers $T_1, \cdots, T_n$ corresponding to n outcomes and we can define frequencies $f_1 = T_1/T, \cdots, f_n = T_n/T$. Then the likelihood function of the multinomial distribution is

$$LF = \frac{T!}{T_1!\ldots T_n!}\pi_1^{T_1}\cdots\pi_n^{T_n} = W(f_1, \cdots, f_n)\pi_1^{T_1}\cdots\pi_n^{T_n}$$

and as $T \to \infty$, which follows from the Stirling approximation,[4]

$$\frac{1}{T}\log W \to H(f_1, \cdots, f_n)$$

In what follows, we shall review the entropy concentration theorem which says that, for a large number of observations, the entropies associated with distributions satisfying the constraints in (2.2) will be concentrated. Let M_T denote the number of elements in C and assign the counting measure $1/M_T$ to each element of C. Associated with each element of C is an entropy deviation from H_{max} where H_{max} can be determined by maximizing H in (2.1) subject to (2.2) and ΔH is a deviation from H_{max}. A certain fraction F of the experimental outcomes of class C will yield an entropy in the range

$$(H_{max} - \Delta H) \leqq H \leqq H_{max} \tag{2.4}$$

Jaynes'(1979) concentration theorem states that if we have a large number of observations, $2T\Delta H$ is distributed over class C as χ^2 with $k = n - N$ degrees of freedom. That is

$$2T\Delta H \doteq \chi^2_k \tag{2.5}$$

where $\doteq$ means approximately equal to.

2.2 Determination of a Maximum Entropy Density Function Given Known Moments

Suppose we obtain approximating densities by choosing a density which

---

Therefore in (2.3), we defined W as the allowable number of permutations for any given sequence of numbers $T_1, \cdots, T_n$.

[4] Mood, Graybill, and Boes (1974) show the Stirling formula in their Appendix A as

$$T! = (2\pi)^{1/2}\exp(-T)T^{T+0.5}\exp[r(T)/12T]$$

where $1 - 1/(12T+1) < r(T) < 1$. Hence,

$$\log(T!) \doteq -T + (T+0.5)\log T \doteq T\log T - T \quad \text{as} \quad T \to \infty$$

where $\doteq$ means approximately equal to.

maximizes entropy subject to moment side conditions. That is, we solve the following problem.

$$\max_f W = -\int f(x)\log f(x)dx \tag{2.6}$$

satisfying $$\int x^m f(x)dx = \mu_m, \qquad m=0, 1, \cdots, N$$

with the μ_m having known values. Once the model moments $\mu_0, \cdots, \mu_N$ are known, the problem of (2.6) becomes a mathematical optimization problem subject to given side conditions. We shall assume that a solution exists to this problem.[5]

The Lagrangian method produces a maximum entropy distribution

$$f(x)=\exp\left[\sum_{n=0}^{N} c_n x^n\right] \quad \text{satisfying} \quad \int x^m f(x)dx=\mu_m, \tag{2.7}$$
$$m=0, 1, \cdots, N.$$

The parameters of f(x) can be determined from the moment restriction conditions.

There is another interpretation for (2.7). We can think of it as a polynomial expansion of the logarithmic pdf and we determine the coefficients c_n's mechanically from the given moments. Since an analytical solution of (2.7) for the c_n's is impossible, many researchers introduced numerical method to find the c_n's. For example, see Zellner and Highfield (1988) and Mead and Papanicolaou (1984).

First, we shall review Zellner and Highfield's (1992, 1998) approach, and then explain our own method later. Zellner and Highfield (1982, 1988) adopted the standard Newton method of solution. That is they view $f(x) = \exp\left[\sum_{n=0}^{N} c_n x^n\right]$ as a function of c_n's and expand the moment $\mu_m = \int x^m f(x)dx = \int x^m \exp\left[\sum_{n=0}^{N} c_n x^n\right]dx$ in Taylor series about initial values for the c^0. If an infinite domain is assumed, $x \in (-\infty, +\infty)$, then N should be an even number and c_N

---

[5] See Mead and Papanicolaou (1984) for the existence conditions.

should be negative to satisfy the normalization constraint, $\int_{-\infty}^{+\infty} f(x)dx =$ 1. If $N=4$, for example, we can relate the model moment $\mu(c)$ with some given four moments of the distribution, $\mu'_0, \cdots, \mu'_4$,

$$\mu_m' \Longleftrightarrow \mu_m(c) = \int x^m f(x)dx \qquad \text{for} \qquad m=0, 1, \cdots, 4 \quad (2.8)$$

$$\cong \mu_m(c^0) + \sum_{n=1}^{4} (c_n - c_n^0) \frac{\partial \mu_m}{\partial c_n} \Big|_{c=c^0} \qquad (2.9)$$

$$= \mu_m(c^0) + \sum_{i=1}^{4} (c_n - c_n^0) \mu_{m+n}(c^0) \qquad (2.10)$$

First, we shall review Zellner and Highfield's (1988) approach, and then explain our own method later. Zellner and Highfield (1988) adopted the standard Newton method of solution. That is they view $f(x) = \exp[\sum_{n=0}^{N} c_n x^n]$ as a function of c_n's and expand the moment $\mu_m = \int x^m f(x)dx = \int x^m \exp[\sum_{n=0}^{N} c_n x^n]dx$ in Taylor series about initial values for the c^0. If an infinite domain is assumed, $x \in (-\infty, +\infty)$ then N should be an even number and c_n should be negative to satisfy the normalization constraint, $\int_{-\infty}^{+\infty} f(x)dx = 1$. If N=4, for example, we can relate the model moment $\mu(c)$ with some given four moments of the distribution, $\mu'_0, \cdots \mu'_4$, where we have used $(\partial \mu_m / \partial c_n)_{c=c^0} = \int x^{m+n} \exp[\sum_{n=1}^{4} c_n^0 x_n]dx = \mu_{m+n}(c^0)$. We can rewrite (2.10) in matrix representation,

$$\begin{pmatrix} \mu_0(c^0) & \mu_1(c^0) & \mu_2(c^0) & \mu_3(c^0) & \mu_4(c^0) \\ \mu_1(c^0) & \mu_2(c^0) & \mu_3(c^0) & \mu_4(c^0) & \mu_5(c^0) \\ \mu_2(c^0) & \mu_3(c^0) & \mu_4(c^0) & \mu_5(c^0) & \mu_6(c^0) \\ \mu_3(c^0) & \mu_4(c^0) & \mu_5(c^0) & \mu_6(c^0) & \mu_7(c^0) \\ \mu_4(c^0) & \mu_5(c^0) & \mu_6(c^0) & \mu_7(c^0) & \mu_8(c^0) \end{pmatrix} \begin{pmatrix} c_0 - c_0^0 \\ c_1 - c_1^0 \\ c_2 - c_2^0 \\ c_3 - c_3^0 \\ c_4 - c_4^0 \end{pmatrix} = \begin{pmatrix} \mu'_0 - \mu_0(c^0) \\ \mu'_1 - \mu_1(c^0) \\ \mu'_2 - \mu_2(c^0) \\ \mu'_3 - \mu_3(c^0) \\ \mu'_4 - \mu_4(c^0) \end{pmatrix}$$

(2.11)

For the given initial values of c^0, we can find $\mu_m(c^0)$ for m=0, ⋯, 8 and then find c from (2.11). On the RHS of (2.11), μ'_0, ⋯, μ'_4, are some given moments. Now taking this new c as initial values, we can find $\mu_m(c)$ for m=0, ⋯, 4 and then find new c′ from (2.11). We continue this iterations until the difference in c becomes appropriately small. This iteration method will converge to a unique point as shown by Zellner and Highfield (1988).

We shall introduce a new problem which is distinct from the maximum entropy problem. In the maximum entropy problem (2.6), we found the functional form of the density which maximizes entropy under the given side conditions and then we determined the parameters of the derived density function from the same side conditions. In the following problem (2.12), the functional form of density is already specified and we are determining the coefficients of the specified density function from the given side conditions. Suppose we define a distribution in the following general form

$$f(x)=\exp\left[\sum_{n=0}^{N} c_n x^n\right] \tag{2.12}$$

satisfying both

$$\mu_m \equiv \int x^m f(x)dx \qquad \text{for} \qquad m=0, 1, \cdots, N \qquad \text{and}$$

$$\mu_m \equiv \int x^m f(x)dx \qquad \text{for} \qquad m=N+1, \cdots, 2N \tag{2.13}$$

Given 2N+1 side conditions for N+1 parameters, there does not necessarily exist a solution of the form (2.12). The existence of a solution is more problematic than existence of a solution to the maximum entropy problem stated on (2.6) and (2.7) because the maximum entropy problem finds N+1 parameters from N+1 restrictions. In the following, we shall assume that a solution exists. In this case, the following theorem 2.1 gives a convenient analytical expression for the c's in terms of the μs. See Appendix A of Ryu (1990) for the proofs of all theorems.

Theorem 2.1 : Suppose a solution exists for the problem stated in (2.12). The following method provides an analytic solution for the model parameters $c_0, \cdots, c_N$ in terms of the known model moments $\mu, \cdots, \mu_{2N}$. First, we shall find an N by 1 vector $c = c_0, \cdots, c_N$ from the following relationship and c_0 will be determined by normalization of the density functions.

$$Bc = d \quad \rightarrow \quad c = B^{-1}d \tag{2.14}$$

where the NxN square matrix B, and the Nx1 vectors c and d are defined as follows. If the domain of x is finite, we can always transform it to [0, 1].

$$B_{mn} \equiv -mn[\mu_{m+n} - \mu_{m+n-1}] \quad \text{where} \quad m, n = 1, \cdots, N \tag{2.15}$$

$$c' = (c_1, \cdots, c_N), \qquad \text{and} \tag{2.16}$$

$$d_m \equiv [m(m+1)\mu_m - m^2\mu_{m-1}] \quad \text{where} \quad m = 1, \cdots, N \tag{2.17}$$

If an infinite domain is assumed, $x \in (-\infty, \infty)$, then N should be an even number and c_N should be negative to satisfy the normalization requirement of the density function. If $x \in [0, +\infty)$, then N can be any positive integer but c_N should be negative to satisfy the normalization requirement. For both cases of $x \in (-\infty, +\infty)$ and $x \in [0, +\infty)$, we define

$$B_{mn} \equiv mn\mu_{m+n} \qquad \text{where} \qquad m, n = 1, \cdots, N$$

$$c' = (c_1, \cdots, c_N), \qquad \text{and}$$

$$d_m = -m(m+1)\mu_m \qquad \text{where} \qquad m = 1, \cdots, N$$

Since B is a positive definite matrix, (2.14) determines $c_1, \cdots, c_N$ and c_0 can be found by normalization of the pdf.

Therefore, Theorem 2.1 says that if more information $(\mu_N, \cdots, \mu_{2N})$ is added to the problem, then we can solve the model parameters $c_0, \cdots, c_N$ analytically. In the following, we shall show that even if we do not know $(\mu_{N+1}, \cdots, \mu_{2N})$, we can solve the model parameters numerically with repeated use of Theorem 2.1. Suppose $\mu_0, \cdots, \mu_N$ have known values but the higher moments $(\mu_{N+1}, \cdots, \mu_{2N})$ are unknown so that we will start with zero values $\mu_{N+1}=\cdots=\mu_{2N}=0$. Using these moments, we can find first round matrix $B^{(1)}$ and $d^{(1)}$. Then first round vector $c^{(1)}$ can be found by

$$B^{(1)}c^{(1)}=d^{(1)} \tag{2.18}$$

We put superscript to show the round number. Using these $c^{(1)}$ values, find the second round model moments

$$\mu_m^{(2)}\equiv\int x^m \exp\left[\sum_{n=0}^{N} c_n^{(1)}x^n\right]dx \quad \text{for} \quad m=1,\cdots,2N \tag{2.19}$$

At each stage, we revise the values of μ_m and B, but we keep $d^{(1)}$ at fixed first round values. Therefore, using these $\mu_m^{(2)}$ values, we can find second round matrix $B^{(2)}$ and second round vector $c^{(2)}$.

$$B^{(2)}c^{(2)}=d^{(1)} \tag{2.20}$$

We continue this iteration process until desired convergence in c or μ is obtained.[6] This process will converge to a unique point.[7]

---

[6] We can establish accuracy up to the certain decimal point or up to the certain number of digits.

[7] We can divide the unique convergence problem and an uniqueness problem. In my experience with this algorithm, convergence has not been a problem that we shall emphasize uniqueness problem. Rewrite second round iteration $B^{(2)}c^{(2)}=d^{(1)}$ as $c^{(2)}=[B^{(2)}]^{-1}d^{(1)}$. If Λ is an NxN diagonal matrix with n^{th} element $1/n$, then

$$\Lambda[c^{(2)}-c^{(1)}]=\Lambda[B^{(2)}]^{-1}d^{(1)}c^{(1)}.$$

If we define

$$e^{(2)}\equiv B^{(2)}\Lambda[[B^{(2)}]^{-1}d^{(1)}-c^{(1)}],$$

then

$$[B^{(2)}]\,\Lambda\,[C^{(2)}-C^{(1)}]=e^{(2)}.$$

If we set $S_n\equiv\frac{C_n}{n}$ and $S=(S_1,\cdots,S_n)'$, then we have a relationship

$$[B^{(2)}][s^{(2)}-s^{(1)}]=e^{(2)} \tag{1*}$$

To solve the problem stated in (2.7) we have seen two approaches. Zellner and Highfield (1988) applied Newton method while this chapter utilizes Theorem 2.1. Both approaches utilized model moments μ_m for $m = 0, \cdots, 2N$ as a technical convenience during the intermediate steps. In Zellner and Highfield's approach, nonlinear relationship is approximated by the Taylor expansion as shown in (2.10). Meanwhile, in the method described in Theorem 2.1, we have a linear relationship between the parameters and the moments. However, to apply Theorem 2.1, we needed information of the higher order model moments $\mu_{N+1}, \cdots, \mu_{2N}$ that we suggested an iteration method. In the later section, we shall come back to this iteration problem and consider the cases where we can avoid this iteration process.

We have seen how to determine a ME density function under the given side conditions with the known model moments. In the following section,

---

Iteration method based on (1^*) is equivalent to the iteration method based on (2.18)−(2.20). Therefore, we shall prove unique convergence of the iteration method of (1^*). Since we know $B^{(2)}$ (as well as $B^{(3)}$, $B^{(4)}$, $\cdots$) is a positive definite matrix, unique convergence of this iteration method can be established if we appeal to Gale and Nikaido theorem (1965). Let us elaborate this in the following. Suppose we have a differentiable mapping $g: S \rightarrow R^N$ where S is a region in R^N, and $g(s) = (g_m(s))$ ($s \in S$, $m = 1, \cdots, N$), $g_m(s)$ being differentiable functions on S with total differenctials $dg_m = \sum_{n=0}^{N} g_{mn}(s) ds_n$ for $n = 1, \cdots, N$. Suppose we choose $x \in [0, 1]$ and define

$g_m(s) = -m[\mu_m(c) - \mu_{m-1}(c)]_{c=\Lambda^{-1}s}$, then

$$g_{mn} = -\partial m(\mu_m - \mu_{m-1}) / \partial s_n = -m(\mu_{m+n} - \mu_{m+n-1})n = B_{mn}$$

where we used $\partial \mu_m / \partial s_n = n \mu_{m+n}$. Therefore $dg_m = \sum_{n=0}^{N} g_{mn}(s) ds_n = \sum_{n=0}^{N} B_{mn} ds_n$ for $n = 1, \cdots, N$. Since we know $B^{(2)}$ (as well as $B^{(3)}$, $B^{(4)}$, $\cdots$) is a positive definite matrix, unique convergence of this iteration method can be established for s if we appeal to Gale and Nikaido theorem (1965). If $x \in (-\infty, +\infty)$, we can derive a similar expression.

we shall relax the assumption of known model moments, and estimate the ME density function with the given sample observations.

2.3 Estimation of the Maximum Entropy (ME) Density Function When Moments are Unknown

Suppose we solved the ME method and found the entropy maximizing density function as

$$f(x \mid c_1, \cdots, c_N) = \exp\left[\sum_{n=0}^{N} c_n x^n\right] \tag{2.21}$$

Since the above density function should be normalized, c_0 can be determined as a function of $c_1, \cdots, c_N$.

$$c_0 = c_0(c_1, \cdots, c_N)$$

The density function described in (2.21) is called as the exponential distribution when we choose N = 1, the normal distribution when N=2, and the Nth degree exponential distribution when N is an arbitrary finite N.

Our first objective is to estimate the model parameters $c_0, \cdots, c_N$ from the given observations of $x_1, \cdots, x_T$. We shall suggest three different approaches, maximum likelihood estimation (MLE), the method of moments (MOM), and Bayesian estimation. Once the parameters are estimated, the loss functions and Bayesian expected loss function will be considered. Our second objective is to find the distribution of the density function $f(x \mid c_1, \cdots c_N)$ from the given observations of $x_1, \cdots, x_T$. We plan to make a detailed research about this issue in the future, but for now we shall give only brief survey how to apply the Monte Carlo method, the Jacobian transformation method, and the Bootstrap procedure to find the distribution of the density function.

Let us begin with several problems related with the parameter estimation. The method of moments introduced by Pearson consists in equating a convenient number of the sample moments to the corresponding moments of the distribution, which are functions of the unknown parameters. However, there are no unique way to define sample moments. If we define

m^{th} moments as $\hat{\mu}_m \equiv (1/M)\sum_{t=1}^{T} x_t^m$, then there is no specific rule for choosing M. It can be T, or T−1 , or something else. By considering as many moments as there are parameters to be estimated, and solving the resulting equations with respect to the parameters, estimates of the latter are obtained. The estimates obtained in this way from a set of T sample values are functions of the sample moments, and certain properties of their sampling distributions may be established under fairly general conditions. If we define the sample moments as $\hat{\mu}_m \equiv (1/T)\sum_{t=1}^{T} x_t^m$, then the distribution of an estimate of this kind will be asymptotically normal for large T, and that the mean of the estimate will differ from the true value of the parameter by a quantity of order 1/T, while the standard deviation will be asymptotically of the form $c/\sqrt{T}$.

However, Fisher pointed out the estimates given by the method of moments are not always the best possible from the efficiency point of view, i.e., they do not have the smallest possible variance in large samples. Nevertheless, on account of its practical expediency the method will often render good service. Sometimes the estimates given by the method of moments may be used as first approximations, from which further estimates of higher asymptotic efficiency may be determined by means of other method. To introduce the Bayesian approach, we may characterize the posterior pdf for the parameter in terms of a small number of measures, say measures of central tendency, dispersion, and skewness. The problem of choosing a single measure of central tendency is a well-known problem in descriptive statistics. In some circumstances we may have a loss function, say $L = L(\theta, \hat{\theta})$, where $\hat{\theta} = \hat{\theta}(x)$ is a point estimate depending on the given sample observations $x' = (x_1, \cdots, x_T)$. Since θ is considered random, L is random. One generally used principle, which generates point estimates and which is in accord with the expected utility hypothesis, is to find the value of $\hat{\theta}$ that minimizes the mathematical expectation of the loss function. This value is called as Bayes estimator. The Bayes estimator becomes the posterior mean, posterior mode, and posterior median when we choose a quadratic loss, zero one loss, and absolute loss functions.

To find the density function at a given point $x = x_0$, we can plug the

MLE or MOM estimator into (2.21). Under certain regularity conditions, MLE is consistent, asymptotically normally distributed, and asymptotically efficient in that the asymptotic variance matrix reaches the Cramer–Rao lower bound. However, even if the estimated parameters are unbiased, the plugged in density in general will be biased because the functional form of the density is nonlinear. For any given point of $x = x_0$,

$$E\hat{f}(x_0 \mid \theta, D) \neq f(x_0 \mid \theta)$$

where D denotes observed sample information. Therefore, unbiasedness and asymptotic efficiency of estimated parameters does not mean unbiasedness and asymptotic efficiency of the estimated density function. In comparison, Bayesian estimation chooses $f^*(x_0)$ which minimizes the expectation of the quadratic loss function.

$$L = [\hat{f}(x_0) - f(x_0 \mid \theta)]^2 \tag{2.22}$$

$$f^*(x_0) = E[f(x_0 \mid \theta)] = \int f(x_0 \mid \theta) f(\theta \mid D) d\theta$$

In the remaining portion of this section, we shall present the technical details of parameter estimation and distribution of the density function.

2.3.1 Estimation of the Exponential Density Function (N=1)

In this subsection, we shall establish the exponential density function which can be derived from the ME method when we choose N=1. We will estimate the model parameters with MLE, MOM, and Bayesian method. From these estimated parameters, we shall find the variances and loss functions. To find the density function, we may plug in MLE or MOM estimated parameters into the density function. In the Bayesian method, the parameters will have certain distribution that we can find the expectation of the density function or the distribution of the density function.

Suppose we choose N=1 and normalize the density function described in (2.21),

$$f(x \mid a) = \frac{1}{a} \exp[-x/a] \qquad \text{where} \qquad x \in [0, +\infty) \tag{2.23}$$

For the given observations of $x_1, \cdots, x_T$, the likelihood function is

$$LF = \prod_{t=1}^{T} f(x_t \mid a) = a^{-T} \exp[-S/a] \quad \text{where} \quad S \equiv \sum_{t=1}^{T} x_t \tag{2.24}$$

To find the MLE

$$\frac{\partial \log LF}{\partial a} = \frac{\partial}{\partial a}\left[-T \log a - \frac{S}{a}\right] = 0 \Rightarrow \hat{a}_{MLE} = \hat{\mu} = \frac{S}{T} \tag{2.25}$$

Similarly we can estimate the method of moment estimator by relating the model moment with the sample moment,

$$\mu = \int x f(x \mid a) dx = \int_0^{+\infty} \frac{x}{a} \exp[-x/a] dx = a \Rightarrow \hat{a}_{MOM} = \hat{\mu}_S$$

where $\hat{\mu}_S = (1/\mathrm{M}) \sum_{t=1}^{T} x_t$. If we choose M=T,

$$\hat{a}_{MLE} = \hat{a}_{MOM} = \hat{\mu} \tag{2.26}$$

To find the variance of these estimators, let us establish a formula,

$$E\left[\sum_{t=1}^{T} x_t\right]^2 = E\left[\sum_{t=1}^{T} x_t^2\right] + E\left[\sum_{t \neq t'}^{t} x_t x_{t'}\right]$$
$$= T2a^2 + T(T-1)a^2 = T(T+1)a^2 \tag{2.27}$$

where we used $\int_0^{+\infty} x^2 (1/a) \exp[-x/a] dx = 2a^2$. Using (2.27),

$$VAR(\hat{a}_{MLE}) = VAR(\hat{a}_{MOM}) = E\left[\frac{1}{T}\sum_{t=1}^{T} x_t - a\right]^2 = \frac{a^2}{T} \tag{2.28}$$

It is interesting to note that above variance is equal to the Cramer–Rao lower bound

$$\text{CR Bound} = \frac{-1}{E[\partial^2 \log LF/\partial a^2]} \tag{2.29}$$
$$= \frac{-1}{E[\partial^2(-T \log a - S/a)/\partial a^2]} = \frac{a^2}{T}$$

We have seen the parameter estimation of MLE and MOM and their variances. Now we want to introduce the Bayesian estimation. Suppose we choose a prior density $\pi(a) \propto 1/a$, then the posterior density function can be found as a multiplication of the prior density with the likelihood function derived in (2.24)

$$f(a \mid D) = \frac{S^T}{\Gamma(T)} a^{-(T+1)} \exp[-S/a] \tag{2.30}$$

where we have used following formula to normalize the posterior density function.[8]

$$\int_0^{+\infty} a^{-(T+1)} \exp[-S/a] da = \frac{\Gamma(T)}{S^T} \tag{2.31}$$

For later purpose, we establish similar formula as

$$\int_0^{+\infty} a^{-T} \exp[-S/a] da = \frac{\Gamma(T-1)}{S^{T-1}} \tag{2.32}$$

$$\int_0^{+\infty} a^{-(T-1)} \exp[-S/a] da = \frac{\Gamma(T-2)}{S^{T-2}} \tag{2.33}$$

Suppose we define the Bayesian estimator as the mean of the posterior density function, then

$$\hat{a}_{BAY} = \int a f(a \mid D) da = \frac{S^T}{\Gamma(T)} \int_0^{+\infty} a^{-T} \exp[-S/a] da = \frac{S}{T-1}$$

where we applied (2.32) for integration. The variance of the $\hat{a}_{BAY}$ can be found in a similar way as we did to derive the variance of MLE, but we skip this process because our object is not comparison of variances of the various parameters.

---

[8] Let $y \equiv 1/a$ and $dy = -da/a^2$. Then we have

$$\begin{aligned} \int_0^{+\infty} a^{-(T+1)} \exp[-S/a] da &= \int_{+\infty}^{0} y^{T+1} \exp[-Sy](-a^2) dy \\ &= \int_0^{+\infty} y^{T-1} \exp[-Sy] dy \\ &= s^{-T} \Gamma(\mathrm{T}) \end{aligned}$$

where we have used definition of the gamma function,

$$\Gamma(\mathrm{T}) = \int_0^{+\infty} x^{(T-1)} \exp[-x] dx.$$

Until now, we have estimated the parameters with MLE, MOM, and the Bayesian method. In the following, we shall find the loss functions related with these estimated parameters.

Suppose we choose a quadratic loss function, then

$$L=(a-\hat{a})^2 \tag{2.34}$$

and we can introduce $\hat{a}_{MLE}$ and $\hat{a}_{MOM}$. The Bayesian expected loss is

$$\begin{aligned} EL &= \int_0^{+\infty} (a-\hat{a}_{BAY})^2 \frac{S^T}{\Gamma(T)} a^{-(T+1)} \exp[-S/a] da \\ &= \frac{S^2}{(T-1)^2(T-2)} \end{aligned} \tag{2.35}$$

where we applied (2.31)-(2.33). If we choose a relative loss function $L=[(a-\hat{\mu})/a]^2$, then we shall get a slightly different result. Now we want to find the distribution and expectation of the ME density function. For any given point $x=x_0$, the density function can be found by plugging in MLE or MOM estimator into the density function

$$\hat{\eta} \equiv \hat{f}(x_0 \mid \hat{a}_{MLE}=\hat{\mu}) = \frac{1}{\mu}\exp\left[-\frac{x_0}{\mu}\right] \tag{2.36}$$

We have noted that unbiasedness and asymptotic efficiency of MLE does not provide unbiasedness and asymptotic efficiency of the estimated density. Therefore, we have introduced Bayesian estimation where we choose the density function which minimizes the quadratic loss function. Since $E[f(x_0 \mid \mu, \sigma)]$ minimizes this quadratic loss function, let

$$\eta \equiv f(x_0 \mid a) = \frac{1}{a}\exp[-x_0/a] \tag{2.37}$$

Using the definition of gamma function, the expectation of the ME density can be found as[9]

---

[9] If $z \equiv (S+x_0)/a$ and $dz=(S+x_0)(-da/a^2)$, then

$$E(\eta) = \int_0^{+\infty} (1/a)\exp[-x_0/a] \frac{S^T}{\Gamma(T)} a^{-(T+1)} \exp[-S/a] da$$

$$E(n)=\frac{S^T}{\Gamma(T)}\int_0^\infty \frac{1}{a}\exp[-x_0/a]a^{-(T+1)}\exp[-S/a]da$$
$$=\frac{TS^T}{(S+x_0)^{T+1}}$$
$$\doteq \frac{1}{\hat{\mu}}\exp\left[-\frac{x_0}{\hat{\mu}}\right] \qquad \text{as} \qquad T\to\infty$$

When sample size is large, the expectation of the ME density is approximately equal to the plugged in density function of MLE and MOM shown in (2.36).

Now let us explain how to estimate the density of η, $g(\eta\,|\,D)$. We can apply the Monte Carlo method because (2.30) can be converted into a gamma function if we introduce $z=S/a$ and $da/dz=-a^2/S$,

$$f(z\,|\,D)=f(a\,|\,D)|_{a=S/z}\cdot\frac{da}{dz}=\frac{1}{\Gamma(T)}z^{T-1}\exp[-z] \qquad (2.39)$$

We can generate random samples of z and find a from z. Then for a given point $x=x_0$, each realization of a^k will produce a value for η^k. We repeat this process to get $\eta^1, \cdots, \eta^k$. Therefore, we can estimate $g(\eta\mid D)$ using the Monte Carlo simulation method or any other density estimation method from the generated values of η^k, $k=1, \cdots, K$.

$$=\frac{S^T}{\Gamma(T)}\int_0^{+\infty} a^{-(T+2)}\exp[-(S+x_0)/a]da$$
$$=[S^T/\Gamma(T)]\int_0^{+\infty}\frac{z^T}{(S+x_0)^{T+1}}\exp[-z]dz$$
$$=\frac{S^T}{\Gamma(T)}\frac{\Gamma(T+1)}{(S+x_0)^{T+1}}$$
$$=\frac{TS^T}{(S+x_0)^{T+1}}$$
$$=(T/S)(1+x_0/S)^{-(T+1)}$$
$$=(T/S)\exp[-(T+1)\log(1+x_0/S)]$$
$$\doteq(1/\hat{\mu})\exp\left[-\frac{x_0}{S/(T+1)}\right]$$
$$\doteq(1/\hat{\mu})\exp[-x_0/\hat{\mu}].$$

To estimate the density function g(η | D), we can apply the Jacobian transformation method. With change of variable technique, we can transform any density function of a into a density function of another variable ξ = h(a) if there exists a one to one transformation between ξ and a. As an example of this technique, consider the following example. Suppose our objective is estimation of the density function of the distribution function $F(x_0 | a) \equiv \int_0^{x_0} f(x | a)dx$ rather than estimation of the density function of the $\eta = f(x_0 | a)$.

$$\begin{aligned} F(x_0 | a) &\equiv \int_0^{x_0} f(x | a)dx \\ &= \int_0^{x_0} \frac{1}{a}\exp[-x/a]dx \\ &= 1 - \exp[-x_0/a] \end{aligned} \tag{2.40}$$

Here we have a one to one transformation between F and a. Now we can rewrite a in terms of F,

$$1 - F = \exp[-x_0/a] \qquad \Rightarrow \qquad \frac{1}{a} = -\frac{1}{x_0}\log(1-F)$$

and the Jacobian is $J \equiv da/dF = \exp[x_0/a](a^2/x_0)$. Therefore, from the posterior density function of a given in (2.30), we can find the density of the distribution F,

$$\begin{aligned} g(F | D) &= f(a | D)_{1/a = -\frac{1}{x_0}\log(1-F)} \cdot \frac{da}{dF} \\ &= \frac{S^T}{\Gamma(T)} a^{-(T+1)} \exp[-S/a] \cdot \frac{a^2}{x_0} \exp[x_0/a] \\ &= \frac{S^T}{\Gamma(T)} \left[-\frac{\log(1-F)}{x_0} \right]^{T-1} \cdot (1-F)^{\frac{S}{x_0}} \cdot \frac{1}{x_0} \exp[x_0/a] \\ &= \left[\frac{1}{\Gamma(T)} \right] \left(\frac{S}{x_0} \right)^T [-\log(1-F)]^{T-1} \cdot (1-F)^{\frac{S-x_0}{x_0}} \end{aligned} \tag{2.41}$$

This density function g(F | D) has a unique maximum at $F = 1 - \exp\left[-\frac{(T-1)x_0}{S - x_0}\right]$ and becomes zero at F=0 and F=1. As a second example of the Jacobian transformation method, we want to find the distribution of ratio of densities at x_0 and x_1. Let

$$\eta_0 \equiv f(x_0 | a) = \frac{1}{a}\exp[-x_0/a]$$

$$\eta_1 \equiv f(x_1 | a) = \frac{1}{a}\exp[-x_1/a]$$

$$\phi \equiv \eta_0/\eta_1 = \exp[-(x_0 - x_1)/a] = \exp[\Delta/a]$$

$$\theta \equiv \log\phi = \Delta a \qquad \text{where} \qquad \Delta \equiv x_1 - x_0$$

We transform the posterior distribution of a into θ with Jacobian method. Using $a = \Delta/\theta$, $da/d\theta = -\Delta/\theta^2$, and the posterior distribution of a given at (2.30),

$$\begin{aligned} f(\theta/D) &= f(a/D)_{a=\Delta/\theta} \cdot \frac{da}{d\theta} \\ &= \frac{S^T}{\Gamma(T)}\left[\frac{\Delta}{\theta}\right]^{-(T+1)} \exp[-S\theta/\Delta] \cdot (-\Delta/\theta^2) \\ &\Rightarrow \frac{1}{\Gamma(T)}\left[\frac{\Delta}{\theta}\right]^{T} \theta^{T-1}\exp[-S\theta/\Delta] \end{aligned} \tag{2.42}$$

In the last expression we omitted negative sign because the range of θ should be reversed from $\theta \in (+\infty, 0]$ to $\theta \in [0, +\infty)$.

We have seen how to estimate parameters with MLE, MOM, and Bayesian method for the given exponential density function. Using these parameters, we have calculated loss and Bayesian expected loss. In the Bayesian approach, the model parameters have certain distribution that we could find the expectation and distribution of the density function at a given point. In the following subsection, we shall repeat above estimations for the normal distribution which corresponds to the N=2 case of the ME estimation of density function.

2.3.2 Estimation of the Normal Density Function (N=2)

If we choose N=2, the ME density of (2.21) will produce a normal density function.

$$f(x | c_1, c_2) = \exp[c_0 + c_1 x + c_2 x] \tag{2.43}$$

$$\Rightarrow \frac{1}{\sqrt{2\pi}\,\sigma}\exp\left[-\frac{1}{2\sigma^2}(x-\mu)^2\right]=f(x\,|\,\mu,\sigma^2)$$

We shall begin with parameter estimation of the above normal density function. We shall introduce MLE, MOM, and Bayesian estimation.

1) MLE : The likelihood function is

$$LF=\left[\frac{1}{\sqrt{2\pi}\,\sigma}\right]^T\exp\left[-\frac{1}{2\sigma^2}\sum_{t=1}^{T}(x_t-\mu)^2\right] \tag{2.44}$$

Then we get MLE of $\hat{\mu}=\frac{1}{T}\sum_{t=1}^{T}x_t$ and $\hat{\sigma}^2=\frac{1}{T}\sum_{t=1}^{T}(x_t-\hat{\mu}^2)$.

2) Method of Moments (MOM) : We define MOM as an approach where we estimate the model parameters by equalizing the model moments with sample moments.

$$\mu\equiv\int xf(x\,|\,\mu,\sigma)dx \quad\Leftrightarrow\quad (1/M)\sum_{t=1}^{T}x_t=\hat{\mu} \tag{2.45}$$

$$\sigma^2\equiv\int(x-\mu)^2f(x\,|\,\mu,\sigma)dx \quad\Leftrightarrow\quad (1/M)\sum_{t=1}^{T}(x_t-\hat{\mu})^2=\hat{\sigma}^2 \tag{2.46}$$

There is no general rule to choose M, but if we choose M=T, then the parameters estimated by MLE and MOM are same. However, above estimation of σ^2 is biased and it can be a serious problem when we have a small number of observations. Therefore, we can introduce an unbiased s^2 so that $E(s^2)=\sigma^2$.

$$s^2\equiv\frac{1}{T-1}\sum_{t=1}^{T}(x_t-\hat{\mu})^2 \tag{2.47}$$

3) Bayesian estimation: The likelihood function in (2.44),

$$LF=\left[\frac{1}{\sqrt{2\pi}\,\sigma}\right]^T\exp\left[-\frac{1}{2\sigma^2}\sum_{t=1}^{T}(x_t-\mu)^2\right] \tag{2.48}$$

$$=\left[\frac{1}{\sqrt{2\pi}\,\sigma}\right]^T\exp\left[-\frac{1}{2\sigma^2}\nu s^2+T(\mu-\hat{\mu})^2\right] \tag{2.49}$$

where $\nu=T-1$, $\hat{\mu}=\sum_{t=1}^{T}x_t/T$ and $\nu s^2=\sum_{t=1}^{T}(x_t-\hat{\mu})^2$. Suppose we choose a prior density $\pi(\mu, \sigma)=1/\sigma$, then the joint posterior pdf can be found from $f(\mu, \sigma \mid D) \propto \pi(\mu, \sigma) l(\mu, \sigma \mid D)$.

$$f(\mu, \sigma \mid D)=C\frac{1}{\sigma^{T+1}}\exp\left[-\frac{1}{2\sigma^2}[\nu s^2+T(\mu-\hat{\mu})^2]\right] \quad (2.50)$$

where

$$C \equiv \left(\frac{\sqrt{T}}{\sqrt{2\pi}}\right)\frac{2}{\Gamma(\nu/2)}\left(\frac{\nu s^2}{2}\right)^{\nu/2} \quad (2.51)$$

The normalization constant in (2.50) was found from the fact that $f(\sigma \mid D)=\int_{-\infty}^{+\infty} f(\mu, \sigma \mid D)d\mu$ has an inverted gamma distribution.

If we define Bayesian estimator as the mean of the posterior density function, then

$$\hat{\mu}_B=\hat{\mu} \quad (2.52)$$

$$\hat{\sigma}_B=\frac{\Gamma\left(\frac{\nu-1}{2}\right)}{\Gamma\left(\frac{\nu}{2}\right)}\left(\frac{\nu s^2}{2}\right)^{1/2} \quad \text{for} \quad \nu>1 \quad (2.53)$$

The marginal posterior pdf for μ is in the form of a univariate Student t pdf with mean $\hat{\mu}$, and the marginal posterior pdf for σ is in the form of a univariate inverted Gamma function. The means of these distributions can be found in Zellner (1971).

Now let us find the quadratic loss and Bayesian expected loss functions.

$$L(\hat{\mu}_{MLE})=L(\hat{\mu}_{MOM})=(\mu-\hat{\mu})^2 \quad (2.54)$$

$$L(\hat{\sigma}^2_{MLE})=L(\hat{\sigma}^2_{MOM})=(\sigma^2-s^2)^2 \quad (2.55)$$

The Bayesian expected loss is

$$E[L(\hat{\mu}_B)]=\int(\mu-\hat{\mu}_B)^2 f(\mu, \sigma \mid D)d\mu d\sigma \quad (2.56)$$

$$=\left(\frac{\nu}{\nu-2}\right)\left(\frac{s^2}{T}\right) \quad \text{for} \quad \nu>2$$

where $f(\mu \mid D)$ is in the form of a univariate Student t distribution and its moments are calculated in Zellner (1971). Similarly we can find

$$E[L(\hat{\sigma}_B)] = \int (\sigma - \hat{\sigma}_B)^2 f(\mu, \sigma \mid D) d\mu d\sigma \tag{2.57}$$
$$= \left(\frac{\nu s^2}{\nu - 2}\right) - \hat{\sigma}_B^2 \text{for} \qquad \nu > 2$$

For any given point $x = x_0$, the density function can be found by plugging in MLE or MOM estimators into the density function,

$$\hat{\eta} \equiv \hat{f}(x_0 \mid \hat{\mu}, s^2) = \frac{1}{\sqrt{2\pi} s} \exp\left[-\frac{1}{2s^2}(x_0 - \hat{\mu})^2\right] \tag{2.58}$$

We have noted that unbiasedness and asymptotic efficiency of MLE does not provide unbiasedness and asymptotic efficiency of the estimated density. Therefore, we have introduced Bayesian estimation where we choose the density function which minimizes $E[f(x_0 \mid \mu, \sigma)]$ the quadratic loss function. Since minimizes the quadratic loss function, we shall find $E[f(x_0 \mid \mu, \sigma)]$ from the definition of η.

$$\eta \equiv f(x_0 \mid \mu, \sigma^2) = \frac{1}{\sqrt{2\pi} \sigma} \exp\left[-\frac{1}{2\sigma^2}(x_0 - \mu)^2\right] \tag{2.59}$$

It will have certain distribution because (μ, σ) are random variables. In the following we shall find $E[f(x_0 \mid \mu, \sigma)]$.

$$f^*(x_0) = E[\eta \mid D] \tag{2.60}$$
$$= \int f(x_0 \mid \mu, \sigma) f(\mu, \sigma \mid D) d\mu d\sigma$$
$$= \int C \frac{1}{\sqrt{2\pi}} \frac{1}{\sigma^{(T+2)}} \exp\left[-\frac{1}{2\sigma^2} B_2\right] d\mu d\sigma$$

where

$$C \equiv \left(\frac{\sqrt{T}}{\sqrt{2\pi}}\right) \frac{2}{\Gamma(\nu/2)} \left(\frac{\nu s^2}{2}\right)^{\nu/2}$$
$$B_2 \equiv (x_0 - \mu)^2 + \nu s^2 + T(\mu - \hat{\mu})^2 = z^2 + B_3$$
$$z \equiv \sqrt{T+1}\, \mu - \frac{(x_0 + T\hat{\mu})}{\sqrt{T+1}}$$

$$B_3 \equiv T\hat{\mu}^2 + \nu s^2 + x_0^2 - \frac{(x_0 + T\hat{\mu})^2}{T+1} = \nu s^2 + \frac{T}{T+1}(\hat{\mu} - x_0)^2$$

Rewrite (2.60)

$$E[\eta \mid D] = \int C \frac{1}{\sqrt{2\pi}} \frac{1}{\sigma^{(T+2)}} \exp\left[-\frac{1}{2\sigma^2} B_3 \right] \cdot$$

$$\cdot \exp\left[-\frac{1}{2\sigma^2} z_2 \right] \frac{dz}{\sqrt{T+1}} d\sigma$$

$$= \int C \frac{1}{\sqrt{T+1}} \frac{1}{\sigma^{(T+1)}} \exp\left[-\frac{1}{2\sigma^2} B_3 \right] d\sigma$$

$$= C \frac{1}{\sqrt{T+1}} \cdot 2^{(T-2)/2} \Gamma\left(\frac{T}{2} \right) B_3^{-T/2} \qquad (2.61)$$

where we have used a formula from Zellner (1971) p.23

$$\int_0^{+\infty} \sigma^{-(T+2)} \exp[-B_3/2\sigma^2] d\sigma = 2^{(T-1)/2} \Gamma\left(\frac{T+1}{2} \right) B_3^{-(T+1)/2}$$

(2.62)

Then

$$E[\eta \mid D] = \left(\frac{\sqrt{T}}{\sqrt{2\pi}} \right) \frac{2}{\Gamma(\nu/2)} \left(\frac{\nu s^2}{2} \right)^{\nu/2} \frac{1}{\sqrt{T+1}}$$

$$\cdot \frac{2^{T/2}}{2} \Gamma\left(\frac{T}{2} \right) \left[\nu^2 + \frac{T}{T+1} (\hat{\mu} - x_0)^2 \right]^{-T/2}$$

$$= \left(\frac{\sqrt{T}}{\sqrt{T+1}} \right) \frac{\sqrt{2}}{\sqrt{2\pi}} \frac{\Gamma\left(\frac{\nu+1}{2} \right)}{\Gamma\left(\frac{\nu}{2} \right)} (\nu s^2)^{\nu/2} \cdot$$

$$\left[\nu s^2 + \frac{T}{T+1} (\hat{\mu} - x_0)^2 \right]^{-T/2} \qquad (2.63)$$

When sample size is large, we can show that is approximately equal to the plugged in density function of MLE and MOM.[10]

---

[10] To show (2.64), we shall derive several useful relationships. (i) If we apply a formula from Zeller (1971) p.372, we can show $(T/2)^{0.5} \Gamma(\nu+1/2)/\Gamma(\nu/2) \rightarrow 1$ *as* $T \rightarrow \infty$. (ii) $\sqrt{T}(\nu s^s)^{-0.5} \doteq 1/s$.

$$E[\eta \mid D] = \hat{\eta} \equiv \frac{1}{\sqrt{2\pi}\, s}\exp\left[-\frac{1}{2s^2}(x_0 - \hat{\mu})^2\right] \tag{2.64}$$

Since $\hat{\mu} \xrightarrow{a.s.} \mu$ and $s \xrightarrow{a.s.} \sigma$, we find

Until now, we have compared the parameter estimation methods of MLE, MOM, and Bayesian method. To find the density function at a given point $x = x_0$, we have introduced plugged in method for MLE or MOM, and minimization of the expectation of the quadratic loss function. However, when sample size is big, density function derived by these three approaches are approximately equal and converges to the true density function.

Now let us estimate the density function of the $\eta = f(x_0 \mid \mu, \sigma)$, at a given point $x = x_0$. We shall explain the Monte Carlo method and the Jacobian transformation method. Since the posterior density function of (2.51) can be decomposed into a multiplication of a normal density and an inverted gamma function,

$$\begin{aligned} f(\mu, \sigma \mid D) &= C\frac{1}{\sigma^{T+1}}\exp\left[-\frac{1}{2\sigma^2}[\nu s^2 + T(\mu - \hat{\mu})^2]\right] \qquad (2.65)\\ &= \frac{1}{\sqrt{2\pi}\,\sigma/\sqrt{T}}\exp\left[-\frac{(\mu - \hat{\mu})^2}{2(\sigma/\sqrt{T})^2}\right] \\ &\quad \cdot \left[\frac{2}{\Gamma(\nu/2)}\left(\frac{\nu s^2}{2}\right)^{\nu/2}\right]\frac{1}{\sigma^{\nu+1}}\exp[-\nu s^2/2\sigma^2] \\ &= P_N\left(\mu \mid \hat{\mu}, \frac{\sigma^2}{T}\right) \cdot P_{IG}(\sigma \mid \nu, s) \end{aligned}$$

The Monte Carlo method is following. We can generate random samples of σ^k, k=1, ⋯, K from the inverted gamma function and then generate μ^k from the normal distribution $\mu = N(\hat{\mu}, \sigma^2/T)$. Using these $\{\mu^k, \sigma^k;$ k= 1, ⋯, K$\}$, we can generate samples of $\{\eta^k;$ k=1, ⋯, K$\}$ and find the density function g(η).

As an alternative way to find the density function g(η), we can apply

(iii) If $A \equiv (\hat{\mu} - x_0)^2/\nu s^2$, then $\exp[\log(1+A)^{-T/2}] \doteq \exp[-(T/2) \cdot A] \doteq \exp[-(\hat{\mu} - x_0)^2/2s^2]$. Using these relationships, we can derive (2.64).

Jacobian transformation method. Suppose σ is known in (2.65). Then the conditional density function of ν for given σ is

$$w = f(\mu|\sigma, D) = \frac{1}{\sqrt{2\pi}\sigma/\sqrt{T}} \exp\left[-\frac{(\mu-\hat{\mu})^2}{2(\sigma/\sqrt{T})^2}\right] \tag{2.66}$$

Therefore for given σ, μ and $(\mu - x_0)$ are normally distributed,

$$(\mu - x_0) = N\left[(\hat{\mu} - x_0), \frac{\sigma^2}{T}\right]$$

and

$$z \equiv \frac{(\mu - x_0)^2}{\sigma^2/T} \tag{2.67}$$

will be distributed as noncentral χ_1^2 with degree of freedom one and noncentrality parameter $\theta = (\hat{\mu} - x_0)^2$. To rewrite z in terms of η, we can use (2.59).

$$z = -2T\log[\sqrt{2\pi}\sigma\eta] \tag{2.68}$$

and Jacobian $dz/d\eta = -2T/\eta$. From the density function of z, we can find the density function of η for the given σ

$$g(\eta|\sigma, D) = P_{NC\chi^2}(z, |1, \theta)|_{z=-2T\log[\sqrt{2\pi}\sigma\eta]} \cdot \frac{dz}{d\eta} \tag{2.69}$$

Since the noncentral χ^2 density has an infinite number of terms, evaluation of (2.69) will be difficult from practical point of view. For unknown values of σ, we can average over the pdf of σ,

$$g(\eta|D) = \int g(\eta|\sigma, D)P_{IG}(\sigma|D)d\sigma \tag{2.70}$$

2.4 Estimation of the Exponential Density Function for N>2

Now let us consider the case of N>2. We have seen that the parameters estimated by MLE and MOM are same when we choose N=1 or N=2. In this section we shall prove that such equality holds for any arbitrary finite N. To find the density function of the Nth degree exponential distribution function, we shall introduce Bootstrap procedure of Boos and Monahan (1986).

Let us begin with the parameter estimation. We shall show that parameters estimated by MLE are equivalent to the parameters estimated by MOM. Suppose we have a density function as given in (2.21)

$$f(x \mid c_1, \cdots, c_N) = \exp\left[\sum_{n=0}^{N} c_n x^n\right] \tag{2.21}$$

where c_0 is a function of $c_1, \cdots, c_N$. The likelihood function is

$$\begin{aligned} LF &= \prod_{t=1}^{T} f(x_t \mid c_1, \cdots, c_N) \\ &= \exp\left[c_0 T + c_1 \sum_{t=1}^{T} x_t + c_2 \sum_{t=1}^{T} x_t^2 + \cdots + c_N \sum_{t=1}^{T} x_t^N\right] \\ &= \exp[T(c_0\hat{\mu}_0 + c_1\hat{\mu}_1 + \cdots + c_N\hat{\mu}_N)] \end{aligned} \tag{2.72}$$

where $\hat{\mu}_m = \frac{1}{T}\sum_{t=1}^{T} x_t^m$. To estimate MLE,

$$\frac{\partial[\log LF]/T}{\partial c_m} = \frac{\partial[c_0\hat{\mu}_0 + \cdots + c_N\hat{\mu}_N]}{\partial c_m} = 0 \text{ for } m = 1, \cdots, N \tag{2.73}$$

Since $\hat{\mu}_0 = 1$, we can rewrite (2.73) as

$$\frac{\partial c_0}{\partial c_m} + \hat{\mu}_m = 0 \tag{2.74}$$

We can show that [11]

[11] Let us prove (2.75). Suppose we normalize the density function which is given in (2.21). From

$$\int f(x \mid c_1, \cdots, c_N)dx = \int \exp[c_0 + \Sigma_{n=1}^{N} c_n x^n]dx = 1,$$

$$\exp[-c_0] = \int \exp\left[\sum_{n=1}^{N} c_n x^n\right]dx \quad \textit{and}$$

$$c_0 = -\log\left[\int \exp\left[\sum_{n=1}^{N} c_n x^n\right]dx\right]$$

$$\frac{\partial c_0}{\partial c_m} = -\frac{\int x^m \exp[\Sigma_{n=1}^{N} c_n x^m]dx}{\int \exp[\Sigma_{n=1}^{N}]dx}$$

$$-\frac{\partial c_0}{\partial c_m}=\mu_m=\int x^m \exp\left[\sum_{n=0}^{N} c_n x^n\right]dx \tag{2.75}$$

such that (2.74) and (2.75) will produce

$$\mu_m=\int x^m \exp\left[\sum_{n=0}^{N} c_n x^n\right]dx \Leftrightarrow \hat{\mu}_m=\frac{1}{T}\sum_{t=1}^{T} x_t^m \quad \text{for} \quad m=1, \cdots, N$$

Therefore, MLE is to find $c_1, \cdots, c_N$ from (2.76). We can find c_0 from normalization of $f(x)$. Since we defined MOM as an approach where we find the model parameters by equating the model moments with the sample moments, that both the method of moment and the maximum likelihood method solve the same (2.76) and the estimated parameters are same.

For $N > 2$, Bayesian posterior density estimation seems to be difficult because c_0 cannot be easily found as a function of $c_1, \cdots, c_N$. To find the distribution of the ME estimated density, we want to apply Bootstrap procedure of Boos and Monahan (1986). Suppose we have i.i.d. observations $x_1, \cdots, x_T$, and find the density with the ME method.

$$f(x \mid c_1, \cdots c_N)=\exp\left[\sum_{n=0}^{N} c_n x^n\right] \tag{2.21}$$

We already explained how to estimate the model parameters from the given observations. Now the Bootstrap procedure is as follows. Suppose we can generate another set of random observations $x_1^1, \cdots, x_T^1$ from the empirical distribution of the originally given observations $x_1, \cdots, x_T$. Then we can estimate another set of the model parameters $c^1=c_1^1, \cdots, c_N^1$and density function $\eta^1=\exp[\sum_{n=0}^{N} c_n^1 x^n]$ from $x_1^1, \cdots, x_T^1$. This forms one value of η_1. We can repeat this process many times to get repeated observations $\eta^1, \cdots, \eta^K$. Boos and Monahan (1986) applied the Dirac kernel method to estimate $g(\eta)$, but we can apply other approaches to estimate the density of η.

$$=-\int x^m \exp\left[\sum_{n=0}^{N}\right]dx=-\mu_m$$

Therefore, we have proved (2.75).

Until now, we have seen how to estimate the ME density function from given observations. To estimate the model parameters, we have introduced MLE, MOM, and Bayesian estimation. Furthermore, to find the distribution of density function at a given point, we applied the Monte Carlo method, Jacobian transformation method, and the Bootstrap method. In the following section, we shall study the large sample properties of the ME density function.

2.5 Asymptotic Properties of the Maximum Entropy Density Function

When we have a large number of observations, estimation of the ME density function becomes easier as the model moments can be conveniently approximated with the sample moments. Also we shall establish that the ME estimated density converges in distribution to the population density and the ME parameters are normally distributed. To show that the model moments can be asymptotically approximated with the sample moments, suppose we assume that logarithm of population density can be well approximated by a finite polynomial expansion of order N. Then model moments will be approximately equal to population moments. In many examples shown by Mead and Papanicolaou (1984), the difference between ME estimated density and chosen population density was at the order of $10^{-2} \sim 10^{-7}$ depending on the choice of population density. If we have a large enough number of observations, sample moments $\hat{\mu}_m$ will converge A.S. to population moments μ_m^0 by SLLN, and the model moments are well approximated by sample moments.

Once we accepted that the model moments can be well approximated by the sample moments, Theorem 2.1 solves the ME density function. There is no need to go for iteration method because iteration will converge quickly if we have a large number of observations and if the population density is smooth. In the example presented in chapter 4, where we have 1001 observations, the effect of iteration was so small that the difference between the sample moments and the model moments was less than 0.00013. Therefore, when sample size is large, we can well approximate the model moments with the sample moments. Furthermore, if we could bring an assumption that logarithm of population density can be well approximated by a finite polynomial expansion of order N, then we can establish consistency and distribution theorems for the ME estimated parameters. In the following two theorems, we shall establish that the ME estimated density converges in distribution to the population density and the ME parameters are normally distributed.

Theorem 2.2 : Let $f_0(x)$ be the population density function integrable in $[0, 1]$ whose moments are $\mu_0^0, \mu_1^0, \cdots$ and let $f_N(x)=\exp[\sum_{n=0}^{N} c_N x^n]$ be the ME estimated density associated with the same moments for N=1, 2,$\cdots$ If g(x) is some continuous function in [0,1], then

$$\lim_{N\to\infty}\int_0^1 g(x)f_N(x)dx = \int_0^1 g(x)f_0(x)dx \tag{2.77}$$

In practice, population moments are unknown, but must be estimated. We can use minimum distance or generalized method of moments estimation to estimate c taking account of sampling error that occurs because μ is replaced by its sample mean. We can exploit results in Chiang (1952), Ferguson (1958) in the statistics literature and Sargan (1958), Chamberlain (1987) and Hansen (1982) in econometrics literature in displaying the asymptotic distribution of the estimator and in discussing asymptotic efficiency. We shall assume a compact domain $x\in[0, 1]$, but extension to $x\in[0, +\infty)$ and $x\in(-\infty, +\infty)$ is immediate. Suppose we define a matrix X_t and vectors y_t and u_t with typical elements

$$[X_t]_{mn} \equiv -mn(x_t^{m+n} - x_t^{m+n-1})$$
$$y_{tm} \equiv m(m+1)x_t^m - m^2 x_t^m$$
$$u_t \equiv y_t - X_t \cdot c$$

From B, c, and d defined in (2.15)−(2.17), we get $B=E[X_t]$, $d=E[y_t]$, and

$$E[u_t] = E[y_t] - E[X_t]\cdot c = d - B\cdot c = 0$$

where we applied (2.14). Using these notation, we can establish the following theorem.

Theorem 2.3: Suppose we assume that the logarithm of a population density is given by a power series of order N, log $f_0(x)=\sum_{n=0}^{N}$. Now we estimate the ME parameters from the sample information.

$$\hat{B}\hat{c}=\hat{d} \Rightarrow \hat{c}=\hat{B}^{-1}\hat{d} \tag{2.14'}$$

where the NxN square matrix $\hat{B}$, and the Nx1 vector $\hat{d}$ are defined as follows. For a compact domain x∈[0, 1],

$$\hat{B}_{mn}\equiv -mn[\hat{\mu}_{m+n}-\hat{\mu}_{m+n-1}] \qquad \text{for} \qquad m,\ n=1,\ \cdots,\ N$$
$$\hat{d}_m\equiv[m(m+1)\hat{\mu}_m-m^2\hat{\mu}_{m-1}] \qquad \text{for} \qquad m=1,\ \cdots,\ N$$

Then the sample estimated parameter vector $\hat{c}$ converges A.S. to $c^0=(c_0^0, \cdots, c_N^0)'$, which is the population mean of the asymptotic distribution of $\hat{c}$, and $x=\sqrt{T}(\hat{c}-c^0)$ has multivariate normal distribution with mean zero and N by N asymptotic covariance matrix $\Sigma=B^{-1}E[u_t u_t']B^{-1}$. The asymptotic covariance matrix .can be estimated consistently

$$\hat{\Sigma}=\hat{B}^{-1}\left[\frac{1}{T}\sum_{t=1}^{T}\hat{u}_t\hat{u}_t'\right]\hat{B}^{-1}$$

with $\hat{u}_t=y_t-X_t\cdot\hat{c}$ where B and $\hat{c}$ are defined in Theorem 2.3.

Theorem 2.3 is a special case of a more general result. We can refer to Hansen (1982) for such general result. From the problem stated in (2.12), we assumed the functional form of density be $f(x)=\exp\left[\sum_{n=0}^{N}c_n x^n\right]$ and we have shown how to derive the model parameters with (2.14) of Theorem 2.1.

$$Bc=d \tag{2.14}$$

where B is a N by N matrix, c and d are N by 1 vectors. Suppose we extend (4) and (5) in the proof of Theorem 2.1 which is described in Ryu (1990), i.e., from m=1, ⋯, N to m=1, ⋯, M where M is greater than N, we can find the following relationship.

$$\tilde{B}c = \tilde{d}$$

where $\tilde{B}$ is a M by N matrix, c is N by 1 vector, and $\tilde{d}$ is M by 1 vector. The elements of $\tilde{B}$, c and $\tilde{d}$ are described below equation (5) of the proof of Theorem 2.1 with m=1, ⋯, M. Here larger choices of M will improve the asymptotic efficiency of the estimator, but may detract from the finite sample properties.

We have discussed how to improve the asymptotic efficiency with additional restrictions imposed for the method of moment parameter estimation. Such improvement in asymptotic efficiency with additionally imposed restrictions is also possible for the MLE or Bayesian estimations. Suppose we define the regression function as a conditional expectation of y for given x. If we impose more restrictions on the joint density f(x,y), then the conditional density will be changed so that MLE is changed. If the joint density is restricted, then we get different regression for the Bayesian method. Therefore efficiency improvement can be obtained in all frames of MOM, MLE, and Bayesian method.

Until now we have seen estimation of the asymptotic ME density function. When sample size is large, the model moments can be approximated with the sample moments so that estimation was relatively simple, and the estimated density function converged in distribution to the true distribution function. In the following section, we shall extend the ME density estimation technique to estimation of the ME regression function.

2.6 Maximum Entropy Estimation of Univariate Regression Functions

In this section, we shall define the ME regression function and then explain how the Cobb-Douglas, translog, and Gallant's Fourier series function can be produced as a special cases of the ME method. A regression function is defined as

$$y(x) \equiv \int y f(y \mid x) = \frac{\int y f(x, y) dx}{f(x)}$$

We can apply the maximum entropy method to find a bivariate joint pdf and find the regression function as a conditional expectation of y for given x value. Appendix D of Ryu (1990) shows how to derive the ME density function when there are many variables. However if we can assume a special case where y can be restricted to be positive, then we can estimate the regression function in a simple way without estimating the joint bivariate density function. In practice, this assumption is not so restrictive because many economic variables, such as output, consumption, and food expenditure are restricted to be positive.[12]

Now suppose we solve a regression problem,

$$y(x) \equiv \int y f(y \mid x) dy = \frac{\int y f(x, y) dy}{f(x)} \quad \text{for} \quad 0 < y < +\infty \tag{2.78}$$

For the numerator of the regression function, we define

$$g(x) \equiv \int y f(x, y) dy = \int y f(y \mid x) dy \cdot f(x) = y(x) \cdot f(x) \tag{2.79}$$

We can think of g(x) as a y averaged density function in x with normalization constant $\int g(x) dx = \int y f(y) dy = \overline{y}$. We shall approximate g(x) by choosing a function which maximizes entropy subject to moment side conditions. We solve the following problem.

$$\underset{g}{\text{MAX}}\, W = -\int g(x) \log(x) dx \tag{2.80}$$

$$\text{satisfying} \qquad \int x^n g(x) dx = \nu_n, \qquad n = 0, 1, \cdots, N$$

---

[12] We have requested y(x) be positive for all x. However, this requirement can be relaxed easily. If we can assume $-A < y(x)$ for any big positive finite constant A, then we can always transform y(x) so that $\tilde{y}(x) = y(x) + A > 0$. Therefore, the only restricition which violates our assumption is when y(x) becomes negative infinite, then linear transformation of y(x) can not make $\tilde{y}(x)$ to be positive. As a simple example of this exceptional case, suppose we have a bivariate joint normal distribution f(x, y), then we know the regression function is $y(x) = \alpha + \beta x$. Therefore, when x approaches negative infinity, y(x) approaches negative infinity if $\beta > 0$. In this case, our required assumption is violated, and we have to estimate a bivariate joint pdf to find a regression function from it.

where ν_n are moments of the function g(x). If we maximize entropy, we shall get an exponential expression for g(x). This is the same problem as (2.7) and we already know how to solve this problem. We shall get the information regarding the nth moment from the sample observations.

$$\nu_n \equiv \int x^n g(x)dx = \int x^n y f(x, y)dxdy \Rightarrow \hat{\nu}_n \equiv \frac{1}{T}\sum_{t=1}^{T} x_t^n y_t \quad (2.81)$$

Therefore, using the sample moments, the parameters $r_1, \cdots, r_N$ can be estimated and r_0 can be found from the following normalization condition.

$$\int g(x)dx = \int y f(x, y)dxdy = \int y f(y)dy = \overline{y} \quad (2.82)$$

where $\overline{y} \simeq \frac{1}{T}\sum_{t=1}^{T} y_t$

Since we already know how to estimate density f(x) of (2.78), we can rewrite the regression expression as

$$y(x) \equiv \frac{g(x)}{f(x)} = \frac{\exp[\sum_{n=0}^{N} r_n x^n]}{\exp[\sum_{n=0}^{N} c_n x^n]} = \exp\left[\sum_{n=0}^{N} s_n x^n\right] \equiv \exp[h(x)]$$

where $s_n \equiv (r_n - c_n)$ and $h(x) \equiv \left[\sum_{n=0}^{N} s_n x^n\right]$. What we have established is that the logarithm of unknown regression function has a polynomial expansion. In estimation of the ME method by (2.83), we found normalization constant c_0 and r_0 separately for the denominator and the numerator. However, the only unknown part in (2.83) is a scale factor to move $y(x)$ up and down. Therefore, rather than finding the normalization constants separately by integration, we can match the mean of the model estimated $\hat{y}(x_t)$ with the mean of sample observation $y(x_t)$. For a large number of observations, we have

$$\frac{1}{T}\sum_{t=1}^{T} y(x_t) \doteq \int y f(x, y)dxdy = \int y f(y)dy = \overline{y}$$

$$\frac{1}{T}\sum_{t=1}^{T} \hat{y}(x_t) \doteq \int y \hat{f}(x, y)dxdy = \int y \hat{f}(y)dy = \tilde{y}$$

where $\doteq$ means approximately equal to. Therefore, it is reasonable to match the model estimated mean of y, $\tilde{y}$, with the population mean $\bar{y}$.

Once we have developed ME estimation of univariate regression functions, we shall study the technical problems related with this method. In particular, we shall consider small sample properties, a concavity restriction, possibility of maximizing entropy subject to other side moment conditions (e.g., Fourier series moments), rules to determine regression expansion size, and relationships to other flexible functional form approaches. Let us begin with a concavity restriction which requires

$$\frac{\partial y(x)}{\partial x} = \exp[h(x)] \cdot h'(x) \geqq 0 \qquad \text{and}$$
$$\frac{\partial^2 y(x)}{\partial x^2} = \exp[h(x)] \cdot [\{h'(x)^2 + h''(x)\}] \leqq 0$$

where $h(x) = \sum_{n=0}^{N} s_n x^n$, $h'(x) = \sum_{n=1}^{N} s_n n x^{n-1}$, and $h''(x) = \sum_{n=2}^{N} s_n n(n-1) x^{n-2}$.

It is interesting to note ME estimated regression is related to many other flexible functional form approaches. If we use moment side conditions up to the first and second order in maximizing entropy, we get Cobb–Douglas and translog functional forms from (2.83). If $x = \log z$,

$$\begin{aligned} \log y(z) &= s_0 + s_1 \log z && \text{for} \quad N=1 \\ \log y(z) &= s_0 + s_1 \log z + s_2 (\log z)^2 && \text{for} \quad N=2 \end{aligned} \tag{2.84}$$

In the following, we shall show that if we use trigonometric moments as side conditions in maximizing entropy, we shall get Gallant's (1981) Fourier series functional form. Now we can ask what difference will it make if we maximize the entropy subject to a different set of side conditions. For example we can introduce ONB side conditions or Fourier series side conditions or combinations of them.

$$\textit{Moment side conditions}: \int x^n f(x)dx = \nu_n, \qquad n = 0, \cdots, N$$

$$\textit{ONB side conditions}: \int P_n(x) f(x) dx = \mu_n, \qquad n = 0, \cdots, N$$

Fourier series side conditions: $\int \exp[\mathrm{inx}] f(x) dx = \xi_n,$

$$n = 0, \pm 1, \cdots, \pm N$$

The choice of the side conditions determines the functional form of the entropy maximizing function. For example, if we maximize the entropy subject to the Fourier series side conditions, we will get a pdf of $f(x) = \exp[\sum_{n=-N}^{+N} c_n \exp(inx)]$ and a regression function, $y(x) = \exp[\sum_{n=-N}^{n=+N} s_n \exp(inx)]$. The details are very technical with no new concepts so that we put the derivation in Appendix B of Ryu (1990). If $\tilde{y}(x) = \log y(x)$, we have a functional form $\tilde{y}(x) = \sum_{n=-N}^{n=+N} s_n \exp[inx]$, which is the same form as Gallant's (1981) Fourier series flexible form.[13] This means that if we use trigonometric moments as side conditions in maximizing entropy, we shall get Gallant's (1981) Fourier series functional form.

Until now, we have seen how various unrelated flexible forms, such as Cobb-Douglas, translog, and Fourier series flexible forms, can be produced as special cases of the ME method. Since Gallant's Fourier series are based upon sin nx or cos nx which are quite flexible functions and they are not very suitable to approximate smooth functions. However, the ME method subject to the moment side conditions can be very useful to describe a smooth function, because by writing the functional form as $y = \exp[\sum_{n=0}^{N} s_n x^n]$, y cannot be very flexible.

Now let us compare small sample properties of the ME method and other approaches justified by asymptotic theorems. A crucial assumption of all the asymptotic approaches is that the sample size is large. If the sample size is small, conclusions based upon an assumed large sample size will no longer be justified. In comparison, the maximum entropy method involves maximizing entropy subject to given moment side conditions. A crucial

---

[13] Gallan't Fourier flexible form includes quadratic trend term in the expansion. If we impose $\int x^n f(x) dx = v_n$ for $n = 1, 2$ and $\int \exp[inx] f(x) dx = \xi$ for $n = 0, \pm 1, \cdots, \pm N$, then the ME method will produce both the trend term and Fourier series terms.

assumption of the ME method is the knowledge of the model moments. However, the functional form and the parameters derived from the maximum entropy method do not lose their justification even if the sample size is small. In this respect, the maximum entropy method can be a potentially important method compared to the other regression methods based on asymptotic theorems.

There are several interesting issues to be discussed. First, we do not know what combination of side conditions is a good choice and in what sense are they good? In certain cases, the side conditions may come from the economic conditions or economic interpretations. Since the choice of the side conditions uniquely determines the functional form of the regression function, we can apply model selection criteria for this problem. If we apply posterior odds ratio method, then we can evaluate the relative merits of two models without assuming that these models are necessarily the only appropriate models.

We have noticed that the translog production function and the Gallant's Fourier series form can be obtained as special cases of the ME method. Though both the ME method and the translog function (or Fourier series form) produced the same functional forms, the parameters of the regression are estimated with different methods. We have introduced MLE, MOM, and Bayesian estimation for the ME method, but the translog approach estimated the parameter with OLS estimation for the regression model of log $y_t = \sum_{n=0}^{N} a_n P_n(x_t) + \varepsilon_t$.

2.7 Model Selection for Maximum Entropy Regression

In this section, we shall discuss the rules to determine regression expansion size. We shall apply posterior odds to determine the regression expansion size. Suppose we want to consider two hypotheses H_i and H_j of different regression expansion size. The posterior probabilities represent the weight of prior belief and sample evidence for a particular hypotheses. Rossi (1985) has used posterior odds to compare the translog cost function with the Fourier flexible function. Similarly, a Bayesian approach to choosing between two nested regressions associated with different regression expansion sizes can be applied as stopping rule for the ONB regression.

Suppose we want to consider two hypotheses H_i and H_j of regression expansion size i and j. The posterior probabilities represent the weight of prior belief and sample evidence for particular hypotheses. The ratio of the posterior probabilities associated with two hypotheses given by, $f(H_i \mid D)$ and $f(H_j \mid D)$ is the posterior odds, denoted by K_{ij} and

$$K_{ij} = \frac{f(H_i \mid D)}{f(H_j \mid D)} = \frac{\Pr(H_i)}{\Pr(H_j)} \cdot \frac{f(D \mid H_i)}{f(D \mid H_j)}$$
$$= \frac{\Pr(H_i)}{\Pr(H_j)} \cdot \frac{\int f(\theta) f(D \mid \theta) d\theta}{\int f(\phi) f(D \mid \phi) d\phi} \tag{2.85}$$

where D stands for data. Therefore posterior odds ratio is the product of the prior odds $\Pr(H_i)/\Pr(H_j)$and Bayes factor $f(H_i)/f(H_j)$ which is the ratio of averaged likelihood functions with the prior pdf's $f(\theta)$ and $f(\phi)$serving as the weighting functions. We do not require that $\Pr(H_i)+\Pr(H_j)=1$. The posterior odds ratio is designed to evaluate the relative merits of two models without assuming that these models are necessarily the only appropriate models

In Appendix C of Ryu (1990), we show how the posterior odds ratio works as a model selection rule. Suppose we have prior knowledge that the regression function has the known functional form of $y(x)=\exp[\sum_{n=0}^{N_0} s_n x^n]$ where we have assumed the expansion length N_0 be an unknown finite constant. To find this unknown N_0, we build two models made of N and N + 1 terms. If we have a large number of observations, we can compare the relative merits of these two models made of N terms vs $N+1$ terms. If $N<N_0$, we can show that posterior odds ratio $K_{N,\ N+1}$ approaches zero under appropriate choice of prior density for parameters s_n. This means we have a high degree of belief that the observed sample was generated from a model made of $N+1$ terms rather than from a model made of N terms. However, if N reaches N_0, $K_{N_0,\ N_0+1}$ will approach infinity. From this, we believe that samples were generated from a model made of N_0 terms rather than one from N_0+1 terms. Mathematical elaboration is described in Appendix C of Ryu (1990). We have compared the

regression models with finite N and $N+1$ terms. If we want to increase this regression expansion size N to infinity and use the posterior odds ratio in (2.85), it is possible with appropriate choice of the prior odds ratio $\Pr(H_i)/\Pr(H_j)$.

Suppose we impose higher prior probability for simple models and lower prior probability for complicated models as Jeffreys (1967) suggests.[14] This means we assume

$$\Pr(H_1) > \Pr(H_2) > \Pr(H_3) > \cdots > \Pr(H_m) > \cdots \tag{2.86}$$

Therefore $\Pr(H_N)/\Pr(H_m) \to 0$ *as* $N \to \infty$ for any fixed m. This means any model (H_N) with a higher number N of terms will have a lower posterior probabilities than one with fewer terms.

In this Chapter, we have introduced the ME method to find density functions and regression functions. As a justification for using the ME method, we have reviewed Jaynes' (1979) concentration theorem. Then we developed ME method and have seen the properties of ME method with special attention to the small sample properties, concavity restrictions, relationships to other flexible functional form approaches, and rule to determine regression expansion size. Until now we have considered the ME method for simple regression. However, an extension to the multiple regression case is immediate and presented in the Appendix D of Ryu (1990) where we discuss three dimensional ME estimation of the density and regression functions.

[14] Jeffereys (1967) shows an example of the simplicity postulate. A physicist would test first whether the whole variation is random as against the existence of a linear trend; then a linear law against a quadratic one, then proceeding in order of increasing complexity. All we have to say that the simpler laws have the greater prior probabilities. This is what Wrinch and Jefferys called the *simplicity postulate.*

Chapter 3

Capabilities and Earnings Inequality[15]

3.1 Introduction

Economists have been intrigued by the relationship between unobserved heterogeneity among individuals and the shape of the observed size distribution of earnings for over two hundred years. In this chapter, capability is a description of how an individual combines various attributes in the labor market to produce market outcomes such as observed earnings.[16] Ability and capability may differ because a given individual may have ability which when combined with other attributes does not result in performing in the labor market in a positive way. Earlier researchers thought that measurable proxies for capability should be normally distributed, while clearly empirical earnings distributions have non-zero skewness and kurtosis, cf. Sahota (1978) and Creedy (1985) for discussion of this early work. The causes of the departure from normality in earnings graduations have been debated for almost a century. So-called "stochastic theories" were predicated on the assumption that stochastic or random occurrences (like luck) played a major role in changing the shapes of the observed distributions.

Pareto (1896) is credited with some of the first empirical work ever done in economics while analyzing income distributions. Gibrat (1931), Champernowne (1953) and Mandelbrot (1960) were among the first to tackle the question of how earnings distributions are generated from a nondeterministic viewpoint, showing how changes in observed earnings graduations could evolve from a stochastic process. Pareto had earlier con-

---

[15] This chapter is based on Ryu and Slottje (1994b).

[16] Sen (1985) refers to capabilities as what a person can do or can be, he explicitly argues against focusing only on income outcomes from a welfare perspective. Here the term is used differently and it is argued that differences in individual capability do result in different market outcomes.

cluded that earnings graduations are stable over time and while there may be random perturbations that occur from year to year, the underlying distribution is stable. For a review of hypotheses on how observed distributions are generated, see Slottje (1989).

The purpose of this chapter is three fold. First, it examines the relationship between observed earnings distributions and unobserved heterogeneity among individuals. The maintained hypothesis is that the underlying latent distribution of capability among individuals follows a normal distribution as Roy (1950) assumed. Secondly, this chapter seeks to analyze whether a relatively simple relationship between the normal distribution and the observed earnings graduation. If so, then this relationship may be stable across different observed earnings graduations. That exercise should be an informative one for several reasons. First, if a relatively straightforward relationship is discussed between the presumed normal distribution of capability and an empirical earnings distribution, then a more fundamental understanding should arise of how the observed earnings distribution evolved in the first place. In addition, if the relationship is stable over different earnings distributions, then timely and relevant information may be forthcoming to policy makers whose task is to change recent increasing inequality trends. However, as will be demonstrated below, even if a simple transformation can not be found to define the mapping from normality to an observed earnings graduation, another issue can be analyzed. The framework developed here will have still allows for the exploration of the relationship between unobserved heterogeneity and the observed earnings distribution. The last purpose of this chapter is to relax the normal distribution assumption for the underlying latent distribution of capability among individuals. Since observations on individual capabilities are not available, the normality assumption of individual capabilities can not be proved. An alternative approach begins from a fixed known transformation function which maps individual capabilities to observed earnings. If the model parameters can somehow be estimated, then the expected earnings for an individual can be tabulated with respect to hypothetical capability and the probability density function for individual capability can be specified.

Section 3.2 discusses the theoretical part of this chapter and introduces the accumulated earnings potential model to discuss the transformation function and necessary assumptions on the distribution function for individual capability. Section 3.3 performs the transformations on U.S. data and compares results. Section 3.4 concludes the study.

3.2 The Theory

The shape of the observed size distribution of earnings depends on individual attributes and on the social configuration of any given economy. Individual differences in capabilities which combine skills, occupational characteristics and intensities of work, levels of education, access to capital markets (allowing an individual to borrow to enhance human capital), and other human capital factors will result in inequalities in earnings. Roy (1950) was among the first to note this. This chapter is interested in a better description of this generating process. In particular, it considers the following problems. How do differences in individual capability affect individual earnings on average? If capability is not observed in a given survey, how then can any meaningful conclusions be drawn? The standard approach has been to let schooling, etc., proxy for capability and then to attack the issue through a human capital model. This chapter seeks a more direct route even though it faces the latent nature of capability.

3.2.1 The Earnings Potential Accumulation Model

We introduce an earnings potential model where the accumulation rate is a function of individual capability and time. If individual earnings are proportional to accumulated earnings potential, then we can represent earnings as a function of capability and time. To explain the earnings potential accumulation model, let each individual begin with a stock of human capital endowment. Individuals differ in their access to credit markets to invest in additional human capital. Depending on family circumstances, individual initiative, and so on, individuals differ in ability to borrow at some interest rate, to invest in themselves. They will receive a return of r on this investment. Thus, r is a function, r(x), of x where x is capability. If the return is paid m times per year at equally divided rates of r/m, then a person with capability x will accumulate earnings potential by

$$R=\lim_{m\to\infty} R(m, T)=R_0 \lim_{m\to\infty}\left(1+\frac{r}{m}\right)^{mT}$$

$$=R_0 \lim_{m\to\infty}\left(1+\frac{r}{m}\right)^{\frac{m}{r}rT}=R_0 e^{rT} \tag{3.1}$$

$$\text{where} \qquad 0\leqq t\leqq T.$$

In general, the accumulation rate r will not be constant over time that the accumulation rate r(x, t) can be considered as a function of x and t. Then

$$R(x, T)=R_0(x)\exp\left[\int_0^t r(x, t')dt'\right] \tag{3.2}$$

Becker (1975) devoted his book to consideration of how the interest rate is increased with higher education from an individual point of view, for example, for fixed x. However, a cross sectional view is also considered in (3.2). If measured earnings can be obtained by multiplying the accumulated potential with a proportional constant P, then earnings are

$$y(x, t)=PR(x, t) \tag{3.3}$$

Rewrite the accumulation rate as

$$r(x, t)=\alpha_1(t)+h(x, t) \tag{3.4}$$

where α_1(t) describes the proportional change in earnings for all x and h(x, t) describes departure from the proportional change in earnings for all x. Therefore, inequality in earnings is not affected by $\alpha_1(t)$, but it depends on h(x, t). To consider the accumulated effect, define

$$A(t)\equiv\int_0^t \alpha(t')dt' \text{ and } H(x, t)\equiv\int_0^t h(x, t')dt' \tag{3.5}$$

Substitute (3.3) and (3.4) into (3.2) to get earnings as:

$$\log y=\log P+\log R=\log P+\log R_0(x)+A(t)+H(x, t) \tag{3.6}$$

Earnings can be decomposed as a multiplication of three parts. First, the initial value of earnings depends on initial capability R_0(x), secondly, earnings grow at a society specific rate $\alpha_1(t)$ so that their accumulated values are exp[A(t)] at time t, and third any departure from uniform growth of earnings is described by exp[H(t)]. The level of inequality in earnings will then change over time due to exp[H(t)]. log y is a monotonic increasing function of x and t, but the functional form for H(x,t) has yet to be specified. The following considers three simple cases of (3.6).

Case 1: Let $\log R_0 = a + bx$ and $H(x, t) = 0$. Then

$$\log y_i(t) = \log P + A(t) + a + bx_i + \varepsilon_i \tag{3.7}$$

where i=1, 2, ⋯, I denotes individuals. If x is normally distributed, then a lognormal distribution exists for all t. In this case, two assumptions are made. One is that x is normally distributed and the other is that earnings are a loglinear function of x.

Case 2: At any given time t, suppose log y is a monotonic increasing function of x or equivalently x is a monotonic increasing function of log y. Introduce a flexible semiparametric polynomial series expansion to describe the transformation function between log y and x.

$$x_i = \sum_{n=0}^{N} a_n(t)[\log y_i(t)]^n + u_i \tag{3.8}$$

If x is assumed to be normally distributed, the parameters can be estimated such that the estimated values $\hat{x} = \sum_{n=0}^{N} \hat{a}_n(t)[\log y_i(t)]^n$ can be distributed as closely as possible to a normal distribution.

Here assume the functional form for the probability density function of x is a standard normal distribution but we are taking the transformation function in a flexible functional form. The semiparametric polynomial series expansion used in (3.8) can approximate any continuous function within the desired level of accuracy by expanding the size N and choosing the parameters appropriately. The transformation function in (3.8) can be specified dependent on the observations of x or equivalently depending on the probability density function of capability. However, without knowledge of x, the transformation function can not be specified. When the distribution of capability is different, the corresponding transformation function will be different. As an example, suppose a uniform distribution is followed by x=[0, 1], then another set of parameters can produce a uniform distribution for $\hat{x}=\sum_{n=0}^{N} \hat{b}_n(t)[\log y_i(t)]^n$. Therefore the transformation function shifts if the assumption is changed for the distribution of x.

Case 3: Let $\log R_0(x)=a+bx$ and $r(x,t)=\alpha(t)+\beta(t)x$. Then (3.2)-(3.4) produce

$$\log y_i(t)=C(t)+D(t)x_i+u_i(t) \tag{3.9}$$

where $C(t)=\log P+a+A(t)$ and $D(t)=b+\int_0^t \beta(t')dt'$. Let $u_i(t)$ be independently distributed with mean zero and common variance σ_1^2. A loglinear transformation function is taken in (3.9), but knowledge is not assumed about the probability density functions for x and u. Though observations are absent on x_i, without loss of generality, it can be assumed that x has mean zero and variance one because any random variable can be transformed to have mean zero and variance one with a proper linear transformation. Then at any given time t, the parameters C(t) and D(t) can be estimated and inequality is determined by the parameter $\hat{D}(t)$ and the distribution of x. As a byproduct of this method, observations can be generated on capability using $\hat{x}_i=[\log y_i(t)-\hat{C}(t)]/\hat{D}(t)$ for i=1, ⋯, I, and the probability density function of x can be estimated from these $\hat{x}_i$ values. In the following two subsections, we elaborate on cases 2 and 3.

3.2.2 A Semiparametric Transformation from Earnings to Capability

Assume that capability is independently and normally distributed:

$$H_0: x \sim N[0, I_0] \text{ with } x_i=f(y_i(t)) \quad \text{for} \quad i=1, 2, \cdots, I \tag{3.10}$$

where x_i is a typical element of the I by 1 vector x and I_0 is an I by I unit matrix. The normality assumption of x can be considered as the result of combining a large number of attributes. Then it can be shown that capability is normally distributed by the central limit theorem.[17] To establish the relationship between observed earnings $[y_i(t)]$ and unobserved capability (x_i), consider the following two transformations. The Box-Cox transformation,

$$x_i = \frac{y_i(t)^{\lambda(t)} - 1}{\lambda(t)} + \xi_i \tag{3.11}$$

and the semiparametric transformation:

$$x_i = \sum_{n=0}^{N} a_n(t)[\ln y_i(t)]^n + \varepsilon_i \tag{3.12}$$

As noted above, some criteria must be relied on in assessing the relationship between the observed earnings distributions and the latent capability distribution. The parameters of the Box-Cox transformation and semiparametric transformation will be determined such that the transformed earnings distribution can be distributed as "closely" as possible to a normal distribution of capability. The criteria used have to gauge the effectiveness of the transformations are the Bera-Jarque (1981) statistic and the Kolmogorov (1933)

---

[17] Suppose each person whose observed earnings is $y_i(t)$ is described by N attributes Z_{Nn}, $n=1, 2, \cdots, N$ and its capability is a weighted sum of these attributes. Let each attribute Z_{Nn} for $n=1, 2, \cdots, N$ be independently distributed from every other attribute. Now apply theorem 5.11 of White (1984). Let $\{Z_{Nn}\}$ be a sequence of independent random scalars with $E(Z_{Nn})=\mu_{Nn}$, $var(Z_{Nn})=\sigma^2_{Nn}$, $\sigma^2_{Nn}\neq 0$, and $E\,|Z_{Nn}|^{2+\delta}<\Delta<\infty$ for some $\delta>0$ and all n. Define $\bar{Z}_N \equiv N^{-1}\sum_{n=1}^{N} Z_{Nn}$, $\bar{\mu}_N \equiv N^{-1}\sum_{n=1}^{N} \mu_{Nn}$ and $\bar{\sigma}^2_N \equiv var\sqrt{N}\sum_{n=1}^{N} \sigma^2_{Nn}$. If $\bar{\sigma}^2_N > \delta' > 0$ for all N sufficiently large, then $\sqrt{N}(\bar{Z}_N - \bar{\mu}_N)/\bar{\sigma}_N$ is asymptotically distributed a N(0, 1). Capability is a weighted sum of N attributes, but weighting factors can be removed by rescaling each attribute and thus capability is described by $\sqrt{N}(\bar{Z}_N - \bar{\mu}_N)/\bar{\sigma}_N$. Therefore, capability has a standard normal distribution if the number of attributes is sufficiently large. For simplicity, consider independently distributed random scalar attributes, but the independence assumption may be relaxed if a sequence of ϕ mixing (or α-mixing) random scalars is considered. See theorem 5.19 of White (1984).

statistic.

As a special case of the χ^2 test, Bera-Jarque (1981) showed that the normality of the given sample observations can be tested based on the following statistic BJ:

$$BJ=T\left[\frac{\hat{\mu}_3^2}{6\hat{\sigma}^6}+\frac{(\hat{\mu}_4-3\hat{\sigma}^4)^2}{24\hat{\sigma}^8}\right]\sim\chi_2^2 \tag{3.13}$$

where

$$\hat{\sigma}^2=\frac{1}{I}\sum_{i=1}^{I}x_i^2,\quad \hat{\mu}_3=\frac{1}{I}\sum_{i=1}^{I}x_i^3 \quad \text{and} \quad \hat{\mu}_4=\frac{1}{I}\sum_{i=1}^{I}x_i^4 \tag{3.14}$$

For derivation of this statistic and comparison with other statistics, see Judge et al. (1988). The Kolmogorov (1933) Statistic is defined by

$$D_I=\sup_{x(\lambda)}|F_I[x(\lambda)]-F_0[x(\lambda)]| \tag{3.15}$$

where $F_I[x(\lambda)]$ is the sample distribution which consists of $x_1(\lambda)$, ···, $x_I(\lambda)$ and $F_0[x(\lambda)]$ is the theoretical distribution under the null hypothesis, i.e., under the normal distribution. To estimate the parameter based on the Box-Cox transformation, compute the Bera-Jarque statistic and Kolmogorov Statistic for various choices of the λ values. Choose as the optimal value the λ value which produces the minimum value of the Bera-Jarque statistic or the minimum value of the Kolmogorov statistic.

For the polynomial series transformation method, N+1 parameters must be selected so that use of the above two selection criteria is not feasible. As an alternative method, introduce a simple least squares procedure. Choose the parameter values a_0, a_1, ···, a_N such that transformed values x_1, ···, x_I can be placed as closely as possible to the theoretical random sample values, x_1^0, ···, x_I^0 whose values are defined by the following integration,

$$\int_{-\infty}^{x_i^0}\frac{1}{\sqrt{2\pi}}e^{-x^2/2}dx=\frac{2i-1}{2I} \tag{3.16}$$

for i=1, 2, ···, I. We then minimize the sum of squared errors:

$$\min_{a_0, \cdots, a_N} \frac{1}{I} \sum_{i=1}^{I} \left[x_i^0 - \sum_{n=0}^{N} a_n(t) \{\ln y_i(t)\}^n \right]^2 \tag{3.17}$$

Transformation from capability to earnings

This subsection considers a sequence of problems. First, it derives a logarithm of earnings distribution from a given sample of observations; second it derives the conditional expectation of capability for a given logarithm of earnings level; third it derives a joint bivariate density of logarithm of earnings and capability, and finally it derives the conditional expectation of logarithm of earnings for a given capability level. The conditional expectation of capability for a given logarithm of earnings level is,

$$E[x_i \mid \ln y_i(t)] = \sum_{n=0}^{N} \hat{a}_n(t)[\ln y_i(t)]^n \tag{3.18}$$

A relationship has been derived between the logarithm of earnings and capability in (3.18) but the distance between the observations of ln y are not equally spaced. It is necessary to define equally spaced $(\ln y)_u$ to derive a joint pdf. Suppose the range of lny is divided into I equally spaced intervals, $(\ln y)_u$ for u=1, 2, ⋯, I and then find the expected level of capability with (3.18). Taking these expected values as mean values, a normal distribution of unknown variance σ^2 can be introduced as a proxy for the conditional probability density function of capability for the given $(\ln y)_u$. The joint probability density function is now

$$\begin{aligned} f[x \mid (\ln y)_u] &= \frac{1}{\sqrt{2\pi}\,\sigma} \exp\left[\frac{(x - E[x \mid (\ln y)_u])^2}{-2\sigma^2} \right] \\ &= \frac{1}{\sqrt{2\pi}\,\sigma} \exp\left[\frac{(x - \sum_{n=0}^{N} \hat{a}_n (\ln y)_u^n]^2}{-2\sigma^2} \right] \end{aligned} \tag{3.19}$$

$$f(x, \ln y) = f(x \mid \ln y) \cdot f(\ln y) \tag{3.20}$$

the variance σ^2 can be selected such that f(x) will be a normal distribution with a unit variance. Now the conditional density of lny for given x is

$$f(\ln y \mid x) = f(x, \ln y)/f(x) \tag{3.21}$$

and the conditional expectation of lny for x can be computed from (3.21). Under a normalization distribution assumption of capability, a transformation function has been established between capability and earnings. As long as the distribution of capability is specified, this method can be used to establish the corresponding transformation function. The next subsection relaxes the assumption of a known distribution of capability, but the transformation function is restricted to have a simple fixed form.

3.2.3 The Loglinear Transformation Function

A loglinear transformation function was proposed in section 2.1 as

$$\log y_i(t) = C(t) + D(t)x_i + u_i(t) \tag{3.22}$$

where u_i is independently distributed with mean zero and common variance σ_1^2. Note that earnings $y_i(t)$ and parameters C(t) and D(t) are functions of time, but the distribution of capability is independent of time. The functional form for the probability density function is not specified for x_i and $u_i(t)$ but assume x_i has mean zero and unit variance. The parameters of (3.9) can be estimated by

$$\frac{1}{I}\sum_{i=1}^{I} \log y_i(t) = \hat{C}(t) \tag{3.23}$$

$$\frac{1}{I}\sum_{i=1}^{I} [\log y_i(t) - \hat{C}(t)]^2 = \hat{D}^2(t)\frac{1}{I}\sum_{i=1}^{I} x_i^2 + \sigma_1^2 \tag{3.24}$$

where approximately equal to is replaced with equality (the variance of x is one and $\frac{1}{I}\sum_{i=1}^{I} x_i^2$ is approximately equal to one, but this difference is not distinguished here). If σ_1^2 is known, $\hat{D}(t)$ can be estimated from (3.21). If σ_1^2 s unknown, compare the following two equations established for two different years t and t′:

$$\begin{aligned} \log y_i(t) - \hat{C}(t) &= \hat{D}(t)x_i + u_i(t) \\ \log y_i(t') - \hat{C}(t') &= \hat{D}(t')x_i + u_i(t') \end{aligned} \tag{3.25}$$

Then

$$\frac{1}{I}\sum_{i=1}^{I}[\log y_i(t)-\hat{C}(t)][\log y_i(t')-\hat{C}(t')]$$
$$=\hat{D}(t)\hat{D}(t')+\sigma_1^2 \qquad (3.26)$$

Then $\hat{D}(t)$, $\hat{D}(t')$, $\hat{\sigma}_1^2$ can be estimated using (3.25), (3.26) and the following equation,

$$\frac{1}{I}\sum_{i=1}^{I}[\log y_i(t')-\hat{C}(t')]^2=\hat{D}^2(t')\frac{1}{I}\sum_{i=1}^{I}x_i^2+\hat{\sigma}_1^2 \qquad (3.27)$$

There are three implications in this model. First inequality in earnings due to capability differences are denoted by the $\hat{D}(t)$. When the slope is steep, small differences in capability will yield large differences in earnings, and thus greater inequality in earnings. Therefore, a direct measure is considered to examine the effect of higher capability on earnings with this loglinear model. Second, samples of capability can be generated using (3.9). Using observations $\log_i$ and estimated $\hat{C}(t)$ and $\hat{D}(t)$, corresponding x_i can be predicted though the error term u_i which will bring some distortion in x_i. Third, comparison can be made of the consequence of assuming a normal distribution when the transformation function has a loglinear form. The normal distribution assumption is used for x in case 1, but not in case 3.

3.3 Empirical Results

Data Generation

The theoretical models are applied to Current Population Survey (CPS) data of measured earnings for 1974 and 1990. These years were selected since 1974 has the lowest measured level of earnings inequality since the great society program of the 1960's and 1990 had the highest measured level of earnings inequality since the same benchmark. Since the data set includes a large number of sample observations, one thousand new samples were generated from the original data. The number of sample sizes could be increased to be generated, but one thousand samples should be adequate to derive the transformation function of earnings or logarithm of earnings. First, an averaging method is introduced to generate one thousand samples. If there are 66,000 individual samples for 1990, these data can be sorted in the order of increasing values, then take the mean value of the first 66 observations as the first sample, and the mean value of second 66 observations as the second sample, etc., but information can be lost in this averaging process. As an alternative method, an ME density estimation method can be applied and randomly generate a sample from this density. See Appendix 3.A for details. Twelve sample moments were calculated from the logarithm of earnings, and then compute six coefficients were computed to derive a corresponding pdf. From this density function and corresponding distribution function, one thousand random samples were generated in a similar way as in (3.16). In the ME density estimation method, specific details of sample characteristics are mapped into the sample moments such that the theoretical samples derived by the ME method are different from those found from the averaged one thousand sample means.

In generating random samples, two modifications are brought to the original data. At the lower tail area, there are so few observations that any density estimation method will not work well. All the observations below an annual earnings level of 148 dollars were removed. In 1974, 607 observations out of 47303 total observations belonged to this group while in 1990, 1064 observations out of 66173 observations belonged to this group. In the upper tail area, it decreases too slowly so that the ordinary cartesian coordinate will not describe the distribution of earnings effectively. Next, take the logarithm of earnings so that the tail observations are brought much closer to the center. The lower cut off of 148 dollars corresponds to $\ln y = 5$.

3.3.1 A Transformation from Earnings to Normally Distributed Capability

Next consider the Box-Cox transformation (3.11) and semiparametric expansion (3.8) to transform earnings to capability. Then test for normality in the projected values with the Bera-Jarque statistics (BJ) and the Kolmogorov statistics (D_I). In all tests reported in Tables 3.1-3.4, before applying the normality tests, the given sample observations were standardized so that the linearly transformed data will have a mean of zero and a variance of one. In Table 3.1, the normality of the Box-Cox transformed

Table 3.1. Normality test for Box−Cox Transformed Earnings, 1974 (I=1000)[a]

λ	BJ	P value[b]	D_I
0.15	25.19	0.0000034	0.102
0.16	22.54	0.0000127	0.103
0.17	20.56	0.0000343	0.103
0.18	19.23	0.0000668	0.104
0.19	18.52	0.0000950	0.105
0.20	18.44	0.0000989	0.105
0.21	18.98	0.0000757	0.106
0.22	20.13	0.0000425	0.107
0.23	21.90	0.0000176	0.107
0.24	24.29	0.0000053	0.108
0.25	27.31	0.0000012	0.109

[a] Current Population Survey data were used for measured earning for 1974.
[b] It is the smallest significance level where the null hypothesis would be rejected. The lower the P value, the smaller the level of agreement between the null hypothesis and the sample data.

CPS data were tested for various values of λ. It was found that $\lambda = 0.20$ produced the lowest BJ value, 18.44. However, the corresponding P value[18] (0.0000989) value is so low that it is difficult to believe that the transformed earnings were generated from a normal distribution. For the Kolmogorov statistic, the D_I value is not in agreement with the BJ statistics. Once the sample observations were standardized, any difference in the tail area is difficult to detect by comparing accumulated distributions of the two distinct distributions. In comparison, BJ statistics should be more effective in detecting the difference in the tail area because skewness and kurtosis are sensitive to tail behavior.

[18] It is the smallest significance level at which the null hypothesis would be rejected. The lower the P value, the less agreement there will be between the null hypothesis and the sample data.

As a second example, consider a semiparametric transformation for the logarithm of earnings as stated in (3.8). To find the parameters $a_0, a_1, \cdots, a_N$, apply any numerical optimization method which minimizes the BJ statistics, but for simplicity, an OLS method was introduced so that the transformed values can be placed as closely as possible to the theoretical values defined in (3.16). In Table 3.2, the BJ statistics for various choices of expansion sizes were tabulated. The fourth order polynomial expansion produced the lowest BJ value, 0.132, and the highest P value, 0.936. However, the Kolmogorov statistics produced more or less similar values and did not work as well as a criterion.

When the expansion size in (3.18) is increased, the approximated values will be closer to the theoretical values x_i^0 in the mean squared error sense but this does not necessarily mean that the estimated third or fourth moments will be closer to those of the population density, the standard normal density. A small departure in the tail area will result in a large departure in moment estimation but a small departure near the central region will

Table 3.2. Normality Test for Polynomial Series Transformed Log Earnings of 1974 (I=1000)

N^a	BJ	P value	D_I
2	10.37	0.006	0.102
3	0.991	0.609	0.108
4	0.132	0.936	0.111
5	0.229	0.892	0.114
6	0.254	0.881	0.113
7	0.409	0.815	0.111
8	0.521	0.771	0.102

[a] N denotes the order of the polynomial series expansion in least squares approximation of

$$\min_{a_0, \cdots, a_n} \frac{1}{I} \sum_{i=1}^{I} \left[x_i^0 - \sum_{n=0}^{N} a_n (\ln y_i(t))^n \right]^2$$

result in a small departure in moment estimation. This variable weight effect can not be detected by examination of the mean squared errors.

In Tables 3.3 and 3.4, the procedures reported in Tables 3.1 and 3.2 for the 1990 data were reported. The $\lambda = 0.19$ and expansion size 4 produced the lowest BJ statistics. Another interesting feature is that the transformed

Table 3.3. Normality Test for Box−Cox Transformed Earnings, 1990 (I=1000)

λ	BJ	P value	D_I
0.15	18.05	0.000120	0.117
0.16	15.79	0.000372	0.116
0.17	14.28	0.000793	0.115
0.18	13.48	0.001181	0.113
0.19	13.37	0.001247	0.113
0.20	13.93	0.000940	0.114
0.21	15.14	0.000514	0.115
0.22	17.00	0.000204	0.116
0.23	19.48	0.000059	0.117
0.24	22.60	0.000012	0.118
0.25	27.35	0.000002	0.120

Table 3.4 Normality Test for Polynomial Series Transformed Log Earnings of 1990 (I=1000)

N	BJ	P value	D_I
2	6.510	0.039	0.116
3	0.670	0.705	0.124
4	0.021	0.989	0.126
5	0.085	0.958	0.130
6	0.177	0.915	0.128
7	0.395	0.821	0.127
8	0.754	0.686	0.120

logarithm of earnings for 1990 is much more closely distributed to a normal distribution than is the transformed logarithm of earnings for 1974.

Now to find the joint pdf of the logarithm of earnings and capability, the relationship between the logarithm of earnings and capability (x) is derived. The use can be extended for the equally spaced points in the logarithmic earnings coordinates. Given these equally spaced points $(\ln y)_u$ for u $=1, 2, \cdots I$, the corresponding vector of capability from the derived joint relationship can be estimated. Then we introduce normally distributed capability around these estimated values with a variance of σ^2. Using this conditional pdf of capability for a given logarithm of earnings, the joint pdf and the conditional pdf of logarithm of earnings for a given level of capability can be derived. The expected earnings level for various capability levels is then calculated. In Table 3.5, the expected earnings for a given capability level are reported. Actually, since the expected value of logarithmic earnings are derived, and its exponential value must be taken as indicated above, this value is a slightly different then expected earnings. In 1974, the expected earnings of an individual with mean capability $(z=0.0)$ is 9,323 dollars, but expected earnings for $x=1.0$ increased to 18,406 dollars, and for $x=2.0$ to 34,505 dollars. Therefore, earnings increase more rapidly as capability increases. More or less similar conclusions can be drawn for the negative x values. Returns decrease slowly as we move to lower x values so that expected earnings for $x=-1$, -2 and $x=-3$ are 3,992, 1,228, and 351 dollars respectively. In 1990, the fat tail effect increased so that expected earnings of the lowest capability level $(x=-3.0)$ doubled relative to 1974, but the expected earnings of the highest capability level $(x=+3.0)$ increased more than 3.2 times relative to 1974. This result suggests that one reason for the increasing trend in inequality has been the higher returns to the most able relative to the return to those with the highest capability levels in 1974.

3.3.2 A Loglinear Transformation without the Normality Assumption for Capability

For comparison, begin with the lognormal distribution of earnings, where

Table 3.5 Expected Earnings for an Individual with capability x

Capability	Earnings (1974)	Earnings (1990)	Capability	Earning (1974)	Earnings (1990)
−3.0	351	711	0.0	9323	24682
−2.9	386	812	0.1	10039	26830
−2.8	434	913	0.2	10749	28981
−2.7	491	1076	0.3	11544	31414
−2.6	553	1243	0.4	11384	34008
−2.5	631	1422	0.5	13271	36606
−2.4	722	1639	0.6	14153	39543
−2.3	820	1887	0.7	15134	42675
−2.2	938	2152	0.8	16127	45811
−3.1	1074	2471	0.9	17233	49358
−2.0	1228	2835	1.0	18406	53140
−1.9	1391	3223	1.1	19574	56928
−1.8	1599	3688	1.2	20890	61211
−1.7	1805	4212	1.3	22288	65779
−1.6	2034	4764	1.4	23684	70353
−1.5	2302	5417	1.5	25258	75524
−1.4	2579	6141	1.6	26932	81033
−1.3	2899	6889	1.7	28606	86545
−1.2	3246	7758	1.8	30495	92765
−1.1	3618	8704	1.9	32502	99378
−1.0	3992	9668	2.0	34505	105973
−0.9	4413	10772	2.1	36755	113387
−0.8	4860	11961	2.2	39129	121226
−0.7	5303	13160	2.3	41619	128990
−0.6	5801	14525	2.4	44060	137641
−0.5	6326	15985	2.5	46734	144686
−0.4	6845	17452	2.6	49306	165227
−0.3	7426	19114	2.7	52066	165225
−0.2	8038	20899	2.9	54822	175175
−0.1	8606	22669	2.9	57382	184700
			3.0	60037	194911

individual capability xi are random samples from the standard normal distribution. The least squares method produces

$$\log y(74) = 9.0484 + 0.9034x + u \qquad R^2 = 0.9503 \qquad (3.28)$$

$$\log y(90) = 10.021 + 0.986x + u \qquad R^2 = 0.9387 \qquad (3.29)$$

where two restrictions are imposed, the normality assumption for x and a loglinear transformation function from x to log y, and thus the produced R^2's are not very high.

In the following, the loglinear functional form assumption is maintained but remove the normality assumption for x. Using known values of mean and variance of x and observations of log y, the parameters of

$$\log y_i(t) = C(t) + D(t)x_i + u_i(t) \qquad (3.9)$$

can be estimated and thus the unobserved values of x can be established with

$$\hat{x}_i = \frac{\log y_i(t) - \hat{C}(t)}{\hat{D}(t)} \qquad (3.30)$$

Random samples using (3.30) for 1974 and 1990 are generated, and referred to as and x(74). The estimated sample moments, $\mu_n = \frac{1}{I}\sum_{i=1}^{I} x_i^n$, are

$\mu_1(74) = 0.0000$	$\mu_1(90) = 0.0000$
$\mu_2(74) = 1.0966$	$\mu_2(90) = 0.9162$
$\mu_3(74) = -0.8422$	$\mu_3(90) = -0.6485$
$\mu_4(74) = 5.2627$	$\mu_4(90) = 3.7871$

The sample moments for 1974 and 1990 are not the same because the generated samples were established assuming the error term u=0. There are various statistical methods to test the identical distribution assumption for samples x(74) and x(90), the following cross regression functions are reported.

$$\log y_i(74) = 9.0506 + 0.8729x_i(74) + u_i \qquad R^2 = 1.000 \qquad (3.31)$$

$$\log y_i(74) = 9.0506 + 0.9527 x_i(90) + u_i \qquad R^2 = 0.9953 \qquad (3.32)$$

$$\log y_i(90) = 10.023 + 0.9526 x_i(74) + u_i \qquad R^2 = 0.9953 \qquad (3.33)$$

$$\log y_i(90) = 10.023 + 1.0450 x_i(90) + u_i \qquad R^2 = 1.000 \qquad (3.34)$$

The regression (3.31) is meaningless because it was established that the x samples from (3.30) is equivalent to (3.31) with $u_i = 0$. In (3.32), the logarithm of earnings for 1974 is regressed with capability established using 1990 data. If capability is time independent, then (3.32) would be expected to produce high R^2 value.

This subsection can be concluded with the following remarks. First, the x samples generated by (3.30) are more or less similar for 1974 and 1990 so that cross regression functions (3.32) and (3.33) produced high R^2 values though observed earnings and capability belonged to different years. Second, the loglinear regression functions with normally distributed capability, (3.28) and (3.29), are so restrictive that if we remove the normality assumption maintaining the loglinear functional form, then the regression functions, (3. 31) to (3.34), produced larger R^2's values compared to (3.28) to (3.29). Third, even without observations, a regression function could be established and a measure of inequality of earnings could be determined with the magnitude of the slope of x. Comparison of (3.31) and (3.34) shows that a small increase in capability will yield a larger increase in earnings in 1990 relative to 1974.

3.4 Summary and Concluding Remarks

One argument that has been suggested for why inequality has increased is that as the U.S. has become an increasingly technical society (the shift from a manufacturing based economy to an information based economy), the returns to high skill workers have increased over time while the returns to low skill workers have declined; see Levy and Murnane (1992). This chapter has attempted such a "pure" mapping without proxying other factors. The results indicated that the returns to capability have increased to the most skilled. These results are consistent with the findings of other researchers. The consequence being that this model predicts more expected inequality should have been the case over time.

Since capability is an hypothetical variable which can not be observed, it is assumed that each individual is embodied with a large number of attributes and capability was defined as a weighted average of these attributes. The notion that capability can be shown to be normally distributed under certain assumptions was discussed. Once the distribution of capability is specified, the transformation function can be approximated with a semiparametric polynomial series. However, if the distribution of capability is not specified, the transformation function can not be determined. Therefore, a loglinear function was assumed and capability was approximated using observed earnings and the loglinear function.

Appendix 3.A : Derivation of an Earnings Distribution with Maximum Entropy Method

Here consider the use of the maximum entropy method to estimate the logarithm of the earnings distribution. See Zellner and Highfield (1988) and Ryu (1993) for details of this method. For a given set of side conditions, the functional form of a density by choosing an ME density function can be determined. A maximum entropy density function method is introduced because entropy is a measure of lack of information, the distribution of maximum entropy is the least informative and most conservative distribution while distributions of lower entropy are more informative. Define a maximum entropy distribution as a solution to:

$$f(y)=\exp\left[\sum_{n=0}^{N} c_n y^n\right] \quad \text{satisfying} \quad \int y^m f(y)dy=\mu_m, \quad m=0,1,\cdots,N. \tag{3.A.1}$$

The unknown constants C_n's can be computed from known values of μ_m. Furthermore, Ryu (1993) demonstrated that parameter estimation becomes easier if we have more knowledge of moments $\mu_0, \cdots, \mu_{2N}$. Theorem 1 of Ryu (1993) states that the first parameter C_0 is a normalization constant but the remaining parameters $C=\{C_1, \cdots, C_N\}$ can be determined from the following relationship.

$$Bc = d \Rightarrow c = B^{-1}d \tag{3.A.2}$$

where the $N \times N$ square matrix B and the $N \times 1$ vector d are defined as follows. If $y \in (-\infty, +\infty)$ or $y \in [0, +\infty)$, we define

$$B_{mn} \equiv mn\mu_{m+n} \qquad \textit{and} \qquad d_m = -m(m+1)\mu_m$$

where m, n = 1, ⋯, N. Since B is a positive definite matrix, (3.A.2) determines $\{C_1, \cdots, C_N\}$ and C_0 can be found by normalization of the pdf. Here, knowledge of $\mu_0, \cdots, \mu_{2N}$ is assumed. When maximum entropy estimation is applied to derive the unknown earnings distribution, several interesting features can be noted :

$$f(y) = \exp\left[\sum_{n=0}^{4} c_n y^n\right] = \exp\left[\sum_{n=0}^{2} c_n y^n\right] \cdot \exp\left[\sum_{n=3}^{4} c_n y^n\right]$$

If C_2 is negative, the first part corresponds to a normal distribution while the second part corresponds to a filter which modifies the shape of the first part. If interest lies in the distribution of the logarithm of earnings, then

$$f(Y) = \exp\left[\sum_{n=0}^{4} d_n Y^n\right] = \exp\left[\sum_{n=0}^{2} d_n Y^n\right] \cdot \exp\left[\sum_{n=3}^{4} d_n Y^n\right] \tag{3.A.3}$$

where $Y \equiv \log y$. The logarithm of earnings was considered rather than just earnings because the range of the RHS variable can then be extended from $[0, +\infty)$ to $(-\infty, +\infty)$. The first part of the RHS of (3.A.3) corresponds to the lognormal distribution while the second part corresponds to a modification to it.

Chapter 4

Some New Functional Forms For Approximating Lorenz Curves[19]

4.1 Introduction

This chapter introduces two flexible functional form approaches to approximate Lorenz curves. The first approach expands the inverse function of an income distribution in an exponential polynomial series and derives the Lorenz curve from it. The required convexity condition can be imposed using a Bayesian method. The second approach approximates the Lorenz curve with a sequence of Bernstein polynomial functions. The required convexity condition is automatically established in this approach. We compare these approaches with another well known fixed functional form approaches. We evaluate the performance of these functional forms by comparing approximation errors, maximum error, and the estimates of the Gini coefficient produced by various approaches.

Thus, there are two major contributions of this chapter, the flexibility of the forms used provide a good fit to actual empirical income graduations and the forms introduced here are well behaved with respect to their theoretical properties vis á vis the theoretical Lorenz curve.

The specification problem for the Lorenz curve has been analyzed in the income distribution literature. There is a rich literature on the construction of distribution-free statistical Lorenz curve which have been used to analyze the welfare implications of Atkinson's (1970) notion of Lorenz dominance. This work has been very competently done by Beach and Davidson (1983), Beach and Richmond (1985), Bishop et al. (1989), Bishop et al. (1991) and Gastwirth and Gail (1985). The problem with this work, however, is that it has focused on Lorenz ordinates for quintiles, deciles, etc., in a quest

[19] This chapter follows Ryu and Slottje (1996a).

for "crossings" which yield information about welfare change. As such, it does not consider the shape of the entire Lorenz curve, but rather, only provides information about discrete piece-wise segments.

Other researchers have introduced various parametric functional forms to approximate Lorenz curves, but this previous work has provided relatively little motivation or explanation of how these specific functional forms were derived, cf. Kakwani and Podder (1973, 1976) and Basmann et al. (BHJS, 1990), Arnold (1983, 1986, 1987), Arnold et al. (1987), Dagum (1980), and Villasenor and Arnold (1989). This work is surveyed in Ryu and Slottje (1996b). They reported that specific functional forms approximate unknown income distributions well for a particular set of data, but it is not at all clear why the same functional form should fit well for another set of data. Ryu and Slottje (1996b) discuss this in considerable detail. For example, the empirical income distribution of Brazil is very different from that of Japan,[20] and a fixed functional form method may not be an appropriate approach unless the precise nature of the data are known. As Basmann et al. (1990) noted, some functional forms used to approximate Lorenz curves will fit well at the tails but not over the middle portions of the empirical distribution, while other forms have the opposite problem. In addition, the BHJS form may violate theoretical properties of the Lorenz curve.

In this chapter, we introduce two flexible functional form approaches to approximation Lorenz curves, an exponential polynomial expansion and a Bernstein polynomial expansion. Since both approaches provide global consistency under certain conditions, these forms will fit the empirical Lorenz curve well over all ranges of income for large samples of observations. These forms do not violate theoretical properties of the Lorenz curve, as their predecessors do and these forms provide multidimensional improvement in approximating Lorenz curves.

An obvious question is why should a researcher be interested in approximating the Lorenz curve at all when the Lorenz curve can be calculated di-

---

[20] World Development Report (1990) shows the upper 10 per cent of Brazil income earners get 50.6 per cent of total income while the same 10 per cent of income earners in Japan get only 22.4 percent of income.

rectly from the empirical data? There are several reasons to do so. Suppose you have 65,000+ observations of income receiving units (as we do for 1990 CPS data). It is now possible to graphically represent this information quite well with all these thousands of data points with modern personal computers with immense computing power. The problem still remains, however, as to how to describe these empirical Lorenz curve mathematically and statistically and how to summarize the inequality inherent in these empirical Lorenz curves.

If we can summarize 65,100+ observations (1990 CPS data) with an exponential series using four numbers (see Poly L4(z) in Table 4.1), and if the Lorenz curve derived from these numbers approximates the empirical Lorenz curve very well, then our parametric representation is certainly parsimonious and worthwhile. The usefulness of using the approximation will also be shown in the construction of inequality measures. We provide several justifications why the flexible functional form we have chosen to approximate the Lorenz curve is appropriate in the discussion to follow.

As an alternative way to approximate the unknown Lorenz curve, we apply Bernstein polynomials which were introduced by Bernstein in a different application. He introduced this class of polynomials to give a simple proof of the approximation theorem of Weierstrass. A through discussion of this polynomial can be found in Lorenz(1986). We can interpret the Bernstein polynomials as a special case of kernel estimation where the value of the kernel is constant within the interval but jumps as we move from one interval to the next. Two useful features of this approach are global consistency and the automatic establishment of the concavity or convexity restriction. If the underlying function f(z) is continuous in the whole interval [0, 1], then the Bernstein polynomial Bn(z), which will be defined later, converges uniformly to f(z) is convex (or concave), then Bn(z) will be convex (or concave).

An overview of the chapter is as follows. In Section 4.2, an exponential polynomial functional form is formally introduced and in Section 4.3 the Bernstein polynomial is defined and its properties are explained. We applied the above two approaches to U.S. Current Population Survey data and family income data for Korea, and reported the performance of these approaches as well as the well known approaches in section 4.4. Concluding remarks are presented in Section 4.5.

4.2 A Flexible Lorenz Curve with Exponential Polynomials

Let us review Gastwirth's (1971) derivation of the Lorenz curve. See Slottje (1989) for a review of this topic and related discussions. We formally introduce the flexible form Lorenz curve, and provide some justification for using an exponential polynomial form to approximate the inverse distribution function. The Lorenz curve can be derived as a function of the cumulative distribution function, F(X), where X is the random variate representing income and x is a given value of X. Let

$$z \equiv F(x) = \int_0^x f(x')dx'$$

and define the inverse distribution function as

$$F^{-1} \equiv \operatorname*{Inf}_{x}\{x\,;\ F(x) \geqq z\} \tag{4.1}$$

This equation implies that the minimum value of x is chosen so that $F(x) \geqq z$ and insures the existence of F(x). For all values of F(x) we define the Lorenz curve as

$$L(z) \equiv \frac{1}{\mu}\int_0^z F^{-1}(z')dz' \qquad \text{for} \qquad z \in [0, 1] \tag{4.2}$$

where $\mu = \int_x xf(x)dx.$

We have defined a Lorenz curve L(z) as a function of z.

If the distribution function, F(x) is a strictly increasing function of x, the inverse distribution function $x(z) = [F^{-1}(z)]$ is a non negative continuous function of z, we can approximate it with an exponential polynomial series. The exponential polynomial approach is simple to use and was shown in another application to be very useful in approximating unknown probability density functions.[21] Motivated by the strong performance of this approach, we can expand the inverse function of a statistical income distribution function in an exponential polynomial series and derive its Lorenz curve.[22]

$$x(z)=\exp\left[\sum_{n=0}^{\infty}\beta_n z^n\right]=\exp\left[\sum_{n=0}^{N}\beta_n z^n\right]+\varepsilon'(z) \tag{4.3}$$

where N is the order of the polynomial series. Thus from (4.2),

$$\begin{aligned} L(z) &\equiv \frac{1}{\mu}\int_0^z F^{-1}(z')dz' \\ &= \frac{1}{\mu}\int_0^z \exp\left[\sum_{n=0}^{N}\beta_n z'^n\right]dz' + \eta(z) \quad \text{for} \quad z\in[0,1] \end{aligned} \tag{4.4}$$

Therefore, we are approximating the Lorenz curve with

$$L^N(z)=\frac{1}{\mu}\int_0^z \exp\left[\sum_{n=0}^{N}\beta_n z'^n\right]dz' \quad \text{for} \quad z\in[0,1] \tag{4.5}$$

Until now we have assumed knowledge of the true Lorenz curve and existence of the underlying parameter determination method in (4.3) for the given Lorenz curve. In the following, we remove the assumption that we have a priori knowledge of the true Lorenz curve.

4.3 Approximation of the Empirical Lorenz Curve

Suppose we have a sample from a population having a continuous c.d.f. F(x) where x is income. Let this sample be rearranged in order from lowest to greatest values and let the ordered values be $(x_{(0)}, \cdots, x_{(I)})$ where I is the sample size. Let us approximate the Logarithm of $x_{(i)}$ with a power

---

[21] See Zellner and Highfield (1988) and Ryu (1993) for a justification of introducing the exponential polynomial functional form for a probability density function.

[22] The inverse function of an income distribution function can also be considered as another distribution function if the range of income is rescaled to [0, 1]. Since a distribution function is much smoother than a density function, if a certain flexible functional form is found to be useful for describing a density function, then this same functional form can be useful in describing a distribution function, too.

series,

$$\log x_{(i)} = \sum_{n=0}^{N} \beta_n z_i^n + \xi_i \quad \text{where} \quad z_i = 0,\ 1/I,\ 2/I,\ \cdots,\ 1 \qquad (4.6)$$

We use the least squares method to estimate the parameters of (4.6).[23] Let the approximated income of the jth poorest person be

$$\hat{x}(z_j) = \exp\left[\sum_{n=0}^{n} \hat{\beta}_n z_j^n\right]$$

To plot the Lorenz curve, the percentages of the population arranged from the poorest to the richest are represented on the horizontal axis and the percentages of income enjoyed by the bottom z fraction of the population are shown on the vertical axis.

$$\hat{L}(z_i) = \frac{1}{I\hat{\mu}} \sum_{j=0}^{i} \hat{x}(z_i) = \frac{1}{I\hat{u}} \sum_{j=0}^{i} \exp\left[\sum_{n=0}^{N} \hat{\beta}_n z_j^n\right]$$

where $\hat{\mu}$ is the estimated mean income. If we consider the normalization constant L(z=1)=1,

$$\hat{L}(z_i) = C \sum_{j=0}^{i} \exp[\hat{\beta}_0 + \hat{\beta}_1 z_j + \hat{\beta}_2 z_j^2 + \cdots + \hat{\beta}_N z_j^N] \qquad (4.7)$$

where C is determined from the normalization condition. The remaining portion of this section is devoted to provide some justification for deriving the Lorenz curve by the above method (4.6) and (4.7).

4.4 A Comparison of Two Alternative Derivations of the Lorenz Curves

Consider the following two equivalent derivations of the Lorenz curves,

---

[23] This is essentially a curve fitting exercise and the least squares method is widely used. For efficient parameter estimation, the generalized least squares method can be used if the structure of the covariance matrix is known. However, the difference will be negligible when the observed sample size is large.

Approach 1 :

$$L(z) \equiv \frac{1}{\mu}\int_0^z F^{-1}(z')dz' \tag{4.2}$$

$$= \frac{1}{\mu}\int_0^z \exp\left[\sum_{n=0}^{N} \beta_n z'^n\right]dz' + \eta(z) \quad \text{for} \quad z \in [0, 1] \tag{4.4}$$

Approach 2 :

$$L(z) \equiv \frac{1}{\mu}\int_0^{F^{-1}(z)} xf(x)dx \quad \text{for} \quad x \in [0, +\infty) \tag{4.2'}$$

$$z \equiv F(x) = \int_0^x f(x')dx'$$

where $\mu = \int_x xf(x)dx$. The density f(x) can be found using standard density estimation methods, e.g., a nonparametric kernel estimation method.

The two definitions (4.2) and (4.2') are equivalent and each can be obtained from the other using a Jacobian transformation $dz = f(x)dx$ and $x = F^{-1}(z)$. In the following, we provide two reasons why the first approach is preferred to the second approach. Suppose observed income x ranges from one dollar to one million dollars, but most of the observations are in the middle income region (between five thousand and a hundred thousand dollars) with very few observations in the tail areas. In particular, there will be very few observations in the far right tail. Thus, density estimation in both tails will not be accurate whatever method we may use. In particular, the Lorenz curve derived by the second approach may not be very accurate. In the first approach, we consider an inverse distribution function as another distribution function which is monotonic and smoother than the income density function. By introducing the logarithm of the income observations, log x(z) is a monotonic increasing function from zero to 14 for the domain of $z \in [0, 1]$ and this function can be approximated well with a polynomial series. Another reason why we prefer the first approach to the second approach is its notational convenience. The parametric functional forms such as (4.4) and (4.7) are easy to describe. All we need is to report a few numbers and the functional form of the Lorenz curve. In comparison, if we apply a nonparametric density estimation method as in the second approach, we cannot summarize the Lorenz curve with a few numbers so that it is costly to describe the same Lorenz curve.

4.5 Choosing an Exponential Series Expansion Rather Than a Plain Series Expansion

We have introduced an exponential series expansion (4.3) to expand the inverse distribution function, $x(z)=F^{-1}(z)$, rather than using a plain series of the following form,

$$x(z)=\sum_{n=0}^{N} c_n z^n + \Psi(z) \tag{4.8}$$

There are three reasons for this choice. First, the former expansion performs better than the latter expansion. The range of $x(z)$ is so diverse, (the income of poor people is relatively negligible compared to that of the rich people), that the functional form given in (4.8) will be dominated by income of the rich people (near $z=1$) and it will be difficult to describe small change of $x(z)$ for small z values near zero. Second, positivity of estimated income is guaranteed in (4.6) but not in (4.8). Third, when we choose $N=2$ in (4.3), we get a normal distribution for the share function. To show this, define a share function as

$$s(z_i)=x(z_i)/\sum_{i=0}^{I} x(z_i) \qquad \text{for} \qquad z_i=0,\ 1/I,\ 2/I,\ \cdots,\ 1$$

We interpret the share function as a probability density function because the share $s(z_i)$ is the probability associated with the probability density that each dollar of total measured income will end up in the ith group. Since each individual has different attributes and a different locational position, some people will collect more money than others. Each dollar bill will end up in the hand of the ith individual with probability $s(z_i)$ so that this share function can be considered as a discrete pdf. We get a normal distribution for the share function when we consider the series up to the second order, $\log s(z)=b_0+b_1z+b_2z^2$. Therefore (4.3) can be considered as an Nth

order extension of the normal distribution.

4.6 About Expanding the Inverse Distribution Rather Than a Lorenz Curve in a Series

If we expand the Lorenz Curve in a series, we have

$$L(z_i)=a_0+a_1 z_i+\cdots+a_N z_i^N+\xi_i \tag{4.9}$$

However, we avoid this because a Lorenz curve can be obtained from the inverse distribution function F^{-1}, but this function can not be derived from a Lorenz curve. Furthermore, there is no guarantee that the estimated Lorenz curve $L(z_i)$ will be nonnegative. Many summary measures such as the Gini coefficient, Theil's entropy measure, and Atkinson's inequality measure, can be obtained directly from the inverse distribution function, but only the Gini coefficient can be obtained directly from the Lorenz curve and then it is still only an approximation.

4.7 Orthonormal Basis Expansion for Discrete Ordered Income Observations

In this section, we provide some justification for using a polynomial series expansion. Suppose we have a sample from a population having a continuous monotone increasing c.d.f. $F(x)$. Let this sample be rearranged in order from lowest to greatest and let the ordered values be $\{x_{(0)}, x_{(1)}, \cdots, x_{(I)}\}$.

Let us consider discrete Legendre polynomial series. Milne (1973, p.267) introduced a sequence of functions for $i=0, 1, \cdots, I$,

$$Q_{j,I}(i)=\sum_{m=0}^{j}(-1)^m\binom{j}{m}\binom{j+m}{m}\frac{i^{(m)}}{I^{(m)}} \tag{4.10}$$

where $i^{(m)}=i(i-1)\cdots(i-m+1)$. For $j=0, 1, 2, \cdots, I$, we get simple polynomial functions.[24] The orthogonality of these polynomials is

[24] The first three polynomials explicityly written out,

$$Q_{0,I}(i)=1,$$
$$Q_{1,I}(i)=1-2i/I,$$
$$Q_{2,I}(i)=1-6i/I+6i(i-1)/I(I-1), \text{ etc.}$$

$$\sum_{i=0}^{I} Q_{j,I}(i) Q_{k,I}(i) = 0 \qquad \text{if} \qquad j \neq k \tag{4.11}$$

and normalization constant is

$$c_j^2 \equiv \sum_{i=0}^{I} Q^2_{j,I}(i) = \frac{(I+j+1)(j+I)^{(j)}}{(2j+1)I^{(j)}} \tag{4.12}$$

Then a discrete orthonormal bases is defined as

$$P_{j,I}(i) = Q_{j,I}(i)/c_j \tag{4.13}$$

Therefore, $\sum_{i=0}^{I} P_{j,I}(i) P_{k,I}(i) = \delta_{jk}$ where $\delta_{jk} = 1$ if $j = k$ and zero otherwise. Now we rewrite log $x(0)$, log $x(1)$, $\cdots$, log $x(\mathrm{I})$ with an Ith order Legendre polynomial series,

$$\log x_{(i)} = \sum_{j=0}^{I} a_{jI} P_{j,I}(i) \qquad \text{for} \qquad i = 0, 1, \cdots, I \tag{4.14}$$

where

$$a_{j\mathrm{I}} = (a_{jI})_{ONB} \equiv \sum_{i=0}^{I} P_{j,I}(i) \log x_{(i)} \tag{4.15}$$

Therefore, the knowledge of log x(0), $\cdots$, log x(I) is equivalent to knowledge of $a_{0\mathrm{I}}$, $\cdots$, a_{II}. Now let us approximate (4.14) with an Nth order Legendre polynomial series where N is less than I,

$$\log x_{(i)} = \sum_{j=0}^{N} a_{jI} P_{j,I}(i) + \varepsilon(i) \tag{4.16}$$

where L^2 convergence of

$$\log x_i^N = \sum_{j=0}^{N} a_{jI} P_{j,I}(i)$$

to log $x_{(\mathrm{i})}$ is

$$\sum_{i=0}^{I} |\log x_{(i)} - \log x_{(i)}^N|^2 = \sum_{i=0}^{I} \left| \sum_{j=N+1}^{I} a_{jI} P_{j,I}(i) \right|^2 = \sum_{j=N+1}^{I} a_{jI}^2 \tag{4.17}$$

As we increase the number of terms, sum of squared error decreases monotonically.

In the following, we show that the parameter estimation method by the orthnormal basis method (4.15) is equivalent to the least squares method applied to (4.16). To show this, define a matrix

$$X=\begin{bmatrix} P_{0,I}(0) & P_{1,I}(0) & \cdots & P_{N,I}(0) \\ P_{0,I}(1) & P_{1,I}(1) & \cdots & P_{N,I}(1) \\ \vdots & \vdots & \vdots & \vdots \\ P_{0,I}(I) & P_{1,I}(I) & \cdots & P_{N,I}(I) \end{bmatrix} \tag{4.18}$$

Using the orthogonality condition

$$[X'X]_{jk}=\delta_{jk} \tag{4.19}$$

Therefore, apply the least squares method on (4.16),

$$(\hat{a}_{jI})_{LS}=[(X'X)^{-1}X\log x_{(i)}]_j=(a_{ij})_{ONB} \tag{4.20}$$

and the least squares parameters are equivalent to the ONB determined parameters defined on (4.15).

Furthermore, note that Legendre series expansion is equivalent to a power series expansion. By regrouping terms of the Legendre series, we can rewrite it in a power series.

$$\log x_{(i)}=\sum_{j=0}^{I} b_{jI}(i)^j=\sum_{j=0}^{N} b_{jI}(i)^j+\eta(i) \tag{4.21}$$

Until now, we have shown that the model estimated values converges to the observed values at discrete points (z_0, $\cdots$, z_I) as we increase the size of series expansion in (4.21). Our concern is derivation of empirical Lorenz curve at discrete point (z_0, $\cdots$, z_I) as stated in (4.7), but not derivation of the continuous Lorenz curve L(z) which converges to the true Lorenz curve at all points of z=[0, 1]. To establish convergence of the continuous Lorenz curve, we need to impose certain restriction on N with respect to I when I goes to infinity. The details are left as a future research work.

We now summarize the result of this section. We represented a Lorenz curve using a parametric representation method. Though accurate, listing a large number of points on the empirical Lorenz curve, $\hat{L}(z_1)$, $\cdots$, $\hat{L}(z_I)$, is costly, thus we have expanded the logarithm of the inverse distribution function in a polynomial series (4.6) and estimated the parameters of this function with the least squares method. We showed that the estimated Lorenz curve converges globally to the unknown true Lorenz curve in the discrete case.

4.8 A Flexible Lorenz Curve with Bernstein Polynomials

As an alternative way to approximate the empirical Lorenz curve, we expand it in a Bernstein polynomial series. First, we introduce the definition and properties of the Bernstein polynomials. A thorough discussion of this polynomial can be found in Lorenz (1986). For a function L(z) defined on the population coordinate z= [0, 1] the expression

$$B_I(z) \equiv \sum_{\nu=0}^{I} L\left(\frac{\nu}{I}\right)\binom{\nu}{I} z^{\nu}(1-z)^{I-\nu} \tag{4.22}$$

is called the Bernstein polynomial of order I of the function L(z). If L(z) is continuous on [0,1], then we can prove

$$\lim_{I \to \infty} B_I(z) = L(z) \tag{4.23}$$

uniformly[25] in [0,1].

The Bernstein polynomials can be interpreted by the following discussion. The Lorenz curve is defined as an accumulated sum of shares of those whose position in the population coordinate is less than or equal to z. Then the Bernstein's polynomial is the sample correspondence of the Lorenz curve. In particular we can say $B_I(z)$ is the expected value of the accumulated share of those whose position is less than or equal to Z. Suppose we

---

[25] If the function L is bounded, say $|L(z)| \leqq M$ in $0 \leqq z \leqq 1$ and x a point of continutiy, for a given $\varepsilon > 0$ we can find a $\delta > 0$ such that $|z - z'| < \delta$ implies $|L(z) - L(z')| < \varepsilon$. Lorenz(1986) shows

$$|B_I(z) - L(z)| \leqq \varepsilon + M(2I\delta^2)^{-1} < 2\varepsilon \quad \text{as} \quad I \to \infty$$

If L(z) is continuous in [0, 1], then the above inequality hold with a δ independent of x, so that $B_I \to L$ uniformly.

choose a value z, then there exists a corresponding income level, $x = F^{-1}(z)$. When we choose I independent samples from the c.d.f. F(x), the probability of finding ν persons whose incomes are below x is $\binom{I}{\nu} z^{\nu}(1-z)^{I-\nu}$.

However, the accumulated share of ν persons out of the population size I, is defined a $L(\nu/I)$. Therefore, when we find ν persons will be $L(\nu/I)\binom{I}{\nu} z^{\nu}(1-z)^{I-\nu}$, and $B_I(z)$ is the expected value of the accumulated share of those whose position is less than or equal to z. To derive an empirical Lorenz curve, we replace the true Lorenz curve values $L(\nu/I)$ with observed empirical Lorenz curve values, $\hat{L}(\nu/I)$.

The motivation for introducing the Bernstein polynomials is to provide a simple way to approximate a Lorenz curve for all z values. At discrete points, the empirical Lorenz curve is defined as $\hat{L}(z_1)$, $\cdots$ $\hat{L}(z_I)$, but there is no systematic way to interpolate for the values of z between z_i and z_{i+1}. For example, if we have, then (4.22) provides a simple systematic way to represent L(z) for all z. In what follows, we discuss properties of the Bernstein polynomials. Suppose we wish to write (4.22) in the form of a Stieltjes integral in the variable t,

$$B_I(z) = \int_0^1 L(t) d_t K_I(z, t) \tag{4.24}$$

with the kernel

$$K_I(z, t) = \sum_{\nu \leqq It}^{I} \binom{I}{\nu} z^{\nu}(1-z)^{I-\nu} \tag{4.25}$$

which is constant over any interval $\nu/I \leqq t \leqq (\nu+1)/I$, $\nu = 0, 1, \cdots, I-1$, and has a discrete jump

$$\binom{I}{\nu} z^{\nu}(1-z)^{I-\nu} \tag{4.26}$$

at the basic point of interpolation $t = \nu/I$.

Derivatives of the Bernstein polynomials can be found by differentiation. If differentiated k times, we have[26]

$$B_I^{(k)}(z)=I(I-1)\cdots(I-k+1)\sum_{k=1}^{I-k}\Delta^k l\left(\frac{\nu}{I}\right)\binom{I-k}{\nu}z^{\nu}(1-z)^{I-\nu-k} \tag{4.27}$$

where k=1, 2, $\cdots$, I and the function L(z) at $z=\nu/I$ is

$$\Delta^k L(z)\equiv L\left(z+\frac{k}{I}\right)-\binom{k}{1}L\left(z+\frac{k-1}{1}\right)+\cdots+(-1)^k L(z).$$

The importance of the Bernstein polynomials can be shown in the following discussion. In most flexible functional form approaches, global convergence can be established under certain conditions but imposition of an economic restriction such as concavity (or convexity) adds another additional complicated issue. In comparison, both global convergence and concavity (or convexity) are established in the Bernstein polynomial approach. If L(z) increases monotonically and satisfies concavity (or convexity), then (4.27) shows that $B_I(z)$ also increases monotonically and satisfies concavity (or convexity). We now demonstrate the usefulness of these flexible functional forms relative to previous parametric forms and evaluate the performance of our forms relative to these other forms.

In sections 2 and 3, we have introduced two globally flexible functional form approaches and these approaches can be compared with other existing fixed functional form approaches. In comparison, Basmann et al. (1990) and Kakwani and Podder (1973) have introduced a nonlinear functional form to approximate the empirical Lorenz curve. Later, we shall come back to these functions and compare the performance of our method to these

---

[26] If k=1, we obtain

$$\begin{aligned}B_I^{(1)}(z)&=\sum_{\nu=0}^{I}L\left(\frac{\nu}{I}\right)\binom{I}{\nu}\{\nu z^{\nu-1}(1-z)^{I-\nu}\\&\qquad\qquad-(I-\nu)z^{\nu}(1-z)^{I-\nu-1}\}\\&=I\sum_{\nu=0}^{I-1}\left\{L\left(\frac{\nu+1}{I}\right)-L\left(\frac{\nu}{I}\right)\right\}\binom{I-1}{\nu}z^{\nu}(1-z)^{I-\nu-1}\end{aligned}$$

Here $L((\nu+1)/I)-L(\nu/I)$ is the first order difference $\Delta L(\nu/I)$ of the function L(z) evaluated at $z=\nu/I$.

nonlinear parametric forms. There are other related approaches. Beach and Davidson (1983) derived the full variance–covariance structure of the asymptotic normal distribution of a vector of Lorenz curve ordinates. This approach is useful for certain objectives but not directly applicable for derivation of a global Lorenz curve. McDonald (1984) established income density functions based on two generalized beta distributions which include many descriptive models as special or limiting cases. He wanted to show the relationship between various parametric functional forms of hypothetical statistical densities but not to look for a globally well approximating functional form for the Lorenz curve.

4.9 Applications with Actual Data

In this section, we perform four tests to illustrate the usefulness of the exponential polynomial approach (Poly) and the Bernstein approach (Bern) in approximating the empirical Lorenz curve compared to other approaches such as BHJS and Kakwani and Podder's (1973) specification. In the first test, we apply U.S. Current Population Survey (CPS) data for individual income. In the second test, we utilized U.S. cross sectional family income of 1977 also utilized in the study by Basmann et al. (1990). In the third test, we used Korean cross sectional family income data for 1988 surveyed by the Korean Development Institute (KDI). In the fourth test, we generated random samples from a Lognormal distribution, a Gamma distribution, and a Generalized Beta distribution to test the performance of various approximating approaches.

Let us begin with the first test with the U.S. CPS data for individual income. Neglecting very low income observations, we used 65,100 observations ranging from \$159 to \$410,998. The performance of model is evaluated by comparison of model estimation errors at various points, the maximum error criterion, and by examining the Gini coefficient. Model estimation errors are defined as the differences between the model estimated values and the actual empirical Lorenz curve values. The maximum error means the maximum absolute value of the model estimation error, and the Gini coefficient is well known.

Now let us apply (4.14) and (4.15) for the ordered logarithm of income observations. Then choosing an eighth order polynomial series,i

$$\log x^8{}_{(i)} = 2557P_{0,I}(i) - 232.3P_{1,I}(i) - 34.97P_{2,I}(i) - 47.12P_{3,I}(i) - 11.95P_{4,I}(i) - 24.40P_{5,I}(i) - 10.20P_{6,I}(i) - 16.79P_{7,I}(i) \quad (4.28)$$

L^2 Convergence is discussed in (4.17). Compare

$$\sum_{i=0}^{I} |\log x_{(i)}|^2 = \sum_{j=0}^{I} a_{jI}^2 = 6{,}601{,}871 \quad (4.29)$$

with

$$\sum_{j=0}^{1} a_{jI}^2 = 6{,}596{,}796 \qquad \sum_{j=0}^{2} a_{jI}^2 = 6{,}598{,}019$$

$$\sum_{j=0}^{3} a_{jI}^2 = 6{,}600{,}239 \qquad \sum_{j=0}^{4} a_{jI}^2 = 6{,}600{,}382$$

$$\sum_{j=0}^{5} a_{jI}^2 = 6{,}600{,}978 \qquad \sum_{j=0}^{6} a_{jI}^2 = 6{,}601{,}082 \quad (4.30)$$

$$\sum_{j=0}^{7} a_{jI}^2 = 6{,}601{,}363$$

We have shown how to approximate $\log x$ with the ONB expansion and the sum of squared residual decreases as we increase the size of the series expansion. The results of estimation is summarized in Table 4.1. The first column shows the population index z=[0, 1]. If z=0.2, it represents the 20th poorest percentile out of the 100. Similarly, if z=0.9, it represents the 10th richest percentile out of the 100. The second column shows the empirical Lorenz curve. The third column shows the estimated Lorenz curve derived with (4.6) and (4.7). The notation for L4, L6, and L8 means the series in (4.3) includes 4, 6, and 8 parameters. The importance of the parametric representation of the Lorenz curve comes from its convenience in representation. Instead of reporting 65,100 points of the empirical Lorenz curve, we may report only a_0, a_1, $\cdots$, a_7 where a_0 is a normalization constant. The estimated Lorenz curve based upon the third exponential series produced fairly good performance with maximum departure of 0.0135. For the fifth order polynomial series expansion and the seventh order polynomial series expansion, maximum departures are 0.0069 and

Table 4.1 Sample Fitted Lorenz Curve Based on CPS Data[a] (1990)

Z	Empirical L(z)	Poly L4(Z)[b]	Poly L6(z)	Poly L8(z)	Bern10 L(z)[c]	Bern20 L(z)	Bern100 L(z)
0.10	0.0122	0.0109	0.0108	0.0119	0.0183	0.0152	0.0128
0.20	0.0379	0.0345	0.0384	0.0389	0.0489	0.0433	0.0390
0.30	0.0770	0.0749	0.0791	0.0760	0.0925	0.0846	0.0784
0.40	0.1303	0.1328	0.1306	0.1295	0.1500	0.1400	0.1322
0.50	0.1996	0.2062	0.1971	0.2014	0.2231	0.2111	0.2019
0.60	0.2870	0.2936	0.2852	0.2881	0.3141	0.3000	0.2896
0.70	0.3956	0.3967	0.3984	0.3938	0.4268	0.4101	0.3984
0.80	0.5311	0.5252	0.5350	0.5318	0.5683	0.5476	0.5341
0.90	0.7602	0.7040	0.7038	0.7082	0.7514	0.7280	0.7100
0.91	0.7272	0.7266	0.7243	0.7284	0.7728	0.7497	0.7311
0.92	0.7491	0.7503	0.7460	0.7495	0.7948	0.7723	0.7531
0.93	0.7721	0.7754	0.7690	0.7716	0.8176	0.7959	0.7762
0.94	0.7962	0.8019	0.7936	0.7949	0.8411	0.8206	0.8005
0.95	0.8218	0.8299	0.8202	0.8200	0.8654	0.8465	0.8263
0.96	0.8493	0.8597	0.8491	0.8473	0.8905	0.8738	0.8539
0.97	0.8792	0.8914	0.8808	0.8775	0.9164	0.9026	0.8838
0.98	0.9117	0.9252	0.9159	0.9118	0.9433	0.9331	0.9168
0.99	0.9487	0.9613	0.9553	0.9519	0.9711	0.9655	0.9545
1.00	1.0000	1.0000	1.0000	1.0000	1.0000	1.0000	1.0000
Max Error		0.0135	0.0069	0.0045	0.0457	0.0247	0.0058
Gini	0.4352	0.4308	0.4318	0.4320	0.3808	0.4139	0.4324

[a] Based on 1990 cps data of individual income data for the U.S.A.

[b] Poly L4(z) means the inverse distribution function was expanded in an exponential polynomial series of third order which includes four parameters. The Lorenz curve is approximated by $\hat{L}(z)=(1/\hat{\mu})\int_0^z \hat{x}(z')dz'$ for $z \in [0, 1]$ where we used $\hat{X}(Z)=\exp[\Sigma_{n=0}^{3}\hat{\beta}_n z^n]$ and $\hat{\mu}. = \frac{1}{T}\sum_{t=1}^{T} x_t$ with measured income x_t. The parameters $\hat{\beta}$ were estimated by OLS. Similar interpretation can be given for Poly L6(z) and L8(z) where series

expansion includes six and eight parameters respectively.

[c] Bern 10 means the Lorenz curve was approximated by a Bernstein polynomial expansion based upon 10 points, z=0, D.1, ⋯, 1.

0.0045 respectively. At the bottom of these columns, we report the corresponding Gini coefficients based on 65,100 sample observations. The empirical Gini Coefficient is 0.4325 while the Gini coefficients for L4, L6, and L8 are 0.4308, 0.4318, and 0.4320, respectively.

In the sixth column of Table 4.1, result of the Bernstein polynomial approximation is reported. B10 means we used only ten points of the empirical Lorenz curve, i.e., L(0.1), ⋯, L(1.0). Similarly, for B20 and B100, we use 20 or 100 points of the empirical Lorenz curve. Though the performance of B10 is marginal, that of B100 is very satisfactory.

The second performance test which is reported in Table 4.2, we utilized U.S. cross sectional family income of 1977 also utilized in the study by Basmann et al. (1990). They divided U.S. Current Population Survey (CPS) data into 100 income classes and derived the Lorenz curve L(z) from these 100 income classes. As they noted, this allowed them to still maintain enough observations in each cell for reasonable estimation and also to be able to compute empirical Lorenz curves.

In the third performance test reported in Table 4.3, we used Korean cross sectional family income data for 1988. The Korea Development Institute (KDI) surveyed total household income for 5,111 families (excluding Cheju island). Among these families, 4,613 heads of family agreed to meet specially trained surveyors and answered specific items. Others refused to be visited. We also divided these family incomes into 100 income classes.

In the second and third tests, we compared the performance of the exponential polynomial approach (Poly), the Bernstein approach (Bern), Bayesian approach (Bayes), Basmann et al. (1990) nonlinear functional form approach (BHJS), and Kakwani and Podder's [(1973), KP] specification. In what follows, we discuss the Bayesian method, BHJS, and KP.

Since there is no guarantee that the Lorenz curve derived by the exponential polynomial series will be a convex function, we can impose the required convexity using a Bayesian method. To impose convexity on the

Lorenz curve defined in (4.2), require

$$L'(z)=x(z)/\mu \geqq 0 \quad \text{and}$$
$$L''(z)=\frac{1}{\mu}\frac{\partial x(z)}{\partial z} \geqq 0 \quad \text{for} \quad z \in [0, 1]. \tag{4.31}$$

If we define the natural logarithm of income as

$$g(z) \equiv \log x(z) \text{ or equivalently } x(z) \equiv \exp[g(z)], \tag{4.32}$$

then $L'(z)=x(z)/\mu > 0$ with $-\infty < g(z)$ and

$$L''(z)=\frac{1}{\mu}\frac{\partial x(z)}{\partial z}=\frac{1}{\mu}\exp[g(z)]g'(z) \geqq 0 \text{ if } g'(z) \geqq 0 \tag{4.33}$$

Therefore all we need is $g'(z) \geqq 0$ to impose convexity on the Lorenz curve.

In the following discussion, we establish a convexity restricted Bayesian Lorenz curve based on standard Bayesian regression analysis. See e.g., Judge et al. (1985, P.103). Now rewrite (4.6) as

$$g = X\beta + \varepsilon \tag{4.34}$$

where g is a 100 by 1 vector whose elements are $\log x_{(1)}$, $\log x_{(2)}$, $\cdots$, $\log x_{(100)}$ and X is a 100 by N+1 matrix with typical element $[X]_{tj}=z_t^j$. Here x_t is the averaged income of the tth group. Assuming a normal distribution for ε_t[27] in (4.34), we can derive a likelihood function and corresponding posterior density function. We can generate random samples from the posterior density function, by choosing only those convexity restricted Lorenz curves and averaging parameter values of those chosen curves, a convexity restricted Bayesian Lorenz curve can be established based upon the selected parameter average values. See the Bayesian technique developed by Geweke (1986).

The Bernstein polynomial approximation is designed to satisfy the boundary conditions, $B_n(z=0)=L(z=0)$ and $B_n(z=1)=L(z=1)$, but

---

[27] A large number of observations, I, are placed into 100 grid cells and the Lorenz curve is derived using these averaged values.

Table 4.2 Sample Fitted Lorenz Curves Based On Family Income in 1997 (U.S.A.)[a]

Z	Empirical L(z)	Poly L4(Z)	Poly L6(z)	Bayes[b] L4(z)	Bayes L6(z)	Bern[c] L(z)	BHJS[d] L(z)	KP[e] L(z)
0.1	0.0108	0.0164	0.0163	0.0164	0.0163	0.0186	0.0180	0.0199
0.2	0.0528	0.0483	0.0530	0.0483	0.0530	0.0539	0.0537	0.0476
0.3	0.1015	0.0986	0.1037	0.0986	0.1037	0.1030	0.1021	0.0854
0.4	0.1644	0.1663	0.1648	0.1663	0.1647	0.1662	0.1631	0.1363
0.5	0.2424	0.2482	0.2398	0.2482	0.2397	0.2444	0.2385	0.2038
0.6	0.3364	0.3418	0.3342	0.3418	0.3341	0.3385	0.3317	0.2927
0.7	0.4481	0.4482	0.4501	0.4482	0.4501	0.4503	0.4471	0.4086
0.8	0.5814	0.5750	0.5843	0.5750	0.5843	0.5838	0.5910	0.5587
0.90	0.7459	0.7422	0.7432	0.7421	0.7432	0.7487	0.7717	0.7521
0.91	0.7649	0.7726	0.7619	0.7625	0.7619	0.7678	0.7922	0.7743
0.92	0.7846	0.7839	0.7816	0.7838	0.7815	0.7876	0.8131	0.7970
0.93	0.8052	0.8061	0.8022	0.8061	0.8022	0.8083	0.8346	0.8202
0.94	0.8266	0.8295	0.8242	0.8294	0.8241	0.8299	0.8566	0.8440
0.95	0.8491	0.8541	0.8476	0.8540	0.8475	0.8526	0.8791	0.8685
0.96	0.8731	0.8799	0.8728	0.8798	0.8726	0.8768	0.9021	0.8935
0.97	0.8989	0.9072	0.9001	0.9071	0.8999	0.9028	0.9257	0.9192
0.98	0.9276	0.9360	0.9300	0.9359	0.9299	0.9312	0.9499	0.9454

0.99	0.9596	0.9665	0.9631	0.9664	0.9629	0.9631	0.9746	0.9724
Max Error		0.0084	0.0035	0.0083	0.0036	0.0036	0.0301	0.0204
Gini	0.3682	0.3684	0.3682	0.3687	0.3683	0.3645	0.36	0.40

[a] Based on cps data, first used in Basmann et al. (1990), for cross sectional income data for the U.S.A.

[b] Bayes L4(z) means the parameters were estimated by the Bayesian average method described in the text for the functional form of Poly L4(z).

[c] Bern is the same model as Bern 100 of the Table 4.1.

[d] BHJS means the model H_m of Basmann et al. (1990).

[e] Kakwani and Podder's (1973) model.

Table 4.3 Sample Fitted Lorenz Curves Based On Family Income in 1988 (Korea). [a]

Z	Empirical L(z)	Poly L4(z)	Poly L6(z)	Bayes L4(z)	Bayes L6(z)	Bern L(z)	BHJS L(z)	KP L(z)
0.1	0.0138	0.0113	0.0115	0.0113	0.0115	0.0148	0.0144	0.0156
0.2	0.0484	0.0394	0.0485	0.0394	0.0484	0.0491	0.0493	0.0383
0.3	0.0942	0.0893	0.0994	0.0893	0.0994	0.0957	0.0954	0.0706
0.4	0.1542	0.1581	0.1560	0.1581	0.1561	0.1558	0.1514	0.1158
0.5	0.2281	0.2382	0.2233	0.2381	0.2235	0.2296	0.2197	0.1779
0.6	0.3135	0.3241	0.3103	0.3238	0.3105	0.3153	0.3047	0.2625
0.7	0.4135	0.4168	0.4192	0.4164	0.4191	0.4159	0.4135	0.3736
0.8	0.5373	0.5270	0.5424	0.5266	0.5421	0.5394	0.5555	0.5292
0.90	0.6921	0.6856	0.6870	0.6850	0.6865	0.6957	0.7445	0.7320
0.91	0.7108	0.7067	0.7050	0.7061	0.7044	0.7146	0.7666	0.7558
0.92	0.7305	0.7293	0.7243	0.7286	0.7237	0.7343	0.7895	0.7798
0.93	0.7509	0.7534	0.7452	0.7527	0.7446	0.7552	0.8130	0.8048
0.94	0.7728	0.7793	0.7682	0.7786	0.7675	0.7774	0.8373	0.8304
0.95	0.7961	0.8073	0.7937	0.8066	0.7930	0.8014	0.8624	0.8567
0.96	0.8216	0.8376	0.8225	0.8368	0.8216	0.8276	0.8882	0.8838
0.97	0.8494	0.8706	0.8554	0.8697	0.8544	0.8571	0.9149	0.9117
0.98	0.8811	0.9065	0.8937	0.9056	0.8926	0.8992	0.9423	0.9403

0.99	0.9225	0.9459	0.9392	0.9449	0.9379	0.9368	0.9709	0.9698
Max Error		0.0254	0.0167	0.0245	0.0154	0.0143	0.0666	0.0623
Gini	0.4116	0.4105	0.4103	0.4109	0.4105	0.4074	0.3952	0.4411

[a] We have used family income for 1988 collected by the Korea Development Institute. An explanation of each model can be found in the footnotes of Tables 4.1 and 4.2.

does not include an intercept term so that the sum of the model estimation errors may not be zero. We found that the estimated values of the Lorenz curve were always larger than the values of the actual empirical Lorenz curve.[28]

In comparison, BHJS (1990) approximated the Lorenz curve with the following nonlinear form.

$$L(z)=z^{az+b}\exp[-g(1-z^2)-h(1-z)+\mu] \tag{4.35}$$

The parameters are estimated with least squares method on the

$$\log L(z)=az\log z+b\log z-g(1-z^2)-h(1-z)+\mu \tag{4.36}$$

Kakwani and Podder's (1973) specification is a special case of BHJS. Let a =0, b=1, g=0 in (4.35),

$$L(z)=z\exp[-h(1-z)+\mu] \tag{4.37}$$

The parameters are estimated with least squares method on the

$$\log L(z)=\log z-h(1-z)+\mu \tag{4.38}$$

Interpretation of Table 4.2 is as follows. In order to have a meaningful comparison, in using the various approaches we included the same number of parameters (four) and same data are used in the Poly L4(z), Bayes L4 (z), and BHJS. They performed more or less the same for population ranges of z=[0.0,0.9], but BHJS overshoots at the tails (z=0.90, 0.91, ⋯, 0.99) as shown on Table 4.2. When we added more parameters in the regression, Poly L6(z) and Bayes L6(z) performed better than Poly L4(z) and Bayes L4(z). We have introduced a Bayesian approach to impose a convexity restriction, but among the 500 randomly generated Lorenz curves no violation was observed. Therefore, the performance of Poly L4(z) and Poly L6(z) was very similar to that of Bayes L4(z) and Bayes L6(z). Bern

[28] If we approximate a convex function with a weighted averaged sequence, then the approximated value will always be larger than the true function value. In (4.22), we sum over point $z'=\nu/I$ with function values $L(\nu/I)$ and weights $\binom{I}{\nu}z^{\nu}(1-z)^{I-\nu}$.

performed well at the lower portions of the Lorenz curve but the approximation error increased as z increased, though its maximum model estimation error (0.0036 at $z=0.98$) was quite small.

In Table 4.3, we replicated the same procedure as given in Table 4.2 from family income data of Korea. Since the Gini coefficient for Korea (0.41) is larger than the Gini coefficient for the U.S. (0.37), the actual empirical Lorenz curve for Korea is more convex than that of U.S.[29] The richest one percent of individuals in Korea get 7.89 percent of total income while the corresponding portion gets only 4.04 percent in the U.S. As a result, the approximation becomes slightly difficult at the tails for all the models listed in Table 4.3. In the Bayesian approach to impose a convexity restriction, among the 500 randomly generated Lorenz curves no violation was observed.

In Figure 4.1, we introduced box plots made of model estimation errors produced from the various models for U.S. family income in 1977 and for Korean family income in 1988. Chambers et al. (1983) developed the box plot. Construction of our box plots is as follows. For Poly L4(z), we have 100 model estimation errors which are defined as the differences between the hypothetical model values and the actual empirical Lorenz curve values. A horizontal line is drawn through the box at the median of the model estimation errors, the upper and lower ends of the box are at the upper and lower quartiles, and vertical lines ("whiskers") go up and down from the box to the extremes of the model estimation errors. The points that are extreme are plotted by themselves. We can repeat the same process for Poly L6(z) and for the other models. Explanation of each model and source of data are given in the footnote of Table 4.1. Approximation with BHJS produced many outliers because the functional form used in BHJS fit well over the lower portion of the Lorenz curve but not at the tails. Even when

---

[29] The Gini coefficient for Korea has been reported by many researchers. These values ranged between 0.34 and 0.38 which is smaller than our value of 0.41. In the previous surveys, extremely large values of measured income were considered as outliers and removed from the data set. In comparison, our data set collected by KDI includes al the sample observations.

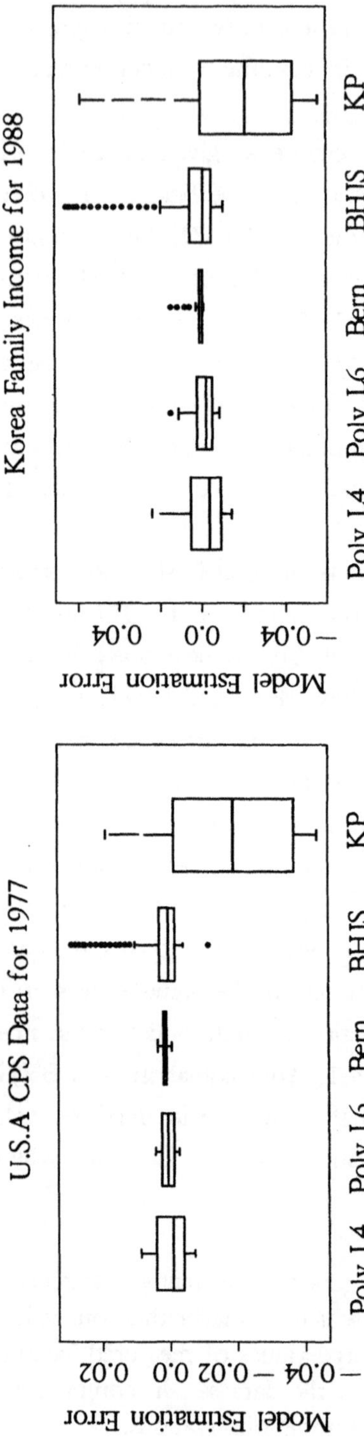

Fig. 4.1. Boxplots of Model Estimation Errors Produced by Various Models

we have a small number of sample classes, we found Poly L4 is still useful as demonstrated by its good performance for the box plot. Kakwani and Podder's (KP) model did not do well. We also repeated the same process for Korean family income in 1988. Its box plot is shown on the right hand side of Figure 4.1. Since family income in Korea is distributed less equitably relative to family income in the U.S., the width of the Poly L4 and for the other approaches became wider and even the Bernstein polynomial approaches produced outliers. As a fourth test, we generated random samples from a Lognormal distribution, a Gamma distribution, and a Generalized Beta distribution and test performance of various approaches for these generated samples. The probability density function of a Lognormal distribution is defined as

$$f(x)=\frac{1}{\sigma x\sqrt{2\pi}}\exp\left[\frac{-1}{2\sigma^2}(\ln x-\mu)^2\right] \qquad \text{for} \qquad x>0 \qquad (4.39)$$

We have chosen $\mu=0$ and $\sigma=1$ to generate 10000 random samples. To generate a random sample from a Gamma distribution, we use the probability density function

$$f(x)=\frac{1}{\Gamma(a)}x^{a-1}e^{-x} \qquad \text{for} \qquad x>0. \qquad (4.40)$$

where we selected a=3 to generate 10000 random samples. To generate a random sample from a Generalized Beta distribution, we use the probability density function

$$f(x;a,b,p,q)=\frac{ax^{ap-1}}{b^{ap}B(p,q)[1+(x/b)^a]^{p+q}} \quad \text{for} \quad x>0. \quad (4.41)$$

We chose the parameter values from McDonald (1984) table III, a=5. 0573, b=13.5815, p = 0.2961, q=0.6708. We generate 10000 random samples. To match the notation of BHJS, we derive the empirical Lorenz curve at z = 0.0, 0.01, 0.02, ···, 0.99, 1.00 with 10000 random samples. Basmann et al. (1990) uses these 100 values to estimate the parameters of their nonlinear function. We compare performance of various approaches based on these 100 values. The box plots based upon these random samples applied to various approximating functions are shown on Figure 4.2. The

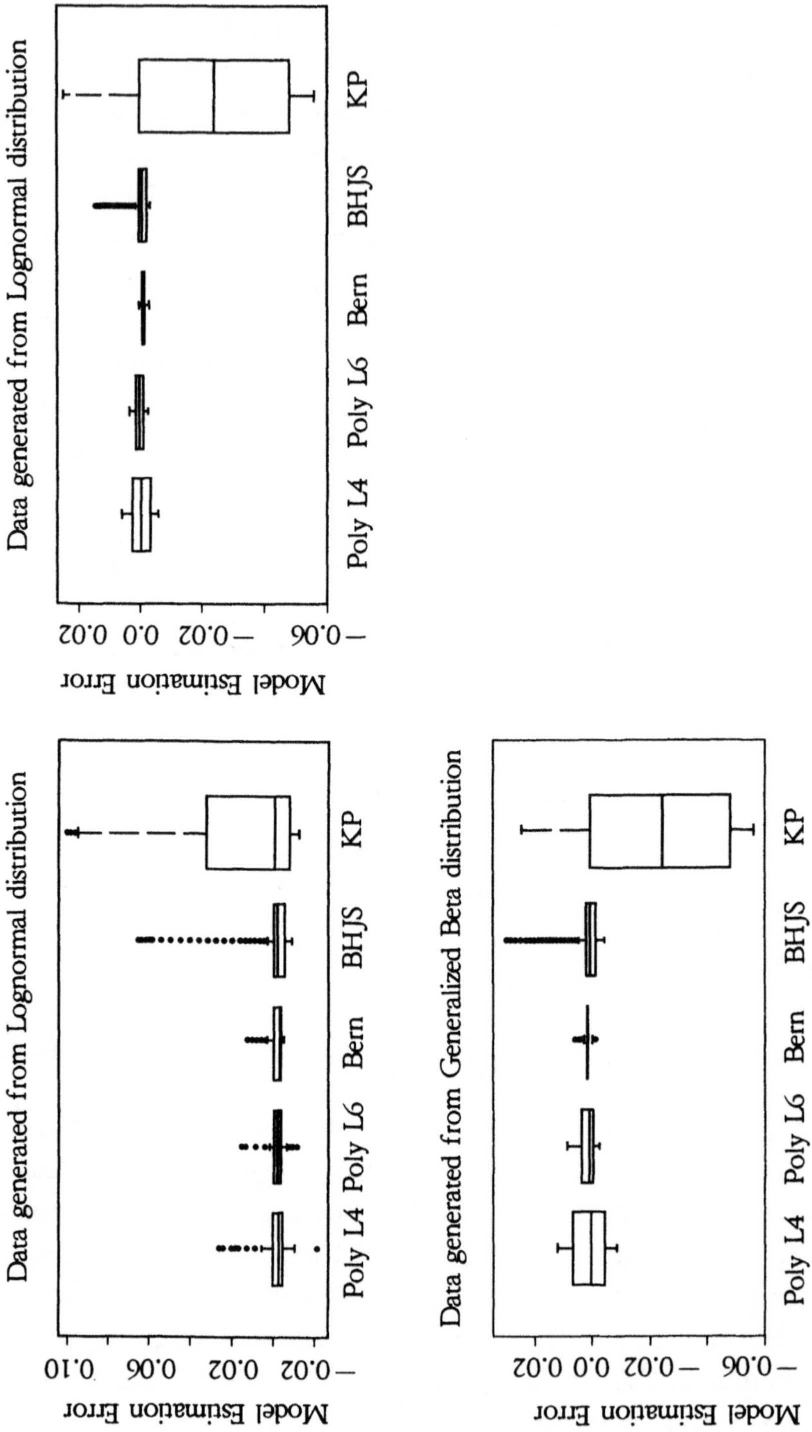

Fig. 4.2. Monte Carlo Exper. with Lognormal, Gamma, and Gen. Beta Distbn

polynomial series expansions and Bernstein series expansion showed good performance but BHJS and Kakwani and Podder's approaches did not.

4.10 Summary and Concluding Remarks

To approximate the empirical Lorenz curve, many researchers have introduced various fixed functional form approaches. These fixed functional form approaches performed relatively well over certain ranges, but the same function performed badly over other ranges of actual data. Therefore, we have introduced two flexible functional form approaches, the exponential polynomial and Bernstein polynomial approaches. We evaluated the performance of these two flexible functional form approaches using CPS income data for 1990. Both approaches performed well at all ranges of the population coordinates.

In the first flexible functional form approach, we expanded the inverse income distribution with a discrete Legendre polynomial series and derived the parameters using the orthonormal basis method. We demonstrated how to choose the size of the discrete Legendre series expansion based upon L^2 convergence of the unexplained part. For convenience in calculation, we have shown that the inverse income distribution values approximated by the orthonormal basis expansion can be obtained by expanding the inverse distribution function in a power series and by estimating the parameters with the least squares method. The equivalence of the two methods holds for small and large batches of sample observations.

In the second flexible functional form approach, we approximated the Lorenz curve with a Bernstein polynomial series. The Lorenz curve is defined as an accumulated sum of shares of those whose position in the population coordinate is less than or equal to $z=F(x)$. In practice, we replace the true Lorenz curve values $L(\nu/I)$ with observed empirical Lorenz curve values, $\hat{L}(\nu/I)$. When we choose I independent samples from the c. d.f. F(x), the probability augmented accumulated share of ν persons whose income will be less than or equal to x is $L(\nu/I)\binom{I}{\nu}z^{\nu}(1-z)^{I-\nu}$ so that the summation of this factor with respect to v, which is defined as the

Bernstein polynomial series $B_I(z)$, corresponds to the expected value of the accumulated share of those whose position is less than or equal to z.

Test results were reported to compare performance of our globally flexible functional form approaches with other fixed functional form approaches introduced by Basmann et al. (1990) and Kakwani and Podder (1973). For sample observations of U.S. CPS family income of 1977 and Korean family income of 1988 as well as random samples generated by the lognormal distribution, gamma distribution, and generalized beta distribution, we have found that these flexible functional form approaches are doing much better than other fixed functional form approaches with respect to approximation error, maximum error and Gini coefficient. For graphical representation of the approximation errors, we introduced the box plots and compared performance of various approaches with respect to the position of horizontal line, upper and lower ends of the box, and positions of outliers.

The necessary convexity condition required for a well-behaved Lorenz curve was established for the exponential power series. We have introduced a Bayesian method to impose the convexity condition. Among the 500 randomly generated Lorenz curves no violation was observed. The fact that Basmann et al.'s approach and results discussed in this chapter find no convexity violations demonstrates that a good choice of functional form virtually eliminates the need to impose convexity. For the Bernstein polynomial series expansion, it preserves convexity as an additional advantage.

Chapter 5

Comparing Income Distributions Using Index Space Representations [30]

5.1 Introduction

The purpose of this chapter is to introduce a new method to compare income distributions. The methodology used here allows us to examine the relationship between the observed income graduation in 1974 and the observed income graduation in 1990 in order to obtain a different perspective on how (and perhaps why) income inequality in the U.S. increased over that 16 years period. The main feature of this chapter is that we introduce an index space representation to compare two income distributions. This concept will be explained below.

We attempt to decompose the normalized income distribution function, i.e., using the derivative of the Lorenz curve which we call the share function, through a sequence of orthogonal polynomial transformations. We then interpret the decomposed functions. From this decomposition, the transition from the actual observed income distribution in 1974 to the actual observed income distribution in 1990 can be considered as a shift of various income distribution components. We selected 1974 as one year to study since this year has been identified by Bishop et al. (1991) and by Slottje (1989) as having the lowest measured (using several different inequality measures) level of family income inequality in the 1970s and 1980s while 1990 has the highest recent measured level of family income inequality.

The chapter proceeds as follows. Section 5.2 lays out the methodology we will use to compare the observed income distribution in 1974 to the observed income distribution in 1990. Section 5.3 presents empirical results and section 5.4 concludes the study.

---

[30] This chapter follows Ryu and Slottje (1997).

5.2 The Theory

The problem of income inequality is often discussed using a particular summary indicator of inequality such as the Gini coefficient, Theil's entropy measure or the Lorenz curve. However, since the Gini coefficient and Theil's measure are summary statistics, detailed information on the extent of income inequality cannot be fully revealed by these summary measures. The Lorenz curve includes more information on the entire distribution but still is lacking in conveying information as to how say the income distribution has changed between 1974 and 1990 beyond a visual comparison of these two curves. In Figure 5.1, we present the empirical Lorenz curves for 1974 and 1990.[31] Examination of these curves reveals that the curve for 1974 unambiguously lies above the curve for 1990, indicating more inequality in 1990. Thus, there is little additional information gained from viewing these curves that wasn't forthcoming from examining the Gini coefficient or Theil's measure. Using quantiles as measures also tells us little about what has transpired within the quantiles between time periods, cf. Slottje (1989). Since the Lorenz curve is a cumulative distribution function (cdf), it possesses an underlying probability density function (pdf) which we call the share function. We establish a semiparametric representation for the derivative of the Lorenz curve and decompose this share function using the Legendre polynomials. In what follows, we explain the motivation for using the pdf rather than the cdf, i.e. using the share function rather than just the Lorenz curve, and we discuss why we decompose the share function into a sequence of orthogonal functions and particularly into the Legendre functions. As Ryu and Slottje (1996a) noted, economists have shown considerable interest in the functional form of the Lorenz curve. The objective being to describe the Lorenz curve with as few parameters as possible and still get a precise approximation. However, with this approximated form of the Lorenz curve, it is difficult to estimate various income inequality measures because most inequality measures require knowledge of the pdf rather than the cdf. Therefore, we introduce the idea of the functional form of the

[31] The domain of population coordinate is $z=[0, +1]$.

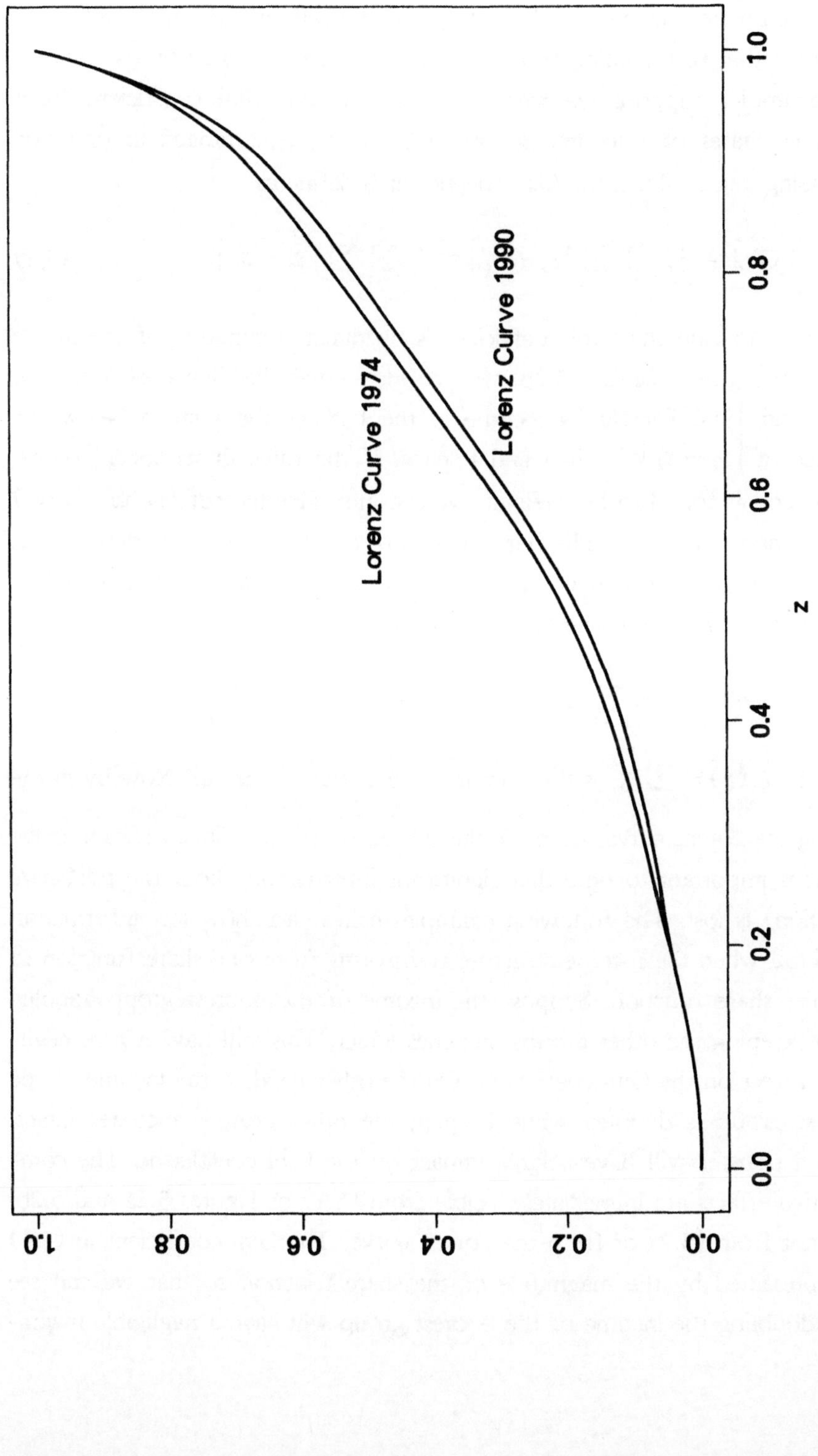

Fig. 5.1. Lorenz Curves for 1974 and 1990

derivative of the Lorenz curve so that various income inequality measures can be estimated. In general, knowledge of the pdf provides more information than that forthcoming from the cdf as will be illustrated by the following example. Suppose we want to determine the Gini coefficient from observed shares of I income groups, $s_1, s_2, \cdots, s_I$, arranged in order of increasing values. Then the Gini coefficient is define as

$$\text{Gini} = \frac{1}{2I}\sum_{i=1}^{I}\sum_{j=1}^{I}|s_j - s_i| = \frac{1}{I}\sum_{i=1}^{I}\sum_{j>i}^{I}|s_j - s_i| \tag{5.1}$$

One way to find the Gini coefficient is by direct summation of the above series. In Figure 5.2a and 5.2b, we present I times the Gini coefficient for 1974 and 1990 for family income in the U.S. as the volume below the surface of $|s_j - s_i|_{j>i}$ in i and j space. If the three dimensional volume calculation is found to be difficult, we can introduce the cdf (Lorenz curve) rather than using the pdf(share function) so that the three dimensional calculation can be converted into a two dimensional area calculation. Equation (5.1) can then be converted into.

$$\text{Gini} = 1 - \frac{2}{I}\sum_{i=1}^{I} L(i) \qquad \text{where} \qquad L(i) \equiv \sum_{j<i} s_j \tag{5.2}$$

Where $L(i) \equiv \sum_{j<i} s_j$ is the Lorenz curve at the ith group. Now by introducing the Lorenz curve, we made the calculation of the Gini coefficient easier but it is important to note that significant information about the pdf(share function) is lost. The following example makes clear how lost information is critical when the income structure transforms from one share function to another share function. Suppose the income of the poorest group doubled while keeping the other groups' incomes intact. This will have a give negligible effect on the Gini coefficient. On the other hand, if the income of the richest group is doubled while keeping the other groups' incomes intact, such a transfer will have a large impact on the Gini coefficient. The comparative effects are immediately visible from (5.1) or Figures 5.2a and 5.2b, but not from (5.2) or from the Lorenz curve. The Gini coefficient in (5.1) is represented by the magnitude of the share function so that we can see that doubling the income of the poorest group will have a negligible magni-

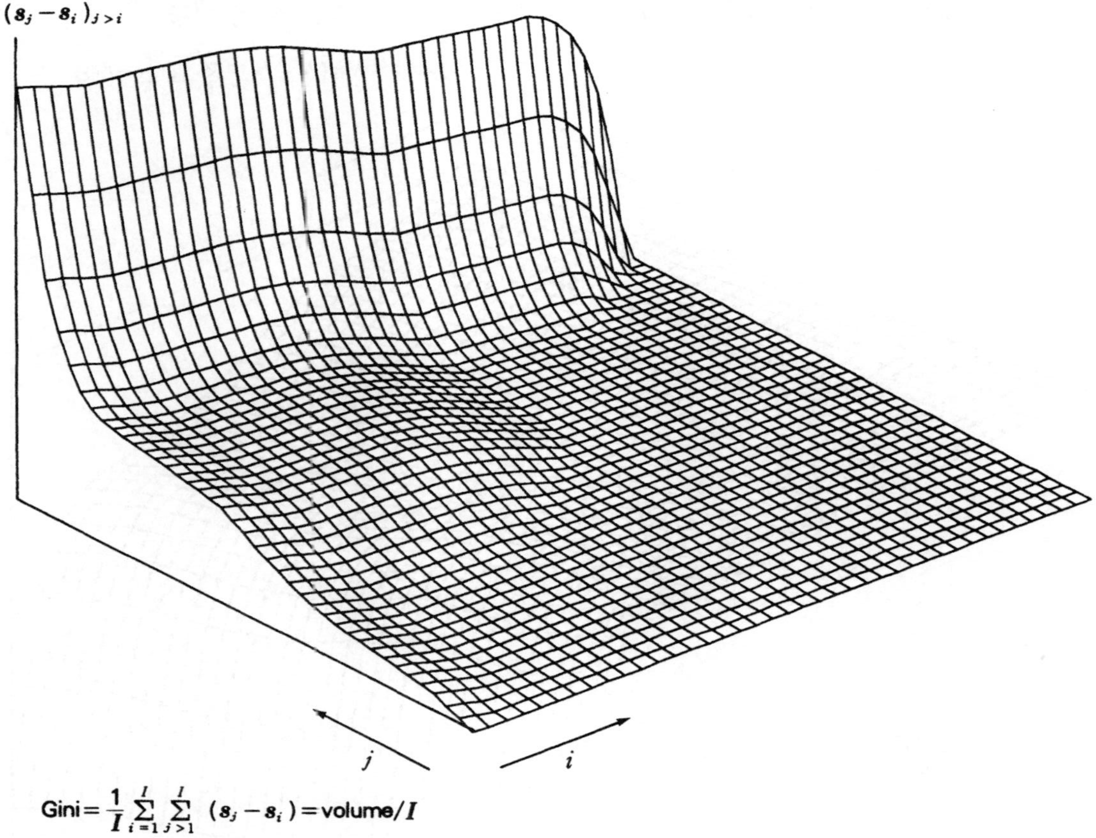

Fig. 5.2a. The Gini Coefficient for 1974 as represented in volume

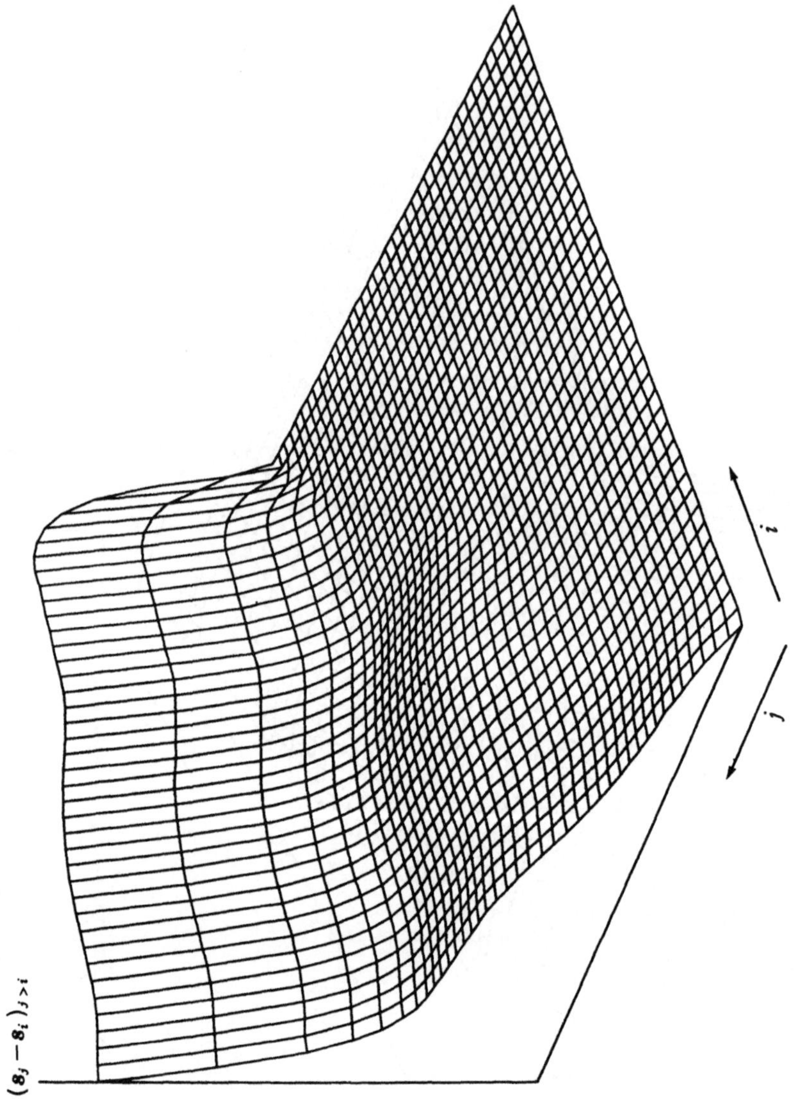

$$\text{Gini} = \frac{1}{I} \sum_{i=1}^{I} \sum_{j>i}^{I} (g_j - g_i) = \text{volume}/I$$

Fig. 5.2b. The Gini Coefficient for 1990 as represented in volume tude effect relative to doubling the income of the richest group.[32] Similarly, we find the Gini coefficients represented as volume in Figures 5.2a and 5.2b are sensitive to the large magnitude change in their peak heights but are not sensitive to a negligible magnitude change from the poorest groups' share. However, the Lorenz curve considers the accumulated share so that any change in individual shares is averaged out during the accumulation process. This is why many inequality measures can better be represented with the share function. The above discussion should now make clear that while the Lorenz curve is a useful vehicle for examining inequality, the share function provides more information on the income distribution and is a better representation on how the income distribution changes over time, as we will demonstrate below.

Once recognizing the importance of using the share function, the next objective is to describe the share function with as few parameters as possible and still get a precise approximation. Furthermore, this functional form should not only be general enough to approximate the empirical share function, but convenient to use. For a good global approximation, we introduce a sequence of functions chosen from a complete set and in order to distinguish between at least two share functions, we have chosen a particular orthonormal basis, the Legendre functions. See Appendix 5.A for more information about the orthonormal basis. We refer to the expansion of a function in an orthonormal basis as an index space decomposition.

As a by product of this approach, we find that there is an analogy between the index space representation which decomposes an arbitrary function through an orthonormal basis, and spectral analysis, which decomposes a given time series in a particular orthogonal function through a Fourier series.

An overview of this section is as follows. In section 5.1, we extend Theil's entropy measure for a continuous version probability density function. In section 5.2, the functional form of the share function is established

---

[32] Doubling the income of the richest group will affect the entire share function but doubling the income of the poorest group will not affect the other group's shares.

using the maximum entropy principle. Decomposition of the share function into a sequence of Legendre functions is demonstrated in section 5.3. Comparison of the index space representation to spectral analysis is discussed in section 5.4.

5.3 Theil's Entropy Measure

To extend Theil's entropy measure for a continuous share function, we define a continuous probability density function based upon the discrete share function and then rewrite Theil's entropy measure using this notation. To derive the share function, we rearrange the given observations of measured income, $y_1, y_2, \cdots y_I$ ordered by increasing income and then divide each measured income by a normalization constant. Esteban (1986) has discussed the share function in detail. The share function is define as

$$s_i \equiv \frac{y_i}{\sum_{i=1}^{I} y_i} \tag{5.3}$$

Replace index i with x_i where we place every individual within $[0,+1]$ at equally spaced distances,

$$s(x_i) = \frac{y(x_i)}{\sum_{i=1}^{I} y(x_i)} \quad \text{for} \quad x_i \equiv \frac{(i-1/2)}{I} \tag{5.4}$$

After dividing the interval $[0, +1]$ in I groups, each group is represented by its center point. In order to interpret the share function as a probability density function (pdf), consider the following example. Suppose there are I individuals in the economy, and dollar bills are falling from the sky, so that each individual will collect falling dollar bills. Since each individual has a different physical condition and different locational position, some people will collect more money than others. Each dollar bill will end up in the hand of the ith individual with probability $s(x_i)$ so that this share function can be interpreted as a discrete pdf. To convert discrete share function, $s(x_i)$, into a continuous share function, $s(x)$ for $x=[0, 1]$, we use $s(x_i) = s(x)/I$. For the continuous probability density function $s(x)$, Shannon (1948) defines entropy as

$$W = -\int s(x)\log s(x)dx. \tag{5.5}$$

Since the above value is negative, the inequality measure is defined with negative entropy.

$$\begin{aligned} H &\equiv -\text{Entropy} \\ &= \int s(x)\log s(x)dx \\ &= \sum_{i=1}^{I} s(x_i)\log[Is(x_i)] \\ &= \log I - \sum_{i=1}^{I} s(x_i)\log[1/s(x_i)] \end{aligned} \tag{5.6}$$

Equation (5.6) is Theil's well known entropy measure. In the continuous case the entropy is written by (5.5) while in the discrete case it is written by the second term of (5.6). The difference is log I. There is an important difference between the continuous and discrete entropies. In the discrete case, the entropy of a set of probabilities $s_1, \cdots, s_I$ has been defined as $w \equiv -\sum_i^I s_i \log s_i$ and it measures in an absolute way the randomness of the random variable. In the continuous case the measurement is relative to the coordinate system. If we change coordinates the entropy will in general change. Theil's entropy measure H is a useful indicator to observe income inequality because H approaches zero for uniformly distributed measured income and H increase to log I as the income distribution becomes more and more unequal. However, it is an averaged indicator so that specific details of the share function $s(x_i)$ are not fully revealed in (5.6). One consequence is that two distinct share functions may produce the same entropy value. Therefore, we shall approximate the functional form of $s(x_i)$ using the maximum entropy principle.[33] Justification for using an entropy principle to derive a pdf can be found in Jaynes (1979).

---

[33] We have indicated that entropy is not uniquely determined in the continuous case, but the measurement is relative to the coordinate system. However, it can be shown that when we change the coordinate system the ME density functions will not be affected except for multiplication by a Jacobi-

5.4 Maximum Entropy Estimation of Share Functions

Zellner and Highfield (1988) solved the following problem where they maximized W subject to side conditions.

$$\max_{s} W = -\int s(x)\log s(x)dx \text{ satisfying } \int x^m s(x)dx = \mu_m \quad (5.7)$$

where $m=0, 1, \cdots, N$ with the μ_m having known values. The Lagrangian method produces the following maximum entropy distribution as a solution,

$$s(x)=\exp\left[\sum_{n=0}^{N} c_n x^n\right] \text{ satisfying } \int x^m s(x)dx = \mu_m \quad (5.8)$$

where $m=0, 1, \cdots, N$. The unknown constants c_n's can be computed from known values of μ_m.

Suppose we choose the functional form of s(x) by the maximum entropy method of Zellner and Highfield. Since Theil's entropy measure is equal to negative entropy for the finite domain x=[0, 1], we are choosing the functional form of s(x) which minimizes Theil's entropy measure, subject to the given side conditions. There are many functions which satisfy the side conditions, but we are choosing a maximum entropy function, or equivalently a minimum Theil's entropy measure function, because entropy is a measure of lack of information. The distribution of maximum entropy is the least informative and most conservative distribution while distribution of lower entropy are more informative. Therefore, we are determining the functional form of a density in a most conservative way be choosing a maximum density function or equivalently a minimum Theil's entropy measure function for the given side conditions.

Interpretation of (5.6) is as follows. If no information on s(x) is provided, i.e., all we know is the normalization constant μ_0, then the maximum entropy density function will be flat for all x. If we are provided with the first and second moments of s(x), then the maximum entropy density

---

an factor. Before a coordinate transformation each small length element (dx) is given equal weight but after a coordinate transformation the new length element (e.g., dy) is given equal weight.

function will be a normal function. If we increase the number of side conditions, our approximated function will be closer and closer to the empirical share function s(x) and its entropy value will converge to the negative value of Theil's measure staged by (5.6).

Ryu (1993) extended the above approach so that side conditions can be imposed for an arbitrary sequence of functions. In particular we choose Legendre polynomial functions, $P_m(z)$, to impose the side conditions. The domain z is [0, +1]. The justification for introducing the Legendre functions will be provided later. Let us first solve,

$$\max W = -\int s(z)\log s(z)dz \text{ satisfying } \int P_m(z)s(z)dz = \xi_m \quad (5.9)$$

where $m=0, 1, \cdots, N$ with the ξ_m having known values. The Lagrangian method produces the following maximum entropy distribution as a solution,

$$s(z) = \exp\left[\sum_{n=0}^{N} a_n P_n(z)\right] \text{ satisfying } \int P_n(z)s(z)dz = \xi_m, \quad (5.10)$$

$m=0, 1, \cdots, N.$

Legendre functions are explained well in many physics textbooks. The normalized Legendre polynomials are defined by the following series,

$$\begin{aligned} &P_0(z)=1 \\ &P_1(z)-\sqrt{3}(2z-1) \\ &P_2(z)=\sqrt{5}(6z^2-6z+1) \\ &P_3(z)=\sqrt{7}(20z^3-30z+12z-1) \\ &P_4(z)=\sqrt{9}(70z^4-140z^3+90z^2-20z+1) \end{aligned} \quad (5.11)$$

for z=[0, +1]. The graph of these functions is presented in Figure 5.3. The sequence of Legendre polynomial functions can be obtained from a power series by rearranging each element function 1, z, z_2, z_3,$\cdots$ so that a new sequence satisfies the following orthogonality condition :

$$\int_0^{+1} P_n(z)P_m(z)dz = \delta_{nm} \quad (5.12)$$

where δ_{nm} is the Kronecker delay and is defined by $\delta_{nm}=0$ if $n \neq m$ and

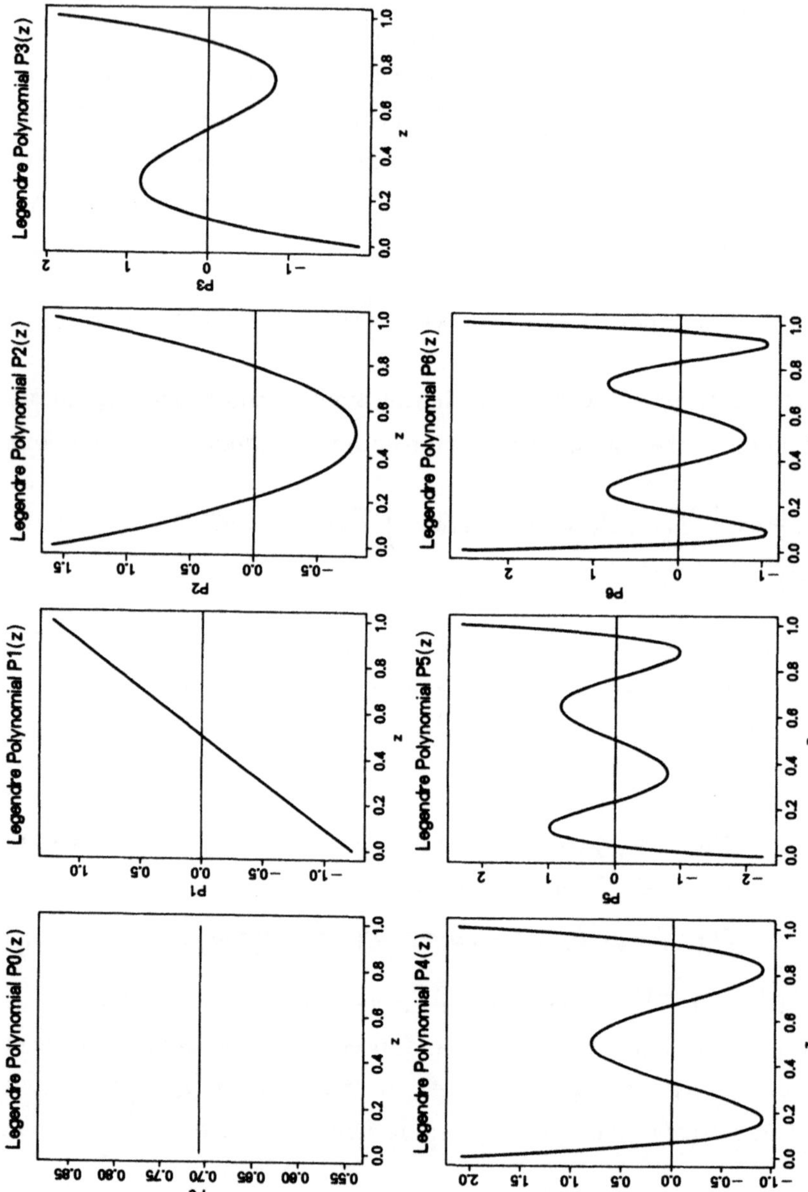

Fig. 5.3. Graph of the Legendre Functions.

$\delta_{nm} = 1$ if n=m. This orthogonalization method is referred to as the Gram-Schmidt method. See Luenberger(1969) for more information.

There are many ways to compute the unknown constants a_n's of (5.10). As is well known, we can use the method of moments (because ξ_m is composed of several moments), the maximum likelihood estimation method, or the Bayesian method. See Ryu (1990) for more details. However, in this chapter, we use the orthogonality property of the Legendre polynomial. Rewriting (5.10), the logarithm of the income share function is expanded in a sequence of Legendre polynomials :

$$\log s(z) = \sum_{n=0}^{N} a_n P_n(z) \tag{5.13}$$

The parameters can then be found using

$$a_n = \int_0^1 \log s(z) P_n(z) dz \tag{5.14}$$

In discrete notation, we have

$$\hat{a}_n = \frac{1}{I} \sum_{i=0}^{I} P_n(z_i) \log s(z_i) \tag{5.15}$$

where the domain z=[0, +1] is divided into I equal intervals. If I and N go to infinity and if certain other conditions are satisfied, then we can prove that the share function approximated by (5.13) will converge to the empirical share function because of the completeness. We require that the size of the chosen series expansion should not be too large relative to I. There are many sources which discuss how to choose a series expansion of size N as a function of sample size I, but we do not go into discussion of asymptotic convergence theory here. Since the observed income distribution in the U.S. is a smooth function, Ryu and Slottje (1996a) showed that good approximations can be obtained with a power series expansion when N is chosen to be four. This result proved to be useful in Monte Carlo experiments for various hypothetical distributions including the lognormal distribution, gamma distribution, and generalized beta distribution. It is interesting to note that the parameters determined by (5.15) are asymptotically equivalent to simple OLS estimation of parameters in

$$\log s(z_i)=\sum_{n=0}^{N} a_n P_n(z_i). \tag{5.16}$$

Using

$$\lim_{I\to\infty}\frac{1}{I}\sum_{i=1}^{I} P_n(z_i)P_m(z_i)=\int_0^1 P_n(z)P_m(z)dz=\delta_{nm}, \tag{5.17}$$

when group size (I) goes to infinity, ordinary least square estimated parameters of (5.16) converses to the parameters stated in (5.15) for n=0, 1, 2, $\cdots$. In the following section, we explain why we expand the share function through the Legendre series.

5.5 Motivation for Decomposing the Share Function Through the Legendre Functions

To obtain a globally good approximation function, we may expand the share function in any complete set of functions. For a finite domain, the Fourier series expansion, the power series expansion, and the Legendre polynomial expansion are widely used. We exclude the Fourier series expansion because the periodicity requirement restricts the share of the poorest to be equal to the share of the richest. The power series expansion and the Legendre polynomial expansion are equivalent except for the orthogonality requirement. Expanding the logarithm of the share function in a Legendre series,

$$\begin{aligned}\log s(z)=&a_0P_0(z)+a_1P_1(z)+a_2P_2(z)+a_3P_3(z)+\cdots\\&+a_N P_N(z)\end{aligned} \tag{5.18}$$

$$\begin{aligned}s(z)=&\exp\left[\sum_{n=0}^{N} a_n P_n(z)\right]\\=&s^0(z)\cdot s^1(z)\cdot s^2(z)\cdot s^3(z)\cdots s^N(z)\end{aligned} \tag{5.19}$$

In equation (5.19), we decomposed the share function as a multiplication of s^0, s^1, s^2, $\cdots$, s^N. To interpret the meaning of decomposed functions, we provide the following example. If everyone has an equal income share s(z)

$= 1/\mathrm{I}$, then we have

$$a_n = -\log 1 \qquad \text{and} \qquad a_1 = a_2 \cdots = a_N = 0 \tag{5.20}$$

Any departure from this situation indicates the presence of the inequality within the society. If inequality in income exists within the society, then the first parameter a_1 is always positive because by definition rich people will have a larger share value while poor people will have a smaller share value. We can approximate (5.19) with :

$$s(z) \doteq e^{a_0 P_0(z)} e^{a_1 P_1(z)} \tag{5.21}$$

$e^{a_0 P_0(z)}$ describes a uniform distribution part and $a_1 P_1(z)$ describes a modification to this uniform distribution. Since $a_1 P_1(z)$ is negative for negative z and positive for positive z, the share of income increases for positive z and the share of income decreases for negative z. To elaborate on this point, suppose $a_1 = 0.5$ and consider the effect on $a_1 P_1(z)$ of (say) five persons located at $z = -0.0$, 0.25, 0.50, 0.75 and $z = 1.0$. Now in the presence of $a_1 P_1(z) = 0.5^* \sqrt{3}\ (2z - 1) = 1.7328 - 0.8660$, the share of these five persons can be shown to have changed by the following mechanism.[34]

without $a_1 P_1(z)$	with $a_1 P_1(z)$
$s(0, 0) = \frac{1}{I}$	$s(0, 0) = \frac{1}{I} \cdot \exp[1.732 * (0.0)] - 0.8660 = \frac{1}{I}(0.4206)$
$s(0.25) = \frac{1}{I}$	$s(0.25) = \frac{1}{I} \cdot \exp[1.732 * (0.25)] - 0.8660 = \frac{1}{I}(0.6486)$
$s(0.50) = \frac{1}{I}$	$s(0.50) = \frac{1}{I} \cdot \exp[1.732 * (0.50)] - 0.8660 = \frac{1}{I}(1.0)$
$s(+0.75) = \frac{1}{I}$	$s(+0.75) = \frac{1}{I} \cdot \exp[1.732 * (0.75)] - 0.8660 = \frac{1}{I}(1.542)$
$s(+1.0) = \frac{1}{I}$	$s(+0.1) = \frac{1}{I} \cdot \exp[1.732 * (1.0)] - 0.8660 = \frac{1}{I}(2.377)$

---

[34] The share function described by $a_0 = -\log \mathrm{I}$, $a_1 = 0.5$, and $a_2 = 0$, $a_3 = 0$, $\cdots$ is not normalized because the sum of shares of all individuals are not constrained to be one. However, this normalization problem can be resolved simply by multiplying everyone's share by a fixed constant so we do not have to worry about the normalization problem in our artificial experiment.

The presence of the positive $a_1P_1(z)$ means we subtract a large share from the poorest, subtract a small amount from the second poorest, do not disturb the median income person, give a small extra share to the second richest person, and give a large extra share to the richest person. In other words, we redistribute a large portion of the income share of the poorest person and give it to the richest individual while we take a small portion of the share of the second poorest person and give it to those better off. Therefore, if this coefficient a_1 increase, income inequality within the society will have worsened substantially.

A similar interpretation can be given for $a_3p_3(z)$. Suppose we have

$$a_0 = -1.414 \log I,\ a_1 = +0.5,\ a_3 = +0.3 \text{ but } a_2 = a_4 = a_5 = \cdots = a_N = 0$$

Now in the presence of $a_3p_3(z) = 0.3^* \sqrt{7}[20z^3 - 30z^2 + 12z - 1] = 15.87z^3 - 23.81z^2 + 9.525z - 0.7937$, the share of these five persons income status will change by the following mechanism :

without $a_3p_3(z)$ with $a_3p_3(z)$

$s(0.0) = \frac{1}{I}(0.4206)$ $\quad s(0.0) = \frac{1}{I}(0.4206)\exp[15.87(0.0)^3 - 23.81(0.0)^2 + 9.525(0.0) - 0.7937 = \frac{1}{I} \cdot (0.4206) \cdot [0.4502]$

$s(0.25) = \frac{1}{I}(0.6486)$ $\quad s(0.25) = \frac{1}{I}(0.6486)\exp[15.87(0.25)^3 - 23.81(0.25)^2 + 9.525(0.25) - 0.7937 = \frac{1}{I} \cdot (0.6486) \cdot [1.408]$

$s(0.50) = \frac{1}{I}(1.0)$ $\quad s(0.50) = \frac{1}{I}(1.0)\exp[15.87(0.50)^3 - 23.81(0.50)^2 + 9.525(0.50) - 0.7937 = \frac{1}{I} \cdot (1.0) \cdot [1.0]$

$s(0.75) = \frac{1}{I}(1.542)$ $\quad s(0.75) = \frac{1}{I}(1.542)\exp[15.87(0.75)^3 - 23.81(0.75)^2 + 9.525(0.75) - 0.7937 = \frac{1}{I} \cdot (1.542) \cdot [0.7044]$

$s(1.0) = \frac{1}{I}(2.377)$ $\quad s(1.0) = \frac{1}{I}(2.377)\exp[15.87(1.0)^3 - 23.81(1.0)^2 + 9.525(1.0) - 0.7937 = \frac{1}{I} \cdot (2.377) \cdot [2.206]$

Now suppose that the income distribution is composed of four stages. In the first stage, we give everyone the same amount of money, 1/I, and then in the second stage, we divide the economy in half. We subtract income from the first half and give it to the other half in such a way that the person at z=0 has his income decreased to 42.06 percent of its original amount, the person at z=1 has his income decreased to 237.7 percent of his original amount, etc. At the third stage, we divide the economy into three groups, but we omitted the effect of $a_2P_2(z)$ in this example. At the fourth stage, we divide the economy into four groups, and decreased the income of the person at z=1 to 45.02 percent, we increase the income of the person at z=1.0 to 220.6 percent, etc. We can interpret these four stages as four income distribution components. Each decomposed Legendre function represents a component of the income distribution.

It is important to note that the effect of $a_0P_0(z)$ is represented by 1/I, the effect of $a_1P_1(z)$ is represented by the values inside the parenthesis, and the effect of $a_3P_3(z)$ is represented by the values inside the brackets. These values are all independent of each other because $\int P_n(z)P_m(z)dz=\delta_{nm}$. These effects are independent because the effect of $a_3P_3(z)$ will be multiplied through the share function without disturbing the values of $a_0P_0(z)$ and $a_1P_1(z)$. This means that even if we add many more terms in the expansion, the values of the lower order terms will not be affected by the addition of the higher order terms. To understand the importance of the orthogonality condition, suppose we expanded the logarithm of the share function in a power series,

$$\log s(z)=\sum_{n=0}^{N} b_n z^n \tag{5.22}$$

When we increase the size of the expansion from N to N+1, the estimated parameters will shift from one value to another.

The presence of the positive a_3 can be discussed in the following qualitative discussion. We take a portion of income from the poorest person(or group) and give it to a less poor person(or group) while we take a portion of income from a better off person (or group) and give it to the richest person or group. See the graph of $P_3(z)$ in Fig. 5.3. Therefore, if the coefficient a_3 increase, it can be seen that income inequality within the society will worsen. All Legendre polynomials of odd power can be interpreted in a similar way. They all worsen income inequality if coefficients increase but as the order of the polynomial function goes up, we have more and more income groups to redistribute their incomes, so that the effect of the higher order terms on the overall level of income inequality will be small.

Interpretation of the even powered Legendre functions if less clear. Very often the coefficients of the Legendre polynomial expansion have alternation signs so that we except a_2 be negative. This means the middle class benefits at the cost of the poor and rich. Therefore, there is no ambiguity in interpreting this $a_2P_2(z)$ component in the sense in which some group gains and in which a group loses but there is still ambiguity in interpreting the effect of this term on overall inequality because both the rich and the poor were gurt. We can give a more or less similar interpretation for all of the $a_4P_4(z)$, $a_6P_6(z)$,$\cdots$ terms.

The importance of the Legendre polynomial expansion of the share function can be shown through the following discussion. Suppose we want to test whether the observed income distributions for 1974 and for 1990 were generated from an identical distribution. However, since we have a large number of sample observations for each year we can easily reject the hypothesis of identical distributions for 1974 and 1990. Therefore, we can readily accept the hypothesis that the income distribution function shifted from 1974 to 1990.[35] This of course is not a startling result. If we draw the Lorenz curve or calculate the Gini coefficient and Theil's entropy measure, we find some shifting in the Lorenz curve and changes in the inequality measures. It is still not clear, however, how the distribution changed from

[35] Suppose we compare the sample moments of the 1974 income distribution with those of the 1990 income distribution. Using the central limit theorem, we can show that the distribution of the sample moments is normal and its variance approaches zero as the sample size increases to infinity. Therefore, the hypothesis of identical distributions for 1974 and 1990 will be rejected unless the sample moments for the 1990 income distribution exactly coincide with those of the 1974 income distribution.

1974 to 1990 from the fact that these overall measures have changed. Therefore, we decompose the derivative of the Lorenz curve, which we call the share function, in a Legendre polynomial series. We interpret each Legendre function as a distribution component of the share function. The zero component $P_0(z)$ corresponds to the uniform distribution, the first component $P_1(z)$ corresponds a distributional component which transfers income from the very poor to the very rich, and so on. As time goes on or as the result of certain economic policies, the coefficient of each component will shift so that the expansion coefficient changes and a redistribution of income occurs. We refer to these effects as component changes in the income distribution.

5.6 A Comparison of Index Space Analysis to Spectral Analysis

We call the Legendre series expansion discussed here an index space representation which is analogous to spectral analysis. As is well known, a time series can be decomposed into a long run component and a short run component, the long run component captures the overall shape or trend in the time series while the short run component captures local perturbations around that trend. The relative importance of each component is described by the magnitude of a Fourier coefficient. This decomposition technique need not be restricted to a Fourier series nor to a time variable. Therefore, we replace the Fourier series with the Legendre series and the time variable with a given z coordinate (normalized rand when every observation in the data batch is rearranged by income size). As a result, we find there is a very good analogy between a spectral analysis approach and the index space representation. For example, a long run component of a time series may indicate that the level of GNP was lower than average for the first half of the period under consideration and then the level of GNP was higher than average for the second half of the period under consideration. One could interpret this as indicating that there was a redistribution of GNP between the first period and the second period. The analogy in index space is that the $a_1 P_1(z)$ component describes how the lower half of income recipients got less income than the average income level and how upper half of income recipients got more income than the average income level. Thus, a_1, $P_1(z)$ accounts for the distribution of income between the poorer group and the richer group. In spectral analysis, low frequency components determine the gross shape of a realized time series curve while in the index space representation, lower index terms determine the gross shape of the observed income distribution. Only low frequency components and low index terms permit a description of the redistribution of income between coarsely separated time or coarsely separated income classes (between the poorest and the richest two groups, for instance).

A short run effect in a time series may describe a yearly fluctuation of GNP without it having much impact upon the goes shape of the GNP series. Or it could describe a redistribution of income between this year and next year. A perfect analogy can be established for the index space representation. If the society is divided into finer and finer income classes, the higher index components will describe the redistribution of income between neighboring classes so that their effect often can be averaged out to zero having no significant effect on the overall income distribution. The Legendre function $Pn(z)$ of large n fluctuates so rapidly that its average over a certain interval of z is small as can be seen by $\int_{z_0}^{z_0+\Delta} P_n(z)dz = 0$ for large n. Therefore, the higher the index terms describe finer and finer decompositions.

5.7 Empirical Results

We applied our approach to Current Population Survey (CPS) data using family income as the income recipient units for 1974 and 1990. Since each data set includes a large number of sample observations, we generate one thousand new samples from the originally given data. We could increase the number of sample sizes to be generated, but one thousand samples will be adequate to derive the functional form of the share function. First, we introduce an averaging method to generate the thousand samples. If there are 66,000 observations for 1990, we can sort by the order of increasing values, then take the mean value of the first 66 observations as the first sample, and the mean value of the second 66 observations as the second sample, etc., but we lose considerable information in this averaging process. As an alternative method, we can apply an ME density estimation method and random sample generation from this density. We calculate twelve sample moments from the logarithm of income, and then compute six coefficients using these moments. See Ryu (1993) for details of the density estimation method. From this density function and corresponding distribution function, one thousand random samples are generated. In ME density estimation, specific sample characteristics are mapped into the sample moments so that the theoretical samples derived by the ME method are different from the averaged one thousand sample means. In generating random samples, we bring two modifications to the original data. At the lower tail area, there are so few samples that any density estimation method will not work well. We removed all the observations below an annual income level of 148 dollars. This figure is the lower terminal. In 1974, 607 observations out of 47303 total observations belonged to this group while in 1990, 1064 observations out of 66173 observations belonged to this group. Our lower terminal of 148 dollars corresponds to $\ln y=5$. For the upper tail area, it decreases so slowly that the ordinary cartesian coordinate will not describe the distribution of income effectively. We take the logarithm of income so that these tail observations are brought much closer to the central region.

In Figure 5.4, we plotted the empirical share curve for 1974 and 1990. The two curves are so closely located to each other that it is difficult to distinguish between them from this figure. Therefore, we expand the logarithm of the share function in a Legendre polynomial series. Based upon one thousand random samples for 1974 and 1990, we find the Legendre coefficients by (5.18):

1974	1990	Difference
$\hat{a}_0=-7.265$	$\hat{a}_0=-7.331$	$\hat{a}_0=-0.066$
$\hat{a}_1=0.8485$	$\hat{a}_1=0.9256$	$\hat{a}_1=0.0802$
$\hat{a}_2=-0.1312$	$\hat{a}_2=-0.1233$	$\hat{a}_2=-0.0079$
$\hat{a}_3=0.2071$	$\hat{a}_3=-0.2146$	$\hat{a}_3=-0.0079$
$\hat{a}_4=0.2277$	$\hat{a}_4=0.2624$	$\hat{a}_4=0.0347$

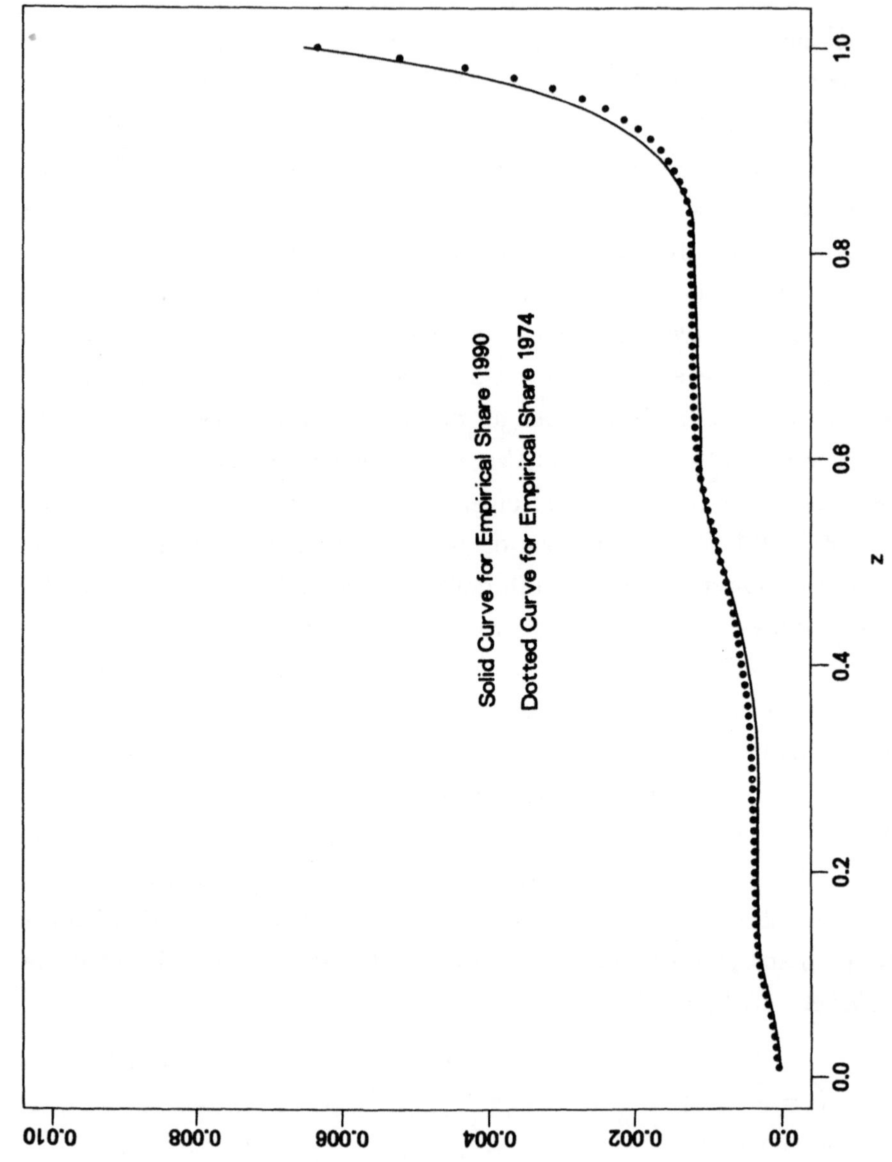

Fig. 5.4. Empirical Share Curves for 1974 and 1990

$\hat{a}_5=0.0545$	$\hat{a}_5=-0.1118$	$\hat{a}_5=-0.0573$
$\hat{a}_6=-7.265$	$\hat{a}_6=-7.331$	$\hat{a}_6=-0.066$

Between the years 1974 and 1990, $\hat{a}_0$ has decreased but $\hat{a}_1$ has increased from 0.8485 to 0.9256 so that income inequality has worsened. To understand the transformation of the share function from 1974 to 1990, let us approximate the Share function with

$$S(z)=\exp[\hat{a}_0 P_0(z)] \cdot \exp[\hat{a}_1 P_1(z)] \tag{5.23}$$

In Figure 5.5a, we plotted $\exp[\hat{a}_0 P_0(z)]$and in Figure 5.5b we plotted $\exp[\hat{a}_1 P_1]$. Multiplying the share elements represented in Figures 5.5a and 5.5b, we find the richest cohort of the income distribution have increased their income share very little during the period of 1974 and 1990 because $\exp[\hat{a}_0 P_0(z)]$ decreased and $\exp[\hat{a}_1 P_1(z)]$ increased. In comparison, the poorest cohort lost ground over the time period because both $\exp[\hat{a}_0 P_0(z)]$ and $\exp[\hat{a}_1 P_1(z)]$ have decreased. Empirically, the richest group increased their share from 0.000638 to 0.000652 while the poorest decreased their share from 0.0000253 to 0.0000145. This important change in the share function is not easily discerned in Figure 5.4, but it is clearly visible in Figure 5.5. Therefore, we can conclude that the poorest cohort lost most, the median income cohort lost moderately, and only the richest cohort gained. To draw such a conclusion, we note that the parameters $\hat{a}_0$ and $\hat{a}_1$ should not depend on the size of the series expansion such that the estimated $\hat{a}_0$ and $\hat{a}_1$ should not be altered as we increase the expansion size. Furthermore, contributions from other factors should be more or less similar for 1974 and 1990 as can be seen from the Figures 5.5c–5.5g. In Figures 5.6 and 5.7, we show how the approximated share functions are changing as we increase the size of the Legendre expansion,

$$s_j(z)=\exp\left[\sum_{n=0}^{j} \hat{a}_n P_n(z)\right] \tag{5.24}$$

for 1974 and 1990. However, we note that it is difficult to distinguish any difference between the share curves for 1974 and 1990 because the y axis measures the share function in a magnitude so finely that details of the

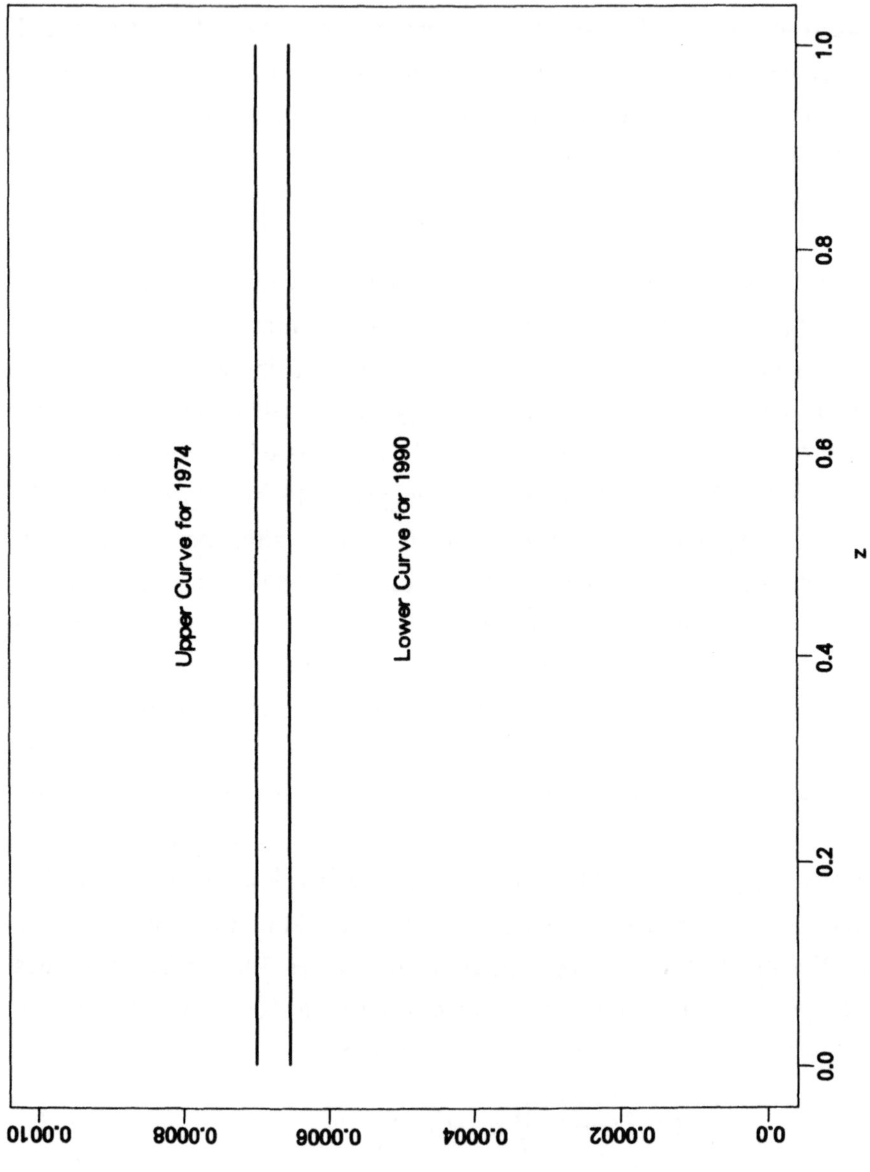

Fig. 5.5a. Zeroth Decomposition component of 1974 and 1990 Share Functions

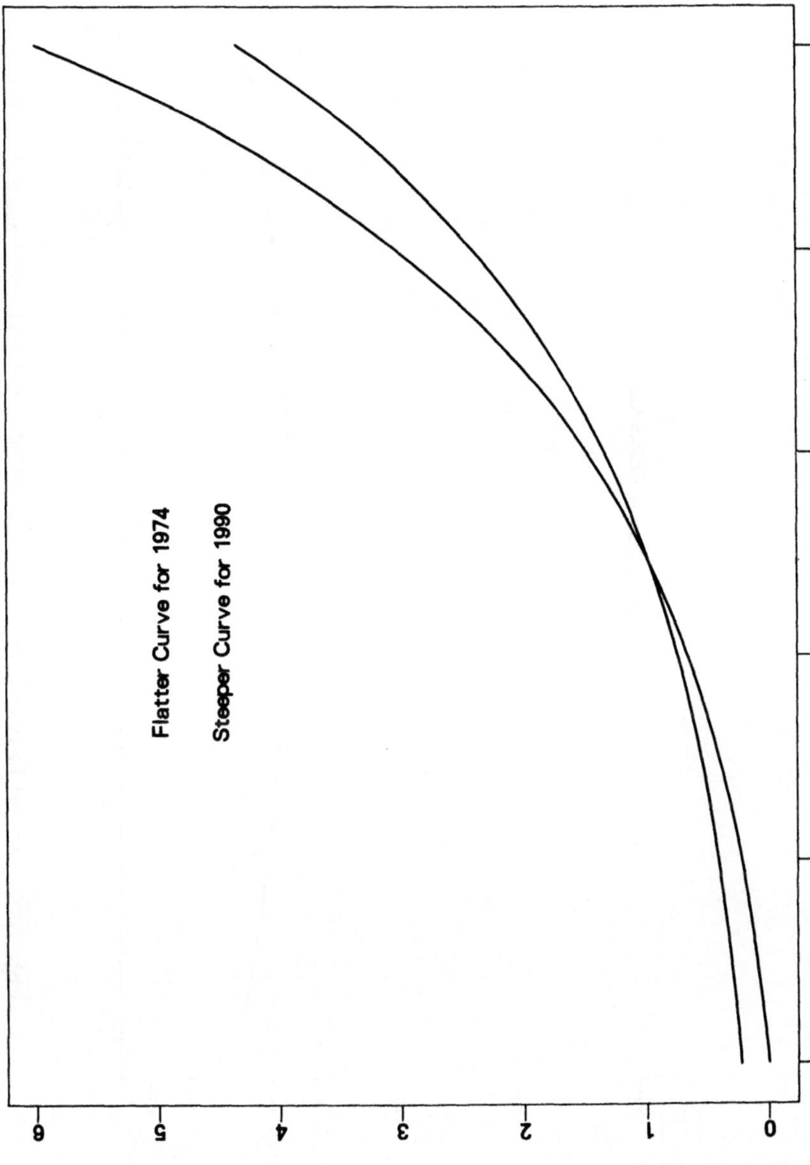

Fig. 5.5b. First Decomposition component of 1974 and 1990 Share Functions

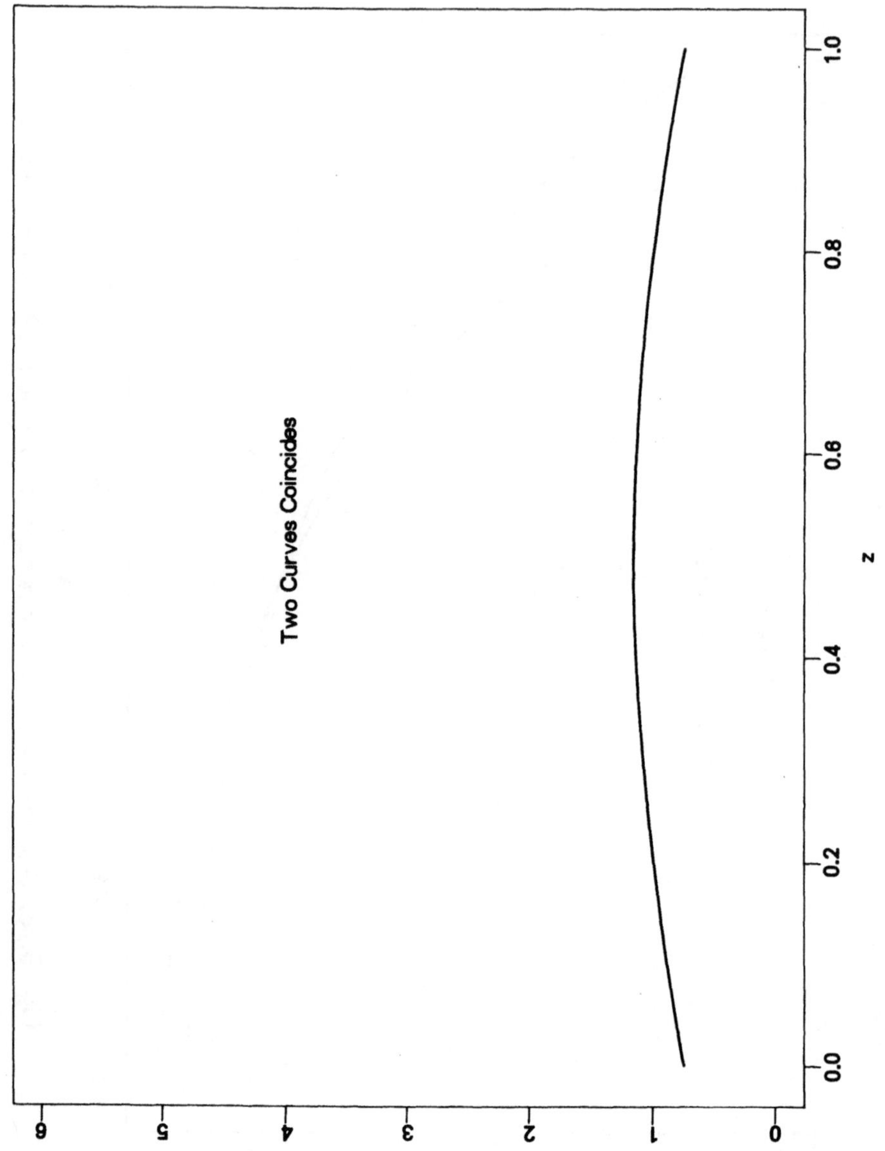

Fig. 5.5c. second Decomposition component of 1974 and 1990 Share Functions

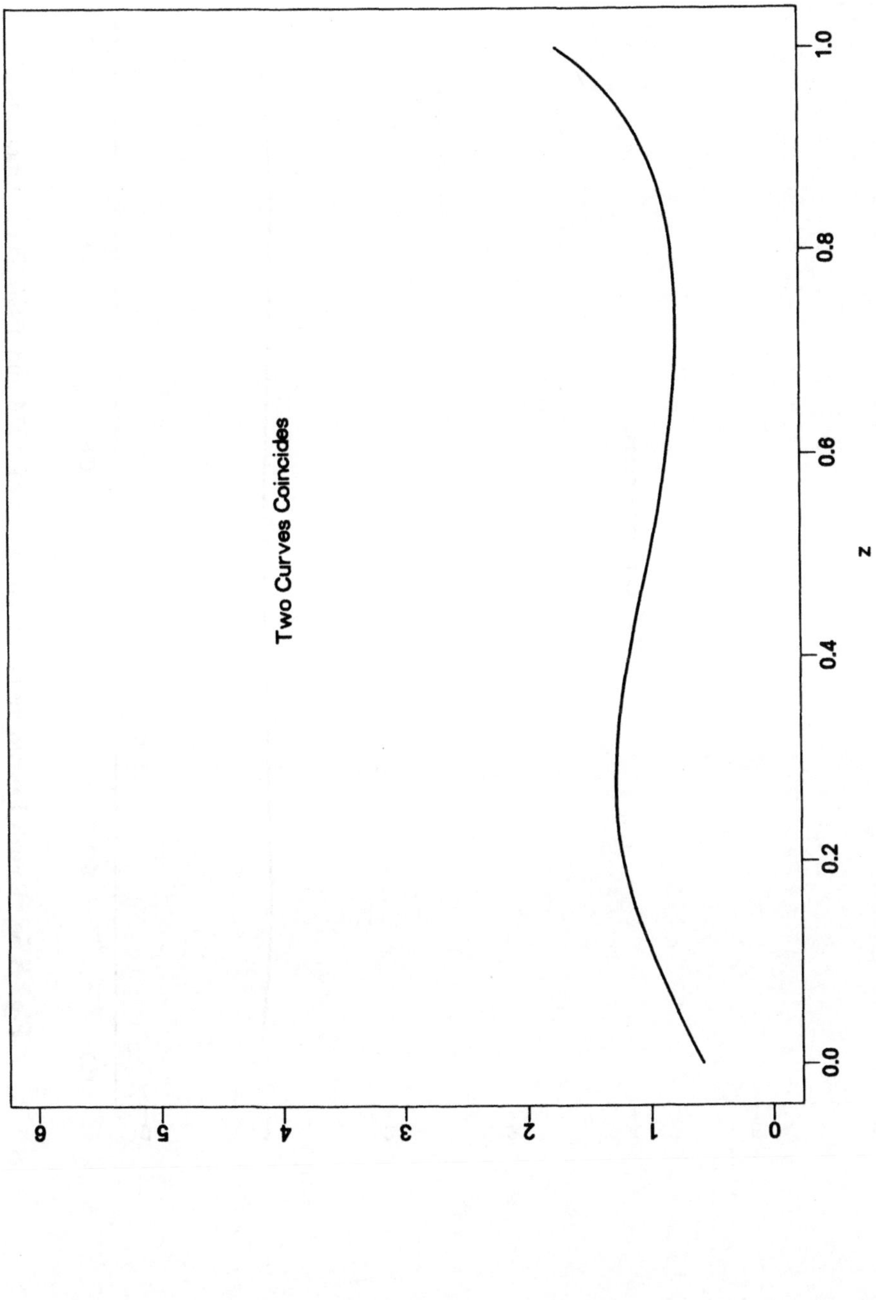

Fig. 5.5d. Third Decomposition component of 1974 and 1990 Share Functions

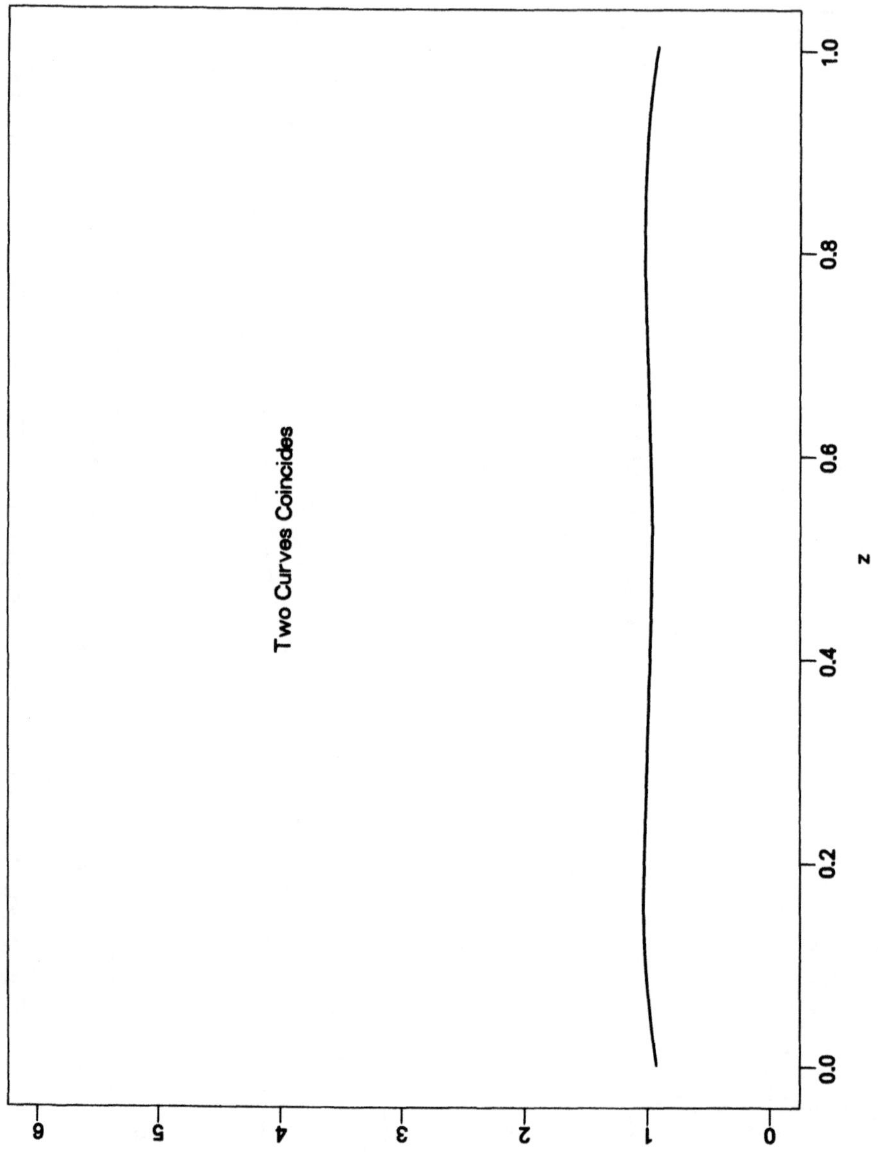

Fig. 5.5e. Fourth Decomposition component of 1974 and 1990 Share Functions

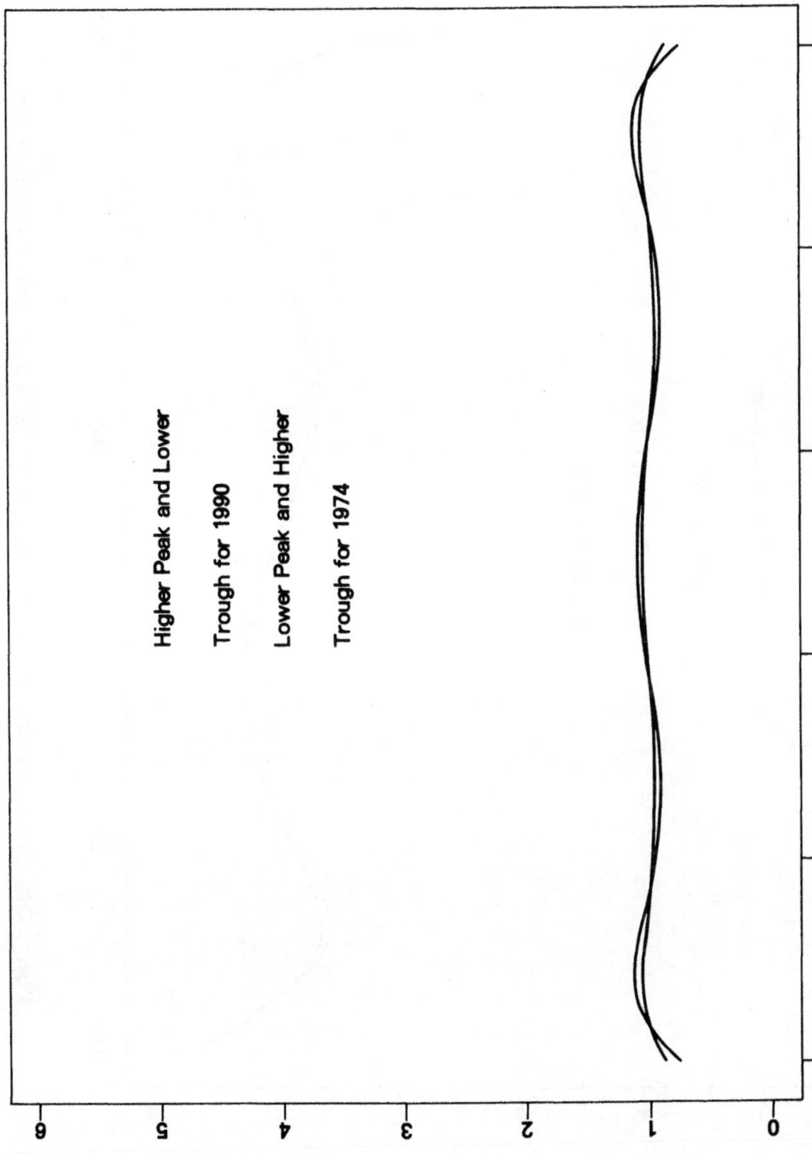

Fig. 5.5f. Fifth Decomposition component of 1974 and 1990 Share Functions

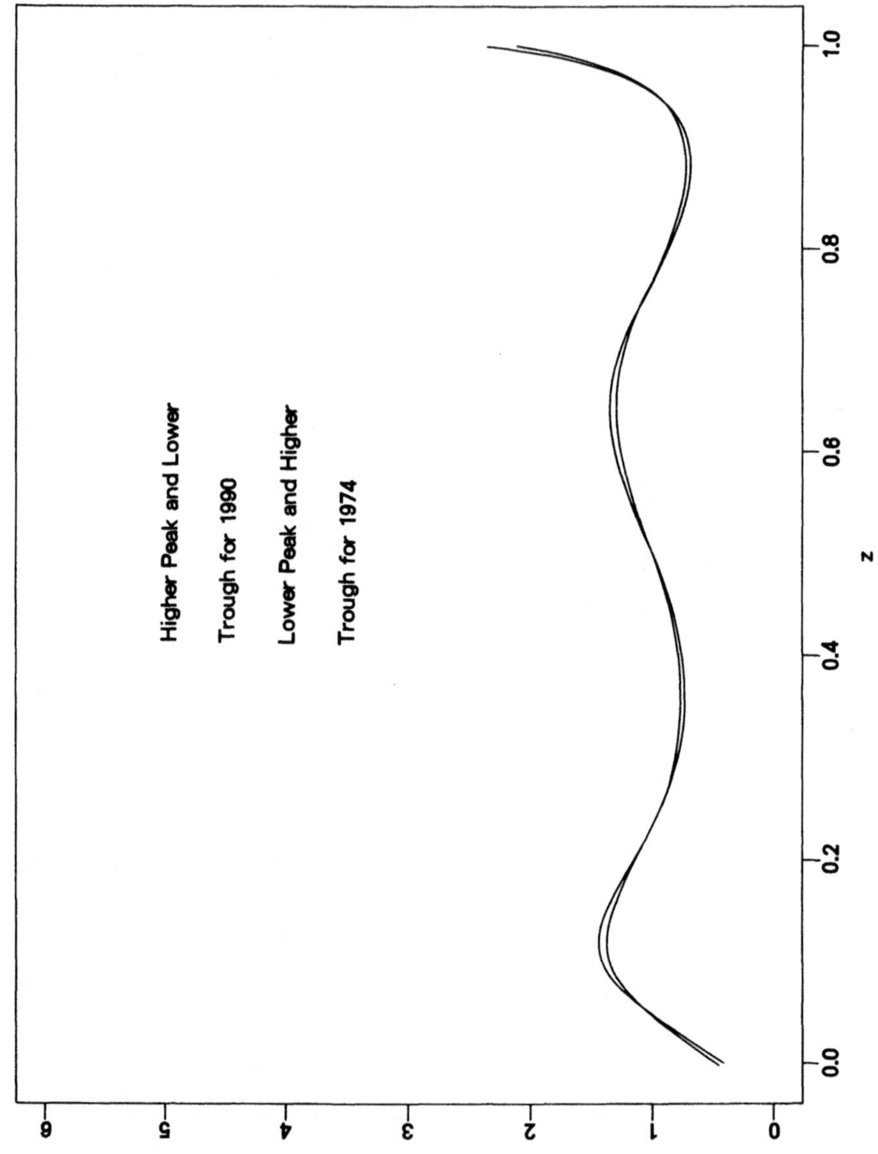

Fig. 5.5g. Sixth Decomposition component of 1974 and 1990 Share Functions

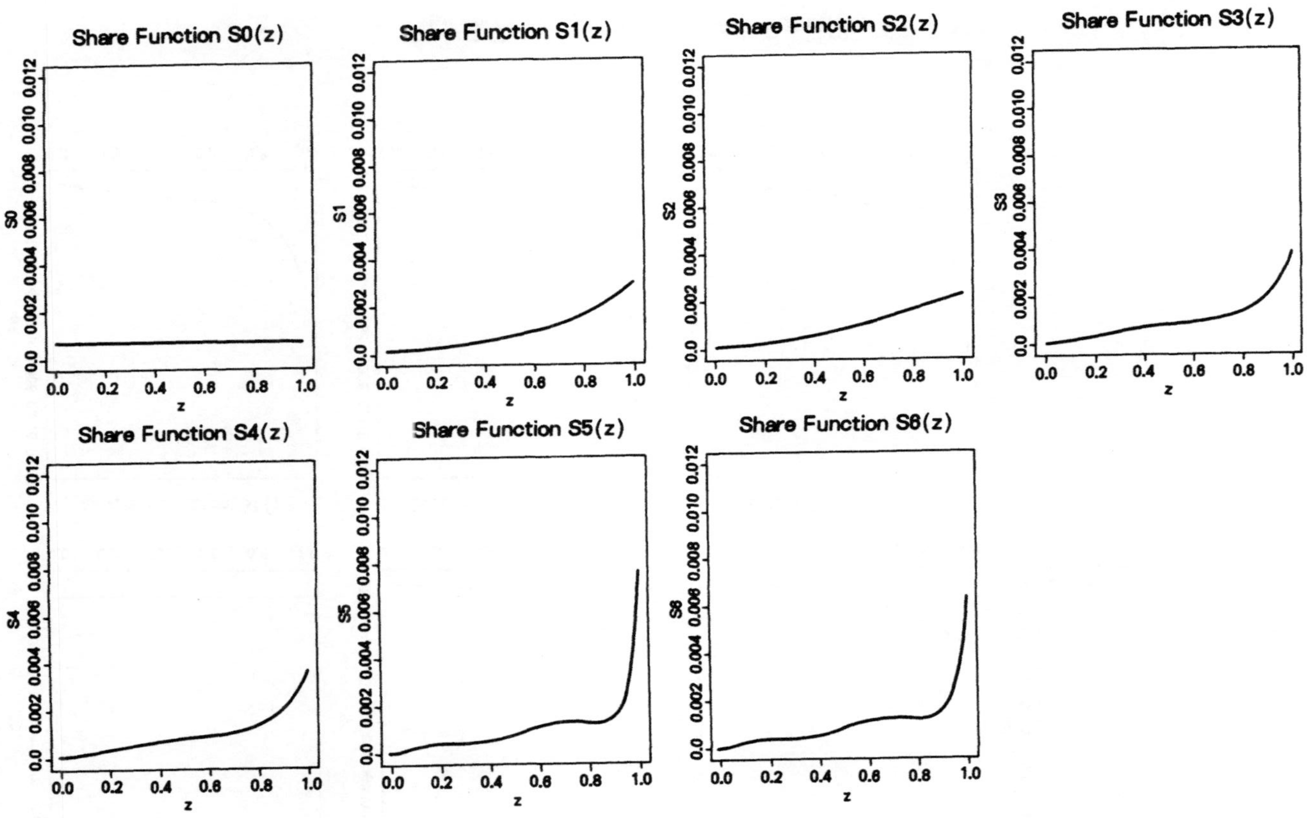

Fig. 5.6. Graph of the Share Functions for 1974.

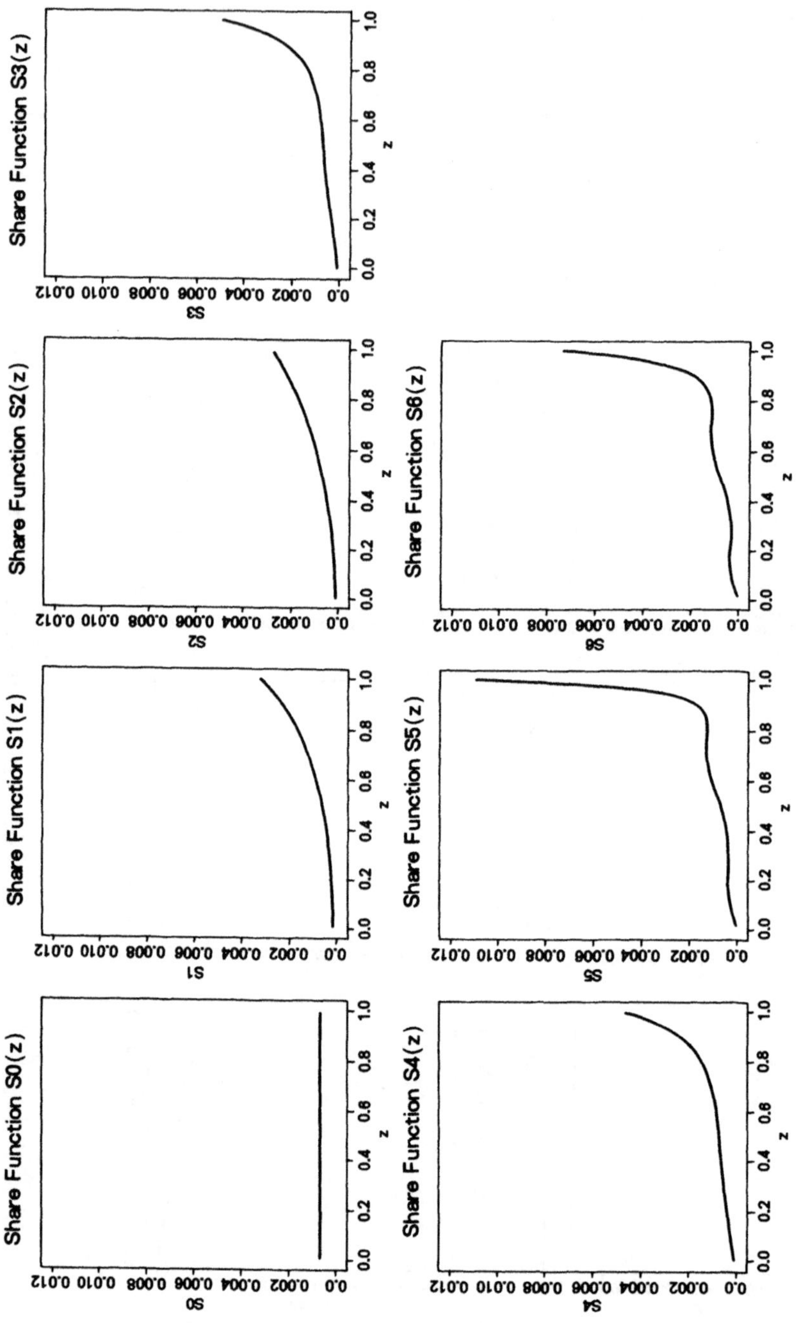

Fig. 5.7. Graph of the Share Functions for 1990.

change for poor people such as the shift from 0.0000253 to 0.0000145 cannot be detected.

For parameter estimation, we noted that OLS estimation of (5.10) asymptotically converges to those derived by orthogonality relationship, (5.9). When we compared the predicted values, the share function approximated by the ordinary least square estimation method. To be more specific, we have observations on the z axis at equal distances so that we are approximating a continuous function with an orthogonal polynomial expansion. There seems to be no reason to introduce the ordinary least square estimation method for this case.

Finally, though the 1990 measured function appears to lie above the 1974 function over the entire range we see that as we increase the precision of the approximation, the poorest cohort lost ground in the relative sense. We see that even though "a rising tide may lift all boats", inequality has increased. Many economists have argued that the rise of the technological information age and the attendant increase in the returns to skill of highly skilled workers and decline in the returns to skill of low skill workers has caused inequality to increase. The change should be reflected in a change in the shape of the income distribution over time. We have found our examination of the 1974 and 1990 observed distributions corroborates that hypothesis.

5.8 Summary and Concluding Remarks

Given a single inequality measure such as the Gini coefficient or Theil's measure, it is hard to describe the underlying share function or to derive a Lorenz curve. Therefore, we have introduced an index space representation for the share function (derivative of the Lorenz function). To obtain a globally good approximating function, we may expand the share function in any complete set of functions, but the Fourier functions oscillate rapidly and may not be adequate to approximate a smooth function. Therefore, we expanded the share function using a Legendre series. Since all the decomposing functions are orthogonal in this expansion, we can interpret the final share function as a result of a sequence of income redistribution between subincome groups beginning from an equal share. Another justification for introducing such a decomposing function is when we regress the share function with respect to the Legendre functions and estimate the parameters with the least squares method, one of the estimated coefficient ($\hat{a}_1$) can be used as an inequality measure. It satisfies all the requirements necessary for an inequality measure. If we can assume that all the parameters except the first two, $\hat{a}_2$, $\hat{a}_3$, $\cdots$ are nearly fixed when the income distribution shifts, then the whole transition mechanism can be summarized by a single income redistribution mechanism $\exp(a_1 P_1(z))$ because the first parameter a_0 corresponds to a normalization constant. Based upon this inequality measure, we can approximate the global shape of the share function and derive the Lorenz curve. Finally the power series expansion and the Legendre polynomial expansion are equivalent except for the orthogonality requirement so that we can expand the logarithm of the share function in a power series function and derive similar results.

The results of our research suggest that while income inequality has increased from 1974 through 1990, the share function of the lowest portion of the observed income distribution and the share function of the top of the observed income distribution have changed the most over the 15 year period. This result is consistent with the findings of others that returns to skill for low skill jobs have declined while they have increased for those at the top of the distribution as technological change has occurred.

Appendix 5.A : A Review of the Concepts of Completeness, Orthonormality, and Basis

Let (X, B, μ)be a measure space where X is a compact space, the set B is a Borel−sigma algebra, and μ is the Lebesgue measure. Define $L^2(X)$ to be the set of all Borel measurable real valued functions f whose squares are integrable on X, i.e., $\int_X |f(x)|^2 dx < \infty$. The set $L^2(X)$ is a normal linear space with norm of $\|f(x)\| = \left[\int_X |f(x)|^2 dx\right]^{1/2}$. There exists in $L^2(X)$ a countable set of elements, which is everywhere dense in the sense that every element of $L^2(X)$ can be approximated arbitrarily closely by elements belonging to this set. In other words, $L^2(X)$ is separable. An orthonormal sequence satisfies

$$\sum_{n=0}^{N(T)} P_n(x)P_m(x)dx=\delta_{nm},\ n,\ m=0,\ 1,\ 2,\ \cdots \tag{5.A.1}$$

where $\delta_{nm}=1$ if $n=m$ and zero otherwise.

The orthogonal sequence P_n in the space $L^2(X)$ is called complete if there is no element $f \neq 0$ of L^2 (X) which is orthogonal to all the elements P_n. In other words, for a complete system of equalities

$$\sum_{n=0}^{N(T)} f(x)P_n(x)dx=0\ (n=0,\ 1,\ 2,\ \cdots) \tag{5.A.2}$$

and for $f(x) \in L^2(X)$ it follows that $f(x)=0$ for almost all $x \in X$.

Suppose we have a countable set of elements in a sequence : g_0, g_1, g_2, $\cdots$, g_n, $\cdots$ We can then construct an orthonormal sequence by the Gram-Schmidt procedure. From the given sequence we delete the function 0 (if it occurs) and all those functions which can be expressed as linear combinations of the preceding ones. When proper normalization is performed, the resulting sequence $P_0(x)$, $P_1(x)$, $P_2(x)$,$\cdots$ is orthonormal.

$$P_0(x)=g_0(x)|\,g_0(x)| \tag{5.A.3}$$

$$Q_n(x)=g_n(x)-\sum_{i=0}^{n-1} P_i(x) \sum_{n=0}^{N(T)} g_n(x)P_i(x)dx,\ n \geq 1 \tag{5.A.4}$$

$$P_n(x)=Q_n(x)/|\,Q_n(x)| \tag{5.A.5}$$

If the orthonormal sequence $P_0(x)$, $P_1(x)$, $P_2(x)$, $\cdots$ satisfies the completeness condition, it is called as an orthonormal basis. We provide two examples of sequences and their corresponding ONBs.

1) Trigonometric expansion : Suppose we have a sequence 1, cos x, sin x, $\cdots$, cos nx, sin nx, $\cdots$ for $x \in [-\pi,\ +\pi]$. Since they are orthogonal, normalization will produce a complete ONB :

$$P_0(x)=\frac{1}{\sqrt{2\pi}},\ P_1(x)=\frac{\cos x}{\sqrt{\pi}},\ P_2(x)=\frac{\sin x}{\sqrt{\pi}},$$

$$P_3(x)=\frac{\cos 2x}{\sqrt{\pi}},\ P_4(x)=\frac{\sin 2x}{\sqrt{\pi}},\ \cdots \tag{5.A.6}$$

2) Legendre expansion : Suppose we have a sequence 1, x, x^2, ⋯ for x∈ [0, + 1], then the Gram - Schmidt orthogonalization will produce a complete ONB :

$$\begin{aligned}
&P_0(x)=1\\
&P_1(x)=\sqrt{3}(2x-1)\\
&P_2(x)=\sqrt{5}(6x^2-6x+1)\\
&P_3(x)=\sqrt{7}(20x^3-30x-12x-1)\\
&P_4(x)=\sqrt{9}(70xy^4-140x^3+90x^2 20x+1)
\end{aligned} \tag{5.A.7}$$

Chapter 6

Coordinate Space vs. Index Space Representations as Estimation Methods : An Application to How Macro Activity Affects the U.S. Income Distribution[36]

This chapter examines the impact of macroeconomic variables on the level of income inequality in U.S. The innovation is that we introduce what is known as an index space representation to do so. In an index space representation, income shares are considered as a linear combination of what are known as index functions. An index function is a polynomial function whose order is specified by the given index. The macroeconomic variables affect the function corresponding to each index function. In early years, we have only quintile data, but we can still derive a well behaved Lorenz curve, Gini coefficient, Theil's entropy measure, standard deviation of the logarithm of the share function, and Atkinson's inequality measure.

6.1 Introduction

There is a relatively sparse literature on the impact of macroeconomic variables on the size distribution of income. This is puzzling given the literally hundreds of papers that have been written on the measurement of and causes of income inequality within countries. One of the primary reasons there is a paucity of literature on the relationship between the macroeconomy and inequality is that the transmission mechanism whereby macroeconomic variables (like inflation) impact income distributions is not understood very well. While the macro approach to analyzing inequality has not been greatly explored, several researchers have examined the issue. Beach (1976, 1977) and Blinder and Esaki (1978) analyzed the relationship in seminal pieces on the subject almost 15 years ago. Nolan (1987), Slottje (1987), Haslag et al. (1989), Jorgenson and Slesnick (1984, 1990), Balke

[36] This chapter follows Ryu and Slottje (1994a).

and Slottje (1993), Haslag and Slottje (1994), Johnson and Shipp (1995) have recently explored the topic. Blank (1989), Blank and Blinder (1986), Blank and Card (1993), Ruggles and Stone (1992) and Ryscavage (1993), and Ryscavage et al. (1992) have all looked at the issue. The traditional method of analysis on this topic has been to regress income shares or a summary statistic of inequality against a broad set of macroeconomic aggregates. We avoid (what amounts to) regressing an empirical Lorenz curve against macroeconomic variables (as those other studies have done) because various inequality measures can be derived directly from a share function but not from a Lorenz curve. Again, none of these aforementioned papers has dealt directly with the major underlying problem of how macroeconomic variables impact the level of inequality in the overall income distribution. Previous work has either examined how the macro aggregates affected quintiles of the income distribution or how the macrovariables impacted a summary measure. Thus, previous work has told us little about how changes in variables like inflation or unemployment affect the overall shape of the income distribution. This chapter suggests a different methodology for analyzing the impact of macroeconomic variables on the level of income inequality. In so doing, we get closer to a description of the transmission mechanism whereby these macro variables affect the size distribution of income.

This chapter examines the effect of macroeconomic variables on the distribution of measured family income. Will an increase in inflation or an increase in the level of unemployment improve or worsen the relative position of a poor family? Several researchers have examined the hypothesis that business cycle fluctuations are correlated with movements in the size distribution of income. Many of the papers just cited studied the effect of the business cycle on the distribution of income while Haslag and Slottje (1994) introduced vector autoregressions to examine the relationships between inequality measures and several macroeconomic variables presumed to proxy a business cycle. This previous work discussed the effect of business cycle fluctuations or the effect of inflation on some summary inequality measure or on the share of certain income groups, e.g., how the share of the poorest quintile of income earners changed when inflation increased. However, it is not clear from an individual point of view how he or she will personally fare when inflation increases because even if the share of income of that income group increased (in which a given individual belongs) the individual's personal income share might decrease. Therefore, we introduce a method which provides more information on how the income share of each family is affected when macroeconomic variables change. Once we have derived the transformation mechanism whereby macrovariables impact the personal income share distribution, which corresponds to the distribution of a normalized measured income, we hope to better understand the transformation mechanism in which macroeconomic variables affect overall income inequality measures such as Theil's (1967) entropy measure, Atkinson's (1970) measure, and the standard deviation of the logarithm of income.

6.2 The Theory

We begin by establishing a semiparametric representation for the share function based upon an orthonormal basis (ONB) expansion. Ryu and Slottje (1994b) demonstrated the usefulness of decomposing the share function in an orthogonal sequence.

Let us review the definition of an orthonormal basis. Suppose we have a sequence in L^2 space. The sequence is called an orthonormal basis if it satisfies orthonormality and completeness. A sequence is called orthonormal if it satisfies $\int p_n(z)p_m(z)dz=\delta_{nm}$ for n, m=0, 1, 2, $\cdots$ where $\delta_{nm}=1$ if n=m and zero otherwise. The orthogonal sequence P_n is called complete if there is no element of L^2 which is orthogonal to all the elements P_n. We provide two examples of sequences and their corresponding ONBs.

1) Trigonometric expansion: Suppose we have a sequence {1, cos z, sin z, $\cdots$, cos nz, sin nz, $\cdots$} for $z\in[-\pi, +\pi]$. Since they are orthogonal, normalization will produce a complete ONB :

$$P_0(z)=\frac{1}{\sqrt{2\pi}},\ P_1(z)=\frac{\cos z}{\sqrt{\pi}},\ P_2(z)=\frac{\sin z}{\sqrt{\pi}},$$

$$P_3(z)=\frac{\cos 2z}{\sqrt{\pi}},\ P_4(z)=\frac{\sin 2z}{\sqrt{\pi}},\ \cdots$$

2) Legendre expansion: Suppose we have a sequence 1, z, z^2, … for $z \in [0, +1]$, then the Gram – Schmidt orthogonalization will produce a complete ONB:

$$
\begin{aligned}
P_0(z) &= 1 \\
P_1(z) &= \sqrt{3}(2z-1) \\
P_2(z) &= \sqrt{5}(6z^2-6z+1) \\
P_3(z) &= \sqrt{7}(20z^3-30z^2+12z-1)
\end{aligned}
\tag{6.1}
$$

We now apply the ONB to the problem at hand.

6.3 An Index Space Representation of the Share Function

Suppose there are I income groups within the society, and we rearrange the given observations of measured income, y_1, y_2, …, y_I, ordered by increasing income and then divide each measured income by a normalization constant.

The share function is defined as

$$s_i \equiv \frac{y_i}{\sum_{i=1}^{I} y_i} \tag{6.2}$$

Replacing index i with z_i where we place every individual within $[0, +1]$ at equally spaced distances,

$$s(z_i) = \frac{y(z_i)}{\sum_{i=1}^{I} y(z_i)} \quad \text{for} \quad z_i \equiv \frac{i}{I} - \frac{1}{2I} \tag{6.3}$$

After dividing the interval $[0, +1]$ in I groups, each group is represented by its center point. We interpret the share function as a probability density function (pdf) because the share $s(z_i)$ is the probability associated with the possibility that each dollar of total measured income will end up in the ith group. Suppose there are I individuals in the economy, and dollar bills are falling from the sky, so that each individual will collect falling dollar bills. Since each individual has different attributes and a different locational position, some people will collect more money than others. Each dollar bill will end up in the hand of the ith individual with probability $s(z_i)$ so that this share function can be interpreted as a discrete pdf.

$$\log s(z)=\sum_{n=0}^{N} a_n P_n(z) \quad \text{or} \quad s(z)=\exp\left[\sum_{n=0}^{N} a_n P_n(z)\right] \tag{6.4}$$

Blinder and Esaki (1978) estimated the change in the share of the quintiles in the distribution of income resulting from a fluctuation in the macroeconomic variables they considered. In this chapter, as an alternative approach, we expand the logarithm of the share function in a sequence of orthogonal polynomials. In the following, we explain the motivation for introducing the particular functional form (6.4).

First, we call the standard approach as introduced by Blinder and Esaki (1978) a histogram approach while our approach (6.4) is a continuous pdf approach. In the histogram approach, Blinder and Esaki are considering the probability that each dollar of total measured income will end up in each quintile group, but in the continuous probability density approach we establish the probability density function (represented as the share function) in a continuous population index z. As is well known, the histogram approach is a rough approximation and the share of an individual cannot be correctly specified if he is located near a boundary, e.g., near the end of the first quintile or near the beginning of the second quintile.

Second, we established the functional form of the share function rather than that of the Lorenz curve because a distribution function can be obtained from a probability density function (share function), but a probability density function can not be derived from a distribution function. Furthermore, many summary measures such as the Gini coefficient, Theil's entropy measure, and Atkinson's inequality measure, can be obtained directly from the share function. In comparison, only the Gini coefficient can be obtained directly from the Lorenz curve and then it is still only an approximation. Third, the motivation for introducing a logarithm (or exponential) function in (6.4) is explained by the following example. In Table 1 of Blinder and Esaki, a one percent increase in the unemployment rate decreases the share of the lowest fifth of income earners by 0.129 percent but increases the share of the highest fifth of income earners by 0.272 percent. In magnitude, the change in the share of the highest fifth seems to be bigger than the change in the lowest fifth, but when considering the relative ratio, there is a substantial difference. Since the share of total income of the poorest quintile is roughly 5 percent while that of the richest quintile is 41 percent on average, the relative change in share due to a one percent increase in the unemployment rate will cause a 2.5 percent decrease in share for the poorest quintile but a 0.66 percent increase in share of the richest quintile. Therefore, the suffering of the poorest fifth may not be adequately described by the standard approach. To get around this problem, we introduced the logarithm of the share function.

We have provided some justification for introducing a particular functional form for the share function as given in (6.4). In the following subsection, we explain further implications resulting from using an orthonormal basis expansion.

6.4 A Comparison of the Index Space Representation with the Coordinate Space Representation

We refer to Blinder and Esaki's approach as a coordinate space representation because they estimated how the quintile shares are affected by changes in the inflation rate and unemployment rate. In this chapter, as an alternative approach, we introduce an index space representation where we expand the logarithm of the share function in a sequence of orthogonal polynomials as stated by (6.4) and consider how the parameters a_n are affected by changes in the inflation rate and unemployment rate.

The following example explains the usefulness of the index space representation. Suppose we have an empirical share function (or any other continuous function) and we want to describe it very accurately but with an eye on cost. A very accurate but most painful way is the coordinate space representation where we could write down millions of points on the empirical share function for all values on the z coordinate. To avoid such complications, we may approximate the share function with kinked linear approximations where we choose only a handful z values and their corresponding values. This is called as a histogram method and utilized in Blinder and Esaki's paper. If five points are chosen, it is called a quintile distribution. In this chapter, as an alternative way to describe the share function (or any other continuous function) we propose a simple parametric functional form. In particular, expand the share function as a linear combination of well known index functions. This is a very convenient way to represent any continuous function because all that is needed is to write down the parameters corresponding to the index functions. As a particular example of this technique, we can expand any time series in a Fourier series and report the parameter values corresponding to frequency decomposed functions. Then we can reproduce the original time sequence simply by adding the frequency functions weighted by these parameters.

Therefore there is an analogy between a spectral analysis and the index space representation. The time coordinate in a spectral analysis corresponds to the z coordinate in the index space representation. In the spectral analysis, long run effects and short run effects are decomposed with low frequency and high frequency functions. In the index space representation, the redistribution of income is decomposed according to the index component. The redistribution between well separated income groups (between very rich and very poor) can be represented with a low index component while redistribution of income between nearby income groups can be described with an high index component. See Ryu and Slottjc (1994b) for more details.

In time series analysis, any modification to the original series can be performed by modifying the frequency component (as can be seen when we remove seasonality from a time series). In the index space representation, the impact of macroeconomic variables on the share function can be understood as a transition of parameter values of the share function.

When we expand a continuous function in an ONB, we have a variety of choices such as the Fourier series, Legendre polynomials, Hermite polynomials, Laguerre polynomials, Bessel functions, etc. However, most of these series expansions are not very useful for expanding a smooth convex function such as a Lorenz curve. Rapid oscillations of the high index term will not be very useful to approximate a smooth curve. A simple polynomial series expansion (power series) could be a better choice. In comparison, it is easy to impose smoothness or convexity for a power series expansion, $f(z)=c_0+c_1z+c_2z^2+\cdots+c_Nz^N$. If the parameters are positive, then f(z) is a smooth and convex function for $z\in[0, 1]$. A power series expansion becomes a Legendre series when we impose orthogonality condition. Further usefulness of the Legendre series can be seen when we estimate the inequality measure. In section 2.4, we shall find that Theil's entropy measure, standard deviation of the logarithm of the share function, and Atkinson's inequality measure can be expressed as a function of parameters of the Legendre series expansion.

6.5 The Impact of Macroeconomic Variables on the Share Function

We have provided justification for expanding the share function in an exponential ONB. In this section, we study the impact of macroeconomic variables on the share function. In particular, we consider the transition mechanism of the share function with respect to the inflation rate (π), unemployment (U), and time variable t. We expand the share function as a function of time variable (t) and population index (z).

For the given year $t=t_0$, if we have observations of $s(t_0, z_i)$ for $i=1, \cdots, I$, then $a_n(t_0)$ can be estimated. For different years, we have different share observations $s(t, z_i)$ and thus different $a_n(t)$ values are estimated. The causes of differences in the income distribution may come from differences in the inflation rate, unemployment rate, or others. As a simple approximation, establish the share function parameters a_n as

$$a_n(t)=\alpha_n+\beta_nD(t)+\gamma_nU(t)+\delta_n\pi(t)+v_nT(t)$$
$$+\xi_nT^2(t)+\phi_nT(t)\cdot D(t)+\varepsilon(t) \tag{6.6}$$

where [D(t)]is a dummy variable, T(t) is a linear time trend, and is a quadratic time trend.

$$\log s(z)=\sum_{n=0}^{N}a_n(t)P_n(z) \tag{6.7}$$

Now it is hopefully clear that Blinder and Esaki's approach is a coordinate space representation while (6.4) – (6.7) is an index space representation, where we study the time varying effect of $a_n(t)$.

As one of the referees pointed, we could have expanded the logarithm of the share function as a linear combination of monomials : 1, z, z^2, ⋯, z^N.

$$\log s(t, z) = \sum_{n=0}^{N} b_n(t) z^n \tag{6.8}$$

$$b_n(t) = \alpha'_n + \beta'_n D(t) + \gamma'_n U(t) + \delta'_n \pi(t) + \upsilon'_n T(t) + \xi'_n T^2(t) + \phi'_n T(t)D(t) + \varepsilon'(t) \tag{6.9}$$

In fitting, it does not matter whether one uses orthogonalized polynomials or the usual monomials as the basis function. A set of N polynomials of degree N whose members are orthogonal under a weight function are just linear combinations of the usual monomials : 1, z, z^2, ⋯, z^N. The coefficient $a_n(t)$ would be different from $b_n(t)$, but the coefficient $a_n(t)$ is also another linear transformation of the coefficient $b_n(t)$. The predicted values are invariant to such linear transformations and thus they are same either one uses (6.5) or (6.8).

In this chapter, we do not emphasize the role of the orthogonality of the chosen index functions. In another paper, Ryu and Slottje (1997) apply the orthogonality condition so that the income distribution can be decomposed into redistribution between the subgroups. We have given a more complete interpretation to the orthogonality condition in that paper.

To estimate the parameters of (6.5) for a given year, we can apply a least squares

$$(\hat{a}_n)_{LS} = [(X'X)^{-1}X' \log s(t, z_j)]_n \tag{6.10}$$

method, where X is a I by N+1 matrix with element $[X]_{in} = P_n(z_i)$. If we apply the orthogonality conditions to (6.10),

$$\lim_{I \to \infty} \frac{1}{I} \sum_{i=1}^{I} P_n(z_i) P_m(z_j) = \int_0^{+1} P_n(z) P_m(z) dz = \delta_{nm}$$

then $X'X$ becomes a unit matrix of order N+1 with diagonal element 1. The least squares method can be simplified as

$$(\hat{a}_n)_{ONB} = \frac{1}{I} \sum_{i=1}^{I} P_n(z_i) \log s(z_i) \tag{6.11}$$

The difference between the OLS estimation and ONB estimation of a_n is further discussed in section 6.7.

6.6 Inequality Measures Associated with the Legendre Polynomial Expanded Share Function

Thus far, we have expanded the logarithm of the share function in a polynomial series and examined the impact of macroeconomic variables upon the income distribution. Once we have established the functional form of the share function, various inequality measures can be estimated based upon the estimated share function. We begin by examining Theil's measure.

1) Theil's entropy measure

Using Shannon's (1948) definition of entropy $W = -\int s(z) \log s(z) dz$, Theil's entropy measure is defined as negative entropy if the domain of z is restricted to [0, 1].

$$\begin{aligned} H &\equiv -\text{Entropy} \\ &= \int s(z) \log s(z) dz \\ &= \sum_{i=1}^{I} s(z_i) \log[I s(z_i)] \\ &= \log I - \sum_{i=1}^{I} s(z_i) \log[1/s(z_i)] \end{aligned} \tag{6.12}$$

where we converted a discrete share function $s(z_i)$ into a continuous share function s(z) using $s(z_i) = s(z)/I$. Applying the series expansion

$$\log s(z) = a_0 P_0(z) + a_1 P_1(z) + \cdots + a_N P_N(z) \text{ for } z = [0, 1]$$

Theil's entropy measure stated in (6.12) can be calculated using (6.11):

$$\begin{aligned} H &= \int s(z) [a_0 P_0 + a_1 P_1(z) + \cdots + a_N P_N(z)] dz \\ &= a_0 E[P_0(z)] + a_1 E[P_1(z)] + \cdots + a_N E[P_N(z)] \end{aligned}$$

where the expectation operator is with respect to the share function.

2) Standard Deviation of the logarithm of the share function

We define the measure as

$$
\begin{aligned}
D &= \int [\log s(z) - \mu]^2 dz \\
&= \int [[a_0 - \mu] + a_1 P_1(z) + \cdots + a_N P_n(z)]^2 dz \\
&= (a_0 - \mu)^2 + a_1^2 + \cdots + a_N^2
\end{aligned}
$$

where μ is the logarithm of a share when every individual has an equal share.

3) Atkinson's (1970) inequality measure

This measure is defined as

$$A = 1 - \frac{s^*}{\mu} \tag{6.14}$$

here μ is the mean share and the equally distributed equivalent level of share s^* is given by

$$U(s^*) = \frac{1}{I} \sum_{i=1}^{I} U(s_i) \tag{6.15}$$

If we choose a particular form of utility function, i.e., a logarithmic utility function of the normalized income which is equal to the share s(z) for the zth individual group,

$$U(s) = \log s(z) = a_0 P_0(z) + a_1 P_1(z) + \cdots + a_N P_N(z) \tag{6.16}$$

We can then introduce (6.16) into (6.15) and use $(1/I) \sum_{i=1}^{I} P_n(z_i) P_0 = \delta_{n0}$,

$$U(s^*) = \log s^* = a_0$$

Then we get

$$s^* = \exp[a_0] \qquad \text{and} \qquad A = 1 - \frac{\exp[a_0]}{\mu}$$

Atkinson also suggested a more general homothetic utility function to describe his inequality measure in a more general way. However, if we had used a more general definition of entropy, then we uncover a monotonic transformation for the entire Atkinson family of indices. See Shorrocks (1980) for details. We emphasize again, that by using the share function approach, we are able to see how changes in the exogenous variables directly impact the overall shape of income distribution through the components of the income distribution measure.

6.7 The Empirical Results

6.7.1 The Performance of the Lorenz Curve Expanded in an Exponential Polynomial Series

Suppose we have an empirical Lorenz curve derived from a large number of income observations. Our first objective is to have this empirical Lorenz curve be well approximated with an exponential polynomial series. Even if we use only five points of the empirical Lorenz curve (quintile data), we can approximate the empirical Lorenz curve at all points of z. Therefore for those early years when we have only quintile data, we can still approximate the unknown Lorenz curve well.

$$L(t, z) = \exp[b_0(t) + b_1(t)z + b_2(t)z^2 + b_3(t)z^3 + b_4(t)z^4] \quad (6.17)$$

The usefulness of the exponential polynomial functional form (6.17) is discussed in Ryu and Slottje (1996a) where they compared its performance with that of the Bayesian approach, the Bernstein polynomial approach, and Basmann, Hayes, Johnson, and Slottje [BHJS (1990)] nonlinear functional form approach. Without knowledge of a good approximating functional form for the Lorenz curve, all we can do with quintile data for early years is to assume an uniform distribution of income within quintile groups and plot the Lorenz curve with a connected kinked lines. This is called as a histogram approach. Our second objective is that the exponential Legendre series approximates the underlying share function well so that the Lorenz curve, derived by integrating this approximated share function, approximates the empirical Lorenz curve well. We perform this experiment with 100 samples reported by Basmann, Hayes, Johnson, and Slottje [BHJS (1990)]. In the following, we compare four different Lorenz curves using the data reported in BHJS.

Model 1 : Empirical Lorenz curve of BHJS

Model 2 : Share function in an exponential ONB

$$s(t, z)=\exp\left[\sum_{n=0}^{6} a_n(t)P_n(z)\right] \Rightarrow L(t, z)=\int_0^z s(t, z')dz' \qquad (6.18)$$

Model 3 : Lorenz curve in an exponential polynomial series

$$L(t, z)=\exp[b_0(t)+b_1(t)z+b_2(t)z^2+b_3(t)z^3+b_4(t)z^4]$$

Parameters are estimated using five points L(t, z=0.2), L(t, z=0.4), L(t, z =0.6), L(t, z=0.8), and L(t, z=1.0).

Model 4 : Quintile Lorenz Curve

$$s(t, z_i)=\text{fixed constant for } i=1, 2, \cdots, 5 \Rightarrow L(t, z)=\int_0^z s(t, z')dz'$$

In the first column in Table 6.1, z represents the population index. If z= 0.2, it represents the 20th poorest percentile out of the 100. Similarly, if z=0.9, it represents the 10th richest percentile out of thc 100. The second column is the actual empirical Lorenz curve (Model 1) reported in BHJS. In the fifth column, a histogram based Lorenz curve (Model 4) is reported where we derived a Lorenz curve assuming all people inside of each quintile group had equal income. The histogram based Lorenz curve always overestimates the empirical Lorenz curve particularly at both ends. Now applying the functional form of an exponential polynomial series expansion for the Lorenz curve, Model 3 is estimated with the least squares method and reported on the fourth column. The Lorenz curve (6.1) is derived using only five points of data (z=0.2, ⋯,1), so that no degree of freedom is left, but approximation with this function is remarkable except near the boundary points (z=0.05 and z=0.95). This is the reason we emphasized this functional form for the Lorenz curve in Ryu and Slottje (1996a). From

Table 6.1 Comparison of Various Lorenz Curves for 1977

Z	Empirical L(z)[a] (Model 1)	Based on ONB Share[b] (Model 2)	Based on Exp. Poly[c] (Model 3)	Based on Histogram[d] (Model 4)
0.05	0.0061	0.0068	0.0140	0.0132
0.10	0.0180	0.0159	0.0231	0.0264
0.15	0.0337	0.0284	0.0358	0.0396
0.20	0.0528	0.0452	0.0528	0.0528
0.25	0.0754	0.0667	0.0742	0.0807
0.30	0.1015	0.0931	0.1001	0.1086
0.35	0.1311	0.1239	0.1302	0.1365
0.40	0.1644	0.1587	0.1644	0.1644
0.45	0.2014	0.1969	0.2022	0.2074
0.50	0.2424	0.2382	0.2435	0.2504
0.55	0.2873	0.2827	0.2881	0.2934
0.60	0.3364	0.3308	0.3364	0.3364
0.65	0.3898	0.3833	0.3888	0.3976
0.70	0.4481	0.4412	0.4461	0.5689
0.75	0.5116	0.5059	0.5098	0.5202
0.80	0.5814	0.5788	0.5814	0.5814
0.85	0.6587	0.6616	0.6632	0.6861
0.90	0.7459	0.7564	0.7578	0.7907
0.95	0.8491	0.8669	0.8687	0.8954
1.00	1.0000	1.0000	1.0000	1.0000
Gini	0.3582	0.3630	0.3527	0.3360
Theil	0.2230	0.2240	0.2116	0.1975
SD[e]	0.6863	0.7086	0.6792	0.5448
Atkinson	0.2292	0.2366	0.2287	0.2014

[a] The Empirical Lorenz Curve is reproduced from BHJS(1990).

[b] The share function is expanded in an exponential Legendre series and a Lorenz curve is obtained by integration of the share function.

[c] Expand the Lorenz Curve in an exponential polynomial series. Quintile data were used to estimate the parameters.

[d] The Lorenz Curve is derived by connecting the quintile points.

[e] Standard deviation of the logarithm of the share function.

this Lorenz curve, we can generate 1000 samples of share observations. Based upon these share values, we can estimate the share function of Model 2 whose parameters are estimated by (6.11). We get a Lorenz curve when this share function is integrated and its values are reported in the third column. The performance of this approach is satisfactory at all ranges of z. We have estimated the parameters with the ONB method ($a_1=0.7772$, $a_2=-0.1267$, $a_3=0.1230$, $a_4=-0.0075$, $a_5=-0.0199$, $a_6=0.0159$). If we had used the least squares method for (3.2), we get ($a_1=0.7769$, $a_2=-0.1267$, $a_3=-0.1230$, $a_5=-0.0198$, and $a_6=0.0158$). Therefore, it does not matter whether we use the orthogonal method (6.11) or a least squares method (6.10).

At the bottom of Table 6.1, we report the estimated income inequality measures, Gini, Theil, standard deviation of the logarithm of the share function (SD), and an Atkinson measure. The share function approach or the exponential ONB expansion approach both performed well but the histogram based approach showed some departure.

In Fig. 6.1, we plotted the empirical Lorenz curve with a smooth curve (Model 1), and the histogram based Lorenz curve with a kinked line (Model 4). This curve is correct at point $z=0.0, 0.2, \cdots, 1.0$, but the connected lines (from the histogram approach) always over estimated the convex Lorenz curve. The dotted line represents the share function based Lorenz curve listed in the third column (Model 2) of Table 6.1. In Fig. 6.2, we show the Lorenz curve (6.17) derived using only quintile data with dotted points (Model 3) and the smooth curve is the empirical Lorenz curve (Model 1).

6.7.2 The Impact of Macroeconomic Variables on the Share Function

Now we turn to the transition mechanism of the share function with respect to the macroeconomic variables. In particular, we utilize quintile data for family income for the years 1947 to 1990. Since CPS microdata (individual income records) only go back to 1968, we are constrained to using the quintile data to obtain a longer series. To accomplish our objective, we derive a Lorenz curve (6.17) for each year using the quintile data and then

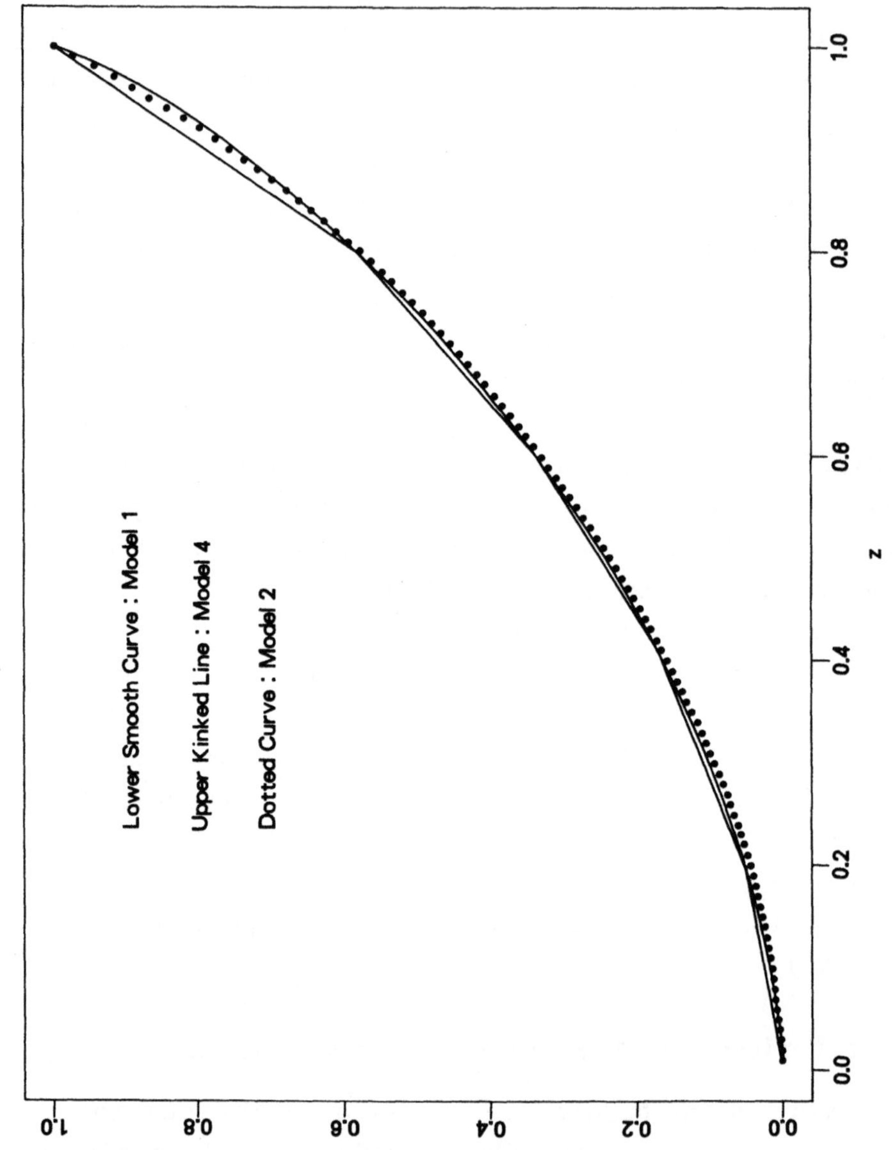

Fig. 6.1. Comparison of Various Lorenz Curves

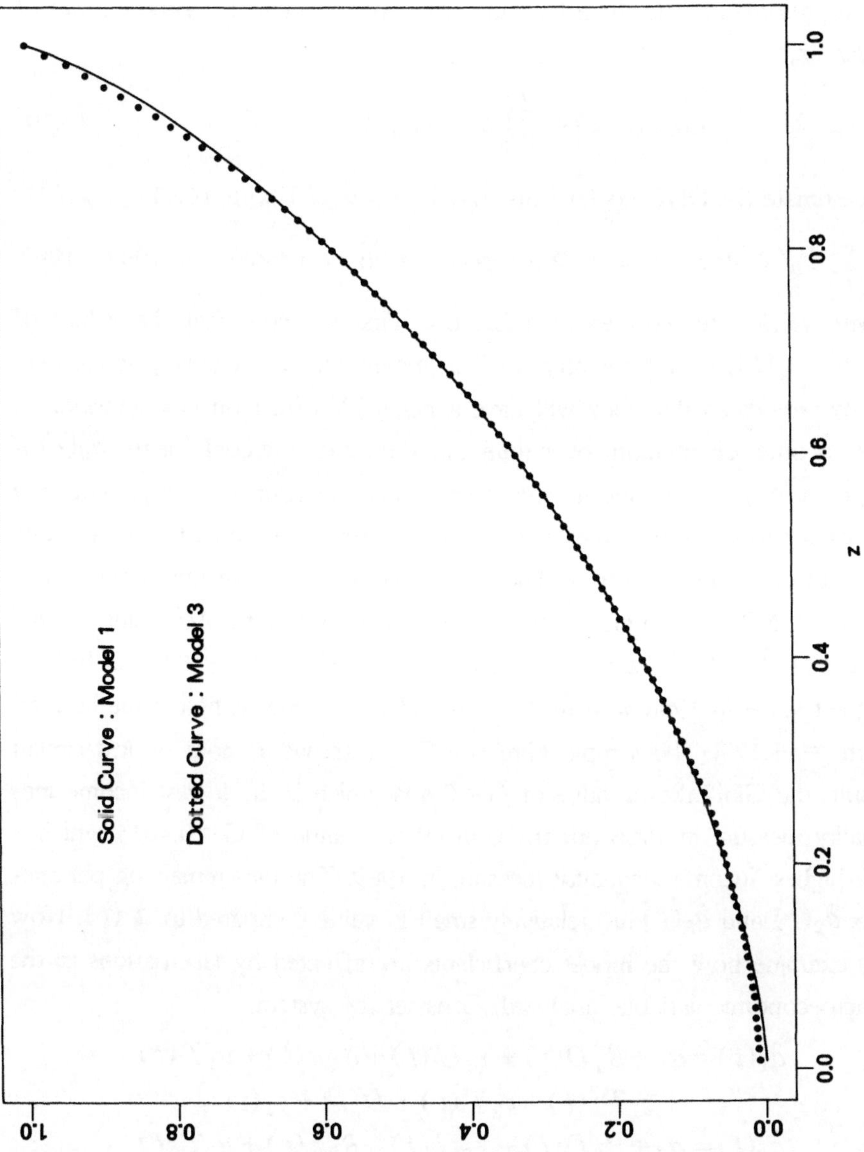

Fig. 6.2. Performance of Exp. Polynomial Lorenz Curve

generate 1000 share observations from the derivative of the derived Lorenz curve.

Approximating the share function with an exponential Legendre series of order six,

$$\log s(t, z) = \sum_{n=0}^{6} a_n(t) P_n(z) \tag{6.19}$$

we estimate the ONB coefficients $\hat{a}_0(t), \cdots, \hat{a}_6(t)$ with (6.11), $\hat{a}_n(t) = \frac{1}{I}\sum_{i=1}^{I} P_n(z_i)\log s(t, z_i)$. We repeat the above process for 1947 – 1990. These values are reported in Table 6.2. First we note that the values of $\hat{a}_4(t)$, $\hat{a}_5(t)$, $\hat{a}_6(t)$ are very small in magnitude and relatively stable over many periods so that they will have a negligible effect on any transition in the income distribution over time. For the remaining coefficients, $\hat{a}_0(t)$ is large in magnitude, but it is a normalizing constant to compensate any changes produced by other coefficients so that one should not give any particular interpretation to it. Therefore, $\hat{a}_1(t)$ is the most important factor in our ONB representation of the income distribution. According to the values of $\hat{a}_1(t)$, we have the lowest value in 1966 with $\hat{a}_1 = 1.030$, but the highest value in 1988 with $\hat{a}_1 = 1.176$ and the second highest value in 1989 with = 1.174. The sample Gini coefficient shows a more or less similar result, the Gini takes a value of G=0.404 which is the lowest income inequality measure in 1966 but the Gini takes a value of G=0.4615 which is the highest income inequality measure in 1989. The two remaining parameters $\hat{a}_2(t)$ and $\hat{a}_3(t)$ are relatively small in value compared to $\hat{a}_1(t)$. Now we examine how the model coefficients are affected by fluctuations in the macroeconomic variables analyzed. Consider the system,

$$\begin{aligned}
\hat{a}_1(t) &= \alpha_1 + \beta_1 D(t) + \gamma_1 U(t) + \delta_1 \pi(t) + v_1 T(t) \\
&\quad + \xi_1 T^2(t) + \phi_1 T(t) \cdot D(t) + \varepsilon_1(t) \\
\hat{a}_2(t) &= \alpha_2 + \beta_2 D(t) + \gamma_2 U(t) + \delta_2 \pi(t) + v_2 T(t) \\
&\quad + \xi_2 T^2(t) + \phi_2 T(t) \cdot D(t) + \varepsilon_2(t) \\
&\ \vdots \qquad\qquad \vdots \\
\hat{a}_N(t) &= \alpha_N + \beta_N D(t) + \gamma_N U(t) + \delta_N \pi(t) + v_N T(t) \\
&\quad + \xi_N T^2(t) + \phi_N T(t) \cdot D(t) + \varepsilon_N(t)
\end{aligned} \tag{6.20}$$

Table 6.2

Estimated ONB Coefficients of Share Functions for 1947 − 1990.

Yaer	$\hat{a}_0$	$\hat{a}_1$	$\hat{a}_2$	$\hat{a}_3$	$\hat{a}_4$	$\hat{a}_5$	$\hat{a}_6$
1947	−10.167	1.101	−0.188	0.254	−0.028	−0.035	0.022
1948	−10.165	1.103	−0.210	0.263	−0.029	−0.035	0.022
1949	−10.188	1.149	−0.240	0.272	−0.038	−0.035	0.022
1950	−10.186	1.145	−0.244	0.278	−0.036	−0.036	0.022
1951	−10.149	1.083	−0.223	0.261	−0.034	−0.035	0.022
1952	−10.158	1.097	−0.223	0.265	−0.040	−0.035	0.022
1953	−10.157	1.107	−0.268	0.266	−0.043	−0.035	0.022
1954	−10.178	1.140	−0.264	0.266	−0.041	−0.034	0.022
1955	−10.158	1.104	−0.245	0.259	−0.033	−0.034	0.022
1956	−10.143	1.078	−0.239	0.254	−0.033	−0.034	0.022
1957	−10.132	1.062	−0.245	0.251	−0.035	−0.034	0.022
1958	−10.141	1.077	−0.245	0.248	−0.034	−0.033	0.022
1959	−10.152	1.093	−0.242	0.250	−0.028	−0.033	0.022
1960	−10.158	1.106	−0.247	0.248	−0.036	−0.033	0.022
1961	−10.173	1.126	−0.234	0.250	−0.031	−0.033	0.022
1962	−10.151	1.091	−0.225	0.234	−0.034	−0.032	0.022
1963	10.150	1.090	−0.227	0.233	−0.030	−0.032	0.022
1964	−10.148	1.084	−0.217	0.224	−0.022	−0.031	0.022
1965	−10.139	1.069	−0.216	0.227	−0.023	−0.032	0.022
1966	−10.118	1.030	−0.197	0.216	−0.021	−0.032	0.022
1967	−10.121	1.037	−0.207	0.218	−0.022	−0.031	0.022
1968	−10.119	1.030	−0.192	0.220	−0.023	−0.032	0.022
1969	−10.119	1.030	−0.192	0.220	−0.023	−0.032	0.022
1970	−10.132	1.053	−0.198	0.221	−0.025	−0.032	0.022
1971	−10.133	1.052	−0.187	0.209	−0.012	−0.031	0.022
1972	−10.139	1.063	−0.189	0.208	−0.017	−0.031	0.022
1973	−10.134	1.055	−0.185	0.201	−0.017	−0.030	0.022
1974	−10.131	1.051	−0.187	0.204	−0.022	−0.031	0.022
1975	−10.140	1.066	−0.193	0.199	−0.012	−0.030	0.022

1976	−10.140	1.066	−0.193	0.199	−0.012	−0.030	0.022
1977	−10.153	1.089	−0.198	0.200	−0.013	−0.030	0.022
1978	−10.154	1.090	−0.196	0.203	−0.011	−0.030	0.022
1979	−10.154	1.090	−0.196	0.203	−0.011	−0.030	0.022
1980	−10.156	1.097	−0.206	0.202	−0.018	−0.030	0.022
1981	−10.169	1.116	−0.203	0.195	−0.012	−0.029	0.022
1982	−10.188	1.148	−0.208	0.213	−0.030	−0.030	0.022
1983	−10.191	1.151	−0.208	0.208	−0.020	−0.030	0.022
1984	−10.193	1.155	−0.204	0.202	−0.021	−0.029	0.022
1985	−10.203	1.168	−0.202	0.210	−0.018	−0.030	0.022
1986	−10.209	1.173	−0.194	0.212	−0.012	−0.030	0.022
1987	−10.209	1.173	−0.194	0.212	−0.012	−0.030	0.022
1988	−10.212	1.176	−0.188	0.208	−0.011	−0.030	0.022
1989	−10.213	1.174	−0.183	0.221	−0.013	−0.031	0.022
1990	−10.212	1.173	−0.185	0.218	−0.016	−0.031	0.022

where U(t) is the overall unemployment rate, $\pi(t)$ is the rate of inflation, T(t) is a linear time trend, $T^2(t)$ is a quadratic time trend, and D(t) is a dummy variable which is zero for 1947−1957 but one for 1958−1990. We included a quadratic time trend because the sample Gini coefficient showed a U shaped curve for 1947−1990. We report the OLS estimated parameters in Table 6.3. We selected the OLS estimation method since it will produce the same results as Zellner's (1962) seemingly unrelated regression method when the right-hand variables are identical in all equations.

When the unemployment rate increases by one percent, the coefficients $a_0(t)$, $a_1(t)$, $a_2(t)$, $\cdots$ change by −0.005, 0.0099, −0.0053, $\cdots$. Similar interpretation can be made of the coefficients when the inflation rate increases by one percent. Since direct interpretation of the above results are difficult, we plotted Fig. 6.3 to see how the share functions transform. When the inflation rate increase by one percent, the income share of the lowest 80 percent of people increased while the share of top 20 percent decreased. In relative terms, the share of the poorest group increased a lot. Similar interpretations can be given for the unemployment rate increase.

Table 6.3 The Effect of Macroeconomic Variables on the ONB Coefficients of the Share Functions. (standard errors in parentheses)

Variables	a_0	a_1	a_2	a_3	a_4	a_5	a_6
Constant	−10.182	1.1228	−0.1968	0.2786	−0.0320	−0.0364	0.0216
	(0.007)	(0.013)	(0.010)	(0.005)	(0.004)	(0.000)	(0.000)
Unemployment	−0.0050	0.0099	−0.0053	0.0002	−0.0009	0.0001	0.0000
	(0.001)	(0.002)	(0.001)	(0.001)	(0.001)	(0.000)	(0.000)
Inflation	0.0021	−0.0035	0.0012	−0.0010	−0.0003	0.0000	0.0000
	(0.000)	(0.001)	(0.001)	(0.000)	(0.000)	(0.000)	(0.000)
Dummy	−0.0143	0.0397	−0.0762	0.0399	−0.0171	−0.0020	−0.0004
	(0.016)	(0.028)	(0.020)	(0.010)	(0.009)	(0.001)	(0.001)
Time	0.0070	−0.0098	−0.0027	−0.0030	0.0000	0.0002	0.0000
	(0.001)	(0.001)	(0.001)	(0.001)	(0.000)	(0.000)	(0.000)
$Time^2$	−0.0002	0.0003	−0.0001	0.0001	−0.0000	−0.0001	0.0000
	(0.000)	(0.013)	(0.000)	(0.000)	(0.000)	(0.000)	(0.000)
Time x Dummy	0.0006	−0.0029	−0.0086	−0.0037	−0.0019	−0.0002	0.0000
	(0.001)	(0.002)	(0.002)	(0.001)	(0.001)	(0.000)	(0.000)
R^2	0.931	0.910	0.839	0.964	0.802	0.968	0.140
Mean of LHS Var	−10.160	1.1002	−0.2120	0.2277	−0.0239	−0.0319	0.0219

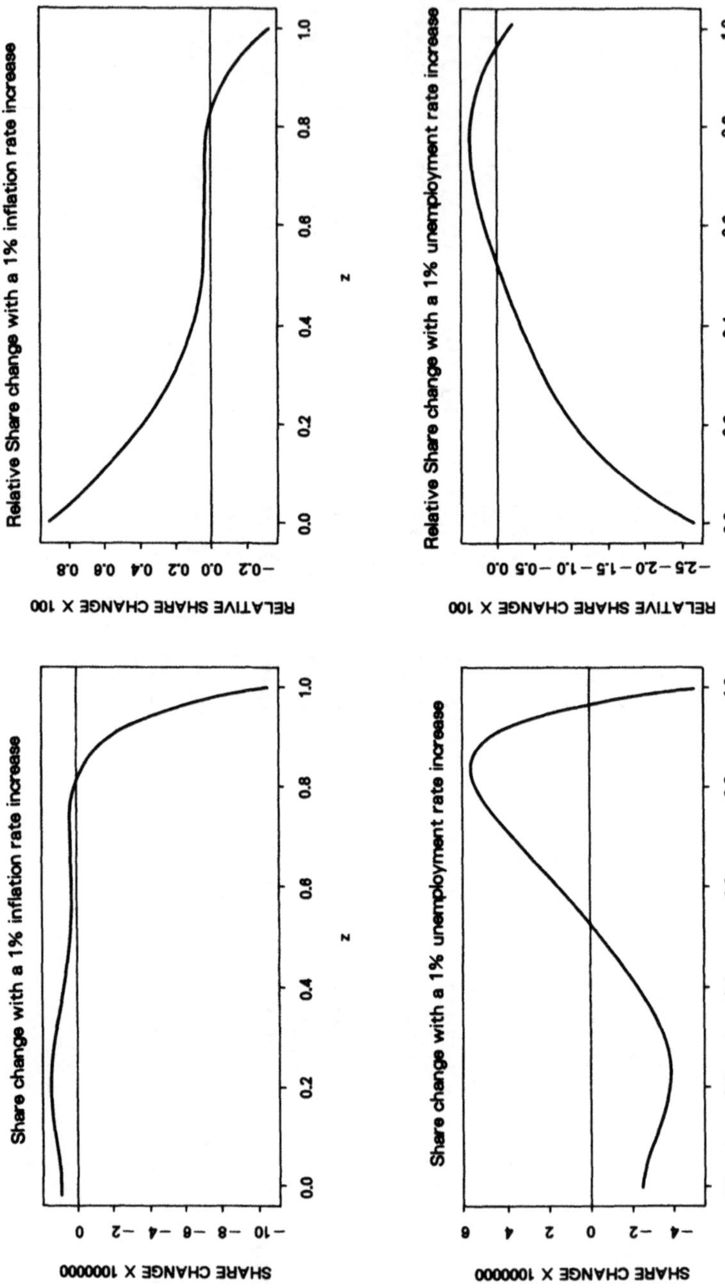

Fig. 6.3. Share Change with a 1% increase in the inflation or unemp. rate.

6.8 Summary and Concluding Remarks

In this chapter, we have introduced a global approximation method to describe the transition mechanism of the share function which describes an underlying income distribution against fluctuations in several macroeconomic variables. The global approximation approach is shown to be useful compared to the standard local approximation method usually considered. Based on knowledge of a good approximating Fig. 6.3 functional form, it is possible to approximate the Lorenz curve globally well even if we have access only to quintile data. By introducing a power series expansion (or equivalently a Legendre polynomial series expansion) to approximate the logarithm of the share function, we could examine the macroeconomic variables impact to the function parameters, and thus transition mechanism of income distribution.

To summarize our results, a one percent increase in the inflation rate increases the income share of the poorest cohort and decreases the income share of the richest group. However, if the change in income share is interpreted as a relative change, then the poorest cohort gained 0.8% in income while the richest lost only 0.2%. Similarly, when the unemployment rate increases, both the richest and poorest groups lose ground. These changes would not have been detectable with the standard methods of analysis. Such fine details can not be detected even in principle using a more traditional approach because usually the share of each quintile of income earners is just regressed against macroeconomic variables.

6.6 Summary and Concluding Remarks

[illegible]

[illegible]

Chapter 7

A New Method for Estimating Limited Dependent Variables : An Analysis of Hunger

7.1 Introduction

The issue of hunger in America was considered resolved in the 1970's after attracting so much attention in the 1960's. President Johnson's War on Poverty was thought to have solved the problem once and for all. The poverty rate in the United States began to fall drastically with the onslaught of the Great Society Programs in the 1960's and continued to do so until the early 1970's when the poverty rate started creeping up again. In the early 1980's the poverty rate again began to level off, only to rise again during the Reagan and Bush eras, cf. Jorgenson (1990).

Concurrent with these trends, there has been a gradual awareness that many of those whom are poor are children. Children have the highest probability of being poor and thus are the most susceptible to being hungry. The Commerce Department reported that one of four children in the U.S. lives in poverty with 5 million children younger than 6 living in families with incomes below the poverty level. Most economists have reached the overall conclusion that the economic status of children has worsened greatly in the last 30 years. Robins (1992) has shown that child support awards have declined over time even as divorce rates increased. A recent study conducted by a Washington research group, the Food Research and Action Center, estimated that hunger afflicts 6.5 million children in the United States. If one accepts their estimates of hunger perception as reasonable, as can be seen in Table 7.1, there is considerable variance across states with respect to the number of hungry children.[37]

---

[37] The problem of course, is that quantifying "hunger" is very difficult since it is a multidimensional problem. This is quite obvious when one peruses the survey used to construct the hunger count (see Table 7.2).

Table 7.1 Hungry Children in the U.S. 1991

State	Percent	Number of Hungry Children
Alabama	16.4	127,455
Alaska	9.3	9,701
Arizona	13.0	81,384
Arkansas	17.1	79,241
California	11.7	647,014
Colorado	10.0	56,984
Connecticut	9.1	39,202
Delaware	11.9	11,603
District of Columbia	18.2	13,395
Florida	14.1	246,294
Georgia	15.4	159,374
Hawaii	11.4	21,875
Idaho	13.4	34,390
Illinois	10.7	276,889
Indiana	10.4	121,279
Iowa	10.0	71,503
Kansas	10.5	44,990
Kentucky	15.1	97,452
Louisiana	15.5	132,993
Maine	14.4	23,555
Maryland	10.0	61,024
Massachusetts	10.8	83,980
Michigan	10.1	224,520
Minnesota	9.0	74,352
Mississippi	19.4	99,035
Missouri	11.8	110,182
Montana	12.1	21,726
Nebraska	10.9	37,165
Nevada	9.9	25,505
New Hampshire	10.0	10,883

Table 7.1 (continued)

New Mexico	16.1	52,416
New York	13.5	412,560
North Carolina	14.8	142,733
North Dakota	12.1	15,081
Ohio	10.6	225,480
Oklahoma	12.8	75,747
Oregon	10.3	55,767
Pennsylvania	11.4	227,703
Rhode Island	11.7	18,458
South Carolina	15.9	97,321
South Dakota	15.2	17,336
Tennessee	15.1	125,183
Texas	13.6	449,833
Utah	11.6	51,703
Vermont	13.0	9,634
Virginia	12.0	100,903
Washington	9.5	89,923
West Virginia	13.7	59,847
Wisconsin	9.2	97,015
Wyoming	8.0	9,538
U.S. TOTAL	12.3	5,502,014

SOURCE: Dallas Morning News, March 27, 1991, p. 26A.

Table 7.2 Questions Asked to Determine Level of Hunger in the U.S.

The following estimates of childhood hunger were calculated in part through a survey of 2,335 randomly selected low-income households from Alabama, California, Connecticut, Florida, Michigan, Minnesota and New York. It included the following questions :

1) Does your household ever run out of money to buy food to make a meal?

2) Do you or adults in your household ever eat less than you feel you should because there is not enough money for food?

3) Do you or adults in your household ever cut the size of meals or skip meals because there is not enough money for food?

4) Do your children ever eat less than you feel they should because there is not enough money for food?

5) Do you ever cut the size of your children's meals or do they ever skip meals because there is not enough money for food?

6) Do your children ever say they are hungry because there is not enough food in the house?

7) Do you ever rely on a limited number of foods to feed your children because you are running out of money to buy food for a meal?

8) Do any of your children ever go hungry because there is not enough money to buy food?

Families answering yes to at least five questions were considered hungry. Survey results nationwide were combined with federal poverty statistics to estimate hunger in each state.

SOURCE : Food Research and Action Center

The purpose of this chapter is twofold. First, we introduce a new econometric method to estimate the impact of political and socioeconomic variables on an ill-defined variable (hunger) and then we examine how the infrastructure of both the legal and political systems, as well as the economic system, are associated with the perceived level of hunger among children across states using our new estimation method. Specifically, there is considerable variance across states with respect to individual state enforcement of child support laws, cf, Good and Pirog-Good (1990). AFDC payments vary by states as do unemployment rates. There is ,of course, considerable debate about the incentive effects of the U.S. welfare system. The political preference structure of a state may also be reflected in that state's tolerance of hunger levels and poverty rates. The methods introduced below will allow us to see how differences in these variables across states are associated with differences in hunger levels across states. In section 7.2 below, we lay out the econometric model. Section 7.3 presents a Bayesian approach for comparing alternative models while section 7.4 presents the empirical results. Section 7.5 concludes the chapter.

7.2 Model Specification

It is presumed that perceived hunger among children in a given state depends on per capita income, unemployment, the enforcement of family law legislation, safety net programs and demographic variables. Per capita income and unemployment may serve as indicators of the economic health of a given state. The level of income support programs and the enforcement of family law legislation in a particular state reflect the preferences of the state's citizens with respect to aversion to hardship towards children. Another words, the extent of these programs in a state may reflect median voter tolerance for such hardship.

Following the tradition of Thurow (1970), Blinder and Esaki (1978) and others, we have specified hunger levels as dependent on broad aggregates. By broadly holding the effects of federal public policy constant we can focus on the role of individual state decision making in analyzing the hunger among children puzzle.

The major finding of this chapter is that educational attainment, as proxied by the high school graduation rate in each state is found to be inversely related to the perceived level of hunger among children across states. The macroeconomic, legislation, policy and demographic variables appear to have negligible effects on the perceived level of hunger across states. In Figure 7.1, contour lines were drawn to specify the magnitude of the percent of children who were considered as hungry. As can be seen, the degree of perceived hunger varied across the states. The state of Mississippi is the "center" of hungry children and the hunger levels spatially correlated with Arkansas, Louisiana, Alabama, Tennessee, Kentucky, and South Carolina. In comparison, most northern states are doing relatively well except for Idaho and Maine. In Figure 7.2, we plotted the contour levels for high school graduation rates in the U.S. The states of Alabama, Tennessee, Kentucky, Mississippi, and Arkansas all have relatively low rates of high school graduation, but most northern states have relatively higher rates except, again, for Idaho and Maine. Comparing figures 7.1 and 7.2, the states with relatively higher (lower) high school graduation rates also are those states with relatively lower (higher) perceived hunger measures.

In the following discussion we present the theoretical model. A standard approach in examining the effect of macroeconomic, political, public policy, and demographic variables on the perceived hunger measures would be to undergo estimation of the form :

$$H_i = \alpha_0 + \alpha_1 Y_i + \alpha_2 U_i + \sum_{j=1}^{n} b_{ij} L_{ij} + \sum_{k=1}^{n} \gamma_{ik} P_{ik} + \sum_{l=1}^{n} \xi_{il} D_{il} + u_i \qquad (7.1)$$

The subscript i denotes variables pertaining to the ith state (i=1, 2, ⋯, 51) and the u_i's are random error terms which are each normally and independently distributed with mean zero and common variance σ^2. On the LHS, the Hunger measure is denoted by H_i. Hunger is defined as the mental and physical conditions of not eating enough food due to insufficient economic resources. Hunger was measured based on the eight questions given in the appendix. If the respondent answered yes to at least five of the questions,

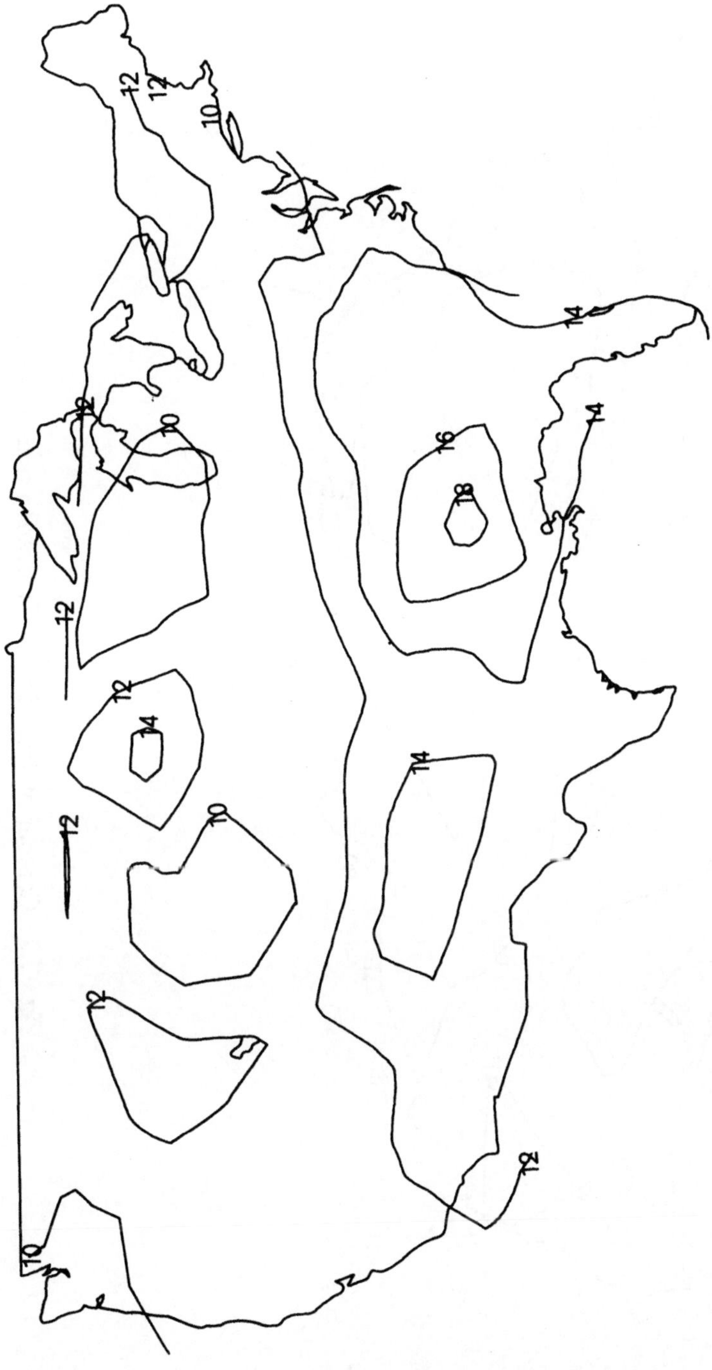

Fig. 7.1. Contour of Hunger rates in the U.S.A.

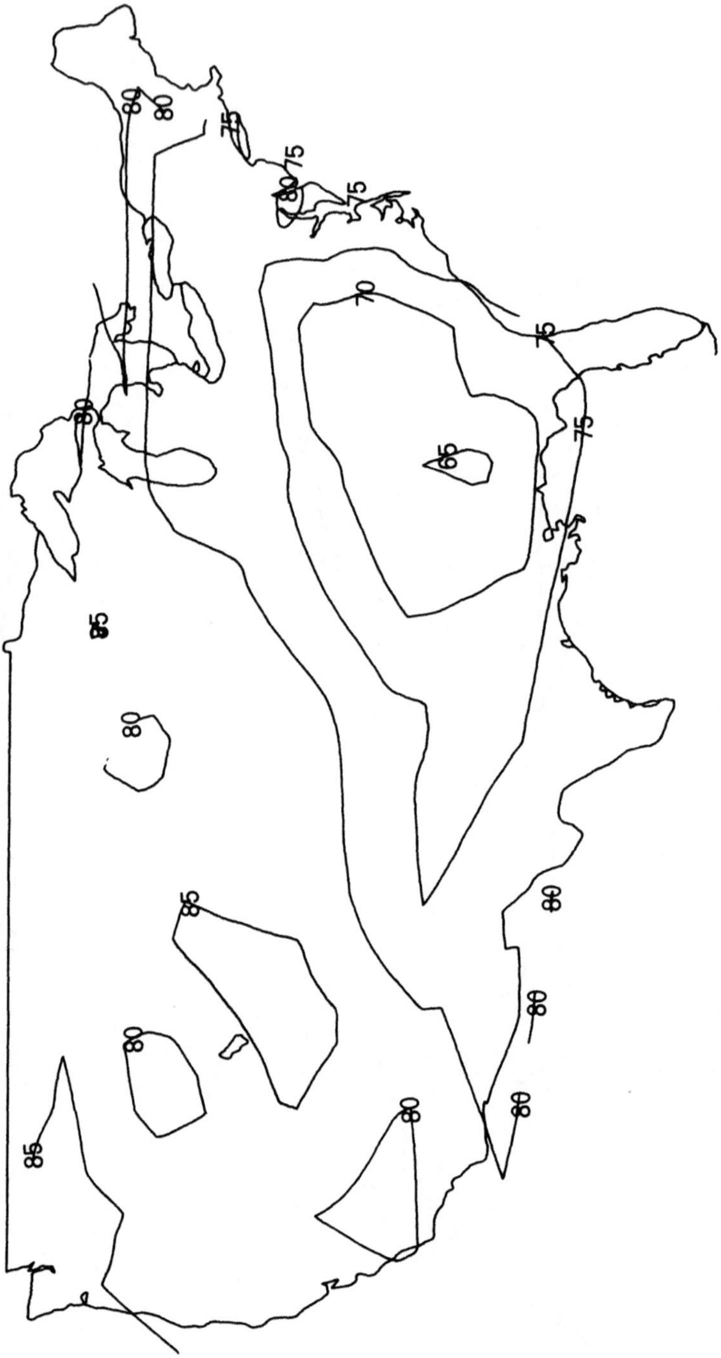

Fig. 7.2. Contour of High School Graduation rates in the U.S.A.

the family was considered to be suffering from hunger. On the RHS, Y_i denotes state per capita disposable personal income, U_i denotes the unemployment rate by state, L_{ij} denotes the legislation variables, P_{ik} denotes policy variables, and D_{il} denotes the demographic variables we consider. The variables definitions employed in the study are listed on the following page. The legislation variables include the proportion of democrats and republicans in each states legislature and the democratic and republican proportion of U.S. representatives in each state. These variables too reflect the preference function for voters and the political structure of a given state. The demographic variables include the proportion of the state population that is black and the percent of the population completing high school or college. The remaining variables listed on the following page are policy variables.[38]

Since all of the Hunger measures are bounded and are difficult to quantify, the assumptions of the General Linear Hypothesis are violated by the truncation of the normal disturbance. To adjust for this we introduce a level of child concern, Q :

$$Q_i = a_0 + a_1 Y_i + a_2 U_i + \sum_{j=1}^{n} b_{ij} L_{ij} + \sum_{k=1}^{n} \gamma_{ik} P_{ik} + \sum_{l=1}^{n} \xi_{il} D_{il} + \varepsilon_i \tag{7.2}$$

where Q is an indicator for the concern citizens in each state hold for their children as reflected in the variable analyzed here. In (7.2), ε_i's are random error terms which are normally and independently distributed each with mean zero and common variance σ^2. The level of child concern Q is a latent variable, and the Hunger measure H is assumed to be a decreasing function of Q with boundary conditions.

---

[38] For the child support stochastic frontier efficiency score, Good and Pirog-Good (1990) did not report the score for Washingtion, D.C., we used the U.S. average for this value for D.C.

Variables Definitions for Variables Analyzed in this Study

UNEMP : Unemployment rate by state.
Source : Bureau of Labor Statistics.

PERDINC : Per capita disposable personal income by state.
Source : Table 711, STAT. ABST., 1991, p.440.

GSPROD : Gross State Product.
Source : Table 710, STAT. ABST., 1991, p.439.

AFDC : Average monthly AFDC payment.
Source : Table 615, STAT. ABST., 1991, p.373.

EDCOL : % completing college by state.
Source : Table 227, STAT. ABST., 1991, p.140.

EDHS : % completing high school by state.
Source : Table 227, STAT. ABST., 1991, p.140.

BLACK : % of state population that is black.

FOODSTP : % of households getting food stamps.
Source : Table 611, STAT. ABST., 1991, p.371.

LEGREP : % of state legislature that is republican.
Source : Table 445, STAT. ABST., 1991, p.265.

LEGDEM : % of state legislature that is democratic.
Source : Table 445, STAT. ABST., 1991, p.265.

REPDEM : Number of U.S. representatives that are democratic.
Source : Table 435, STAT. ABST., 1991, p.260.

REOREP : Number of U.S. representatives that are republican.
Source : Table 435, STAT. ABST., 1991, p.260.

SFSCORE : Stochastic Frontier Efficiency Score.
Source : Good and Pirog-Good (1990), Table 2.

In a world where no children perceive that they are hungry ($H \rightarrow 0$) the level of child concern is very high ($Q \rightarrow \infty$) while when all children perceive that they are hungry ($H \rightarrow 1$) the level of child concern is very low (Q→ −∞). When H(Q) is inverted, we get Q(H), as a monotonic decreasing function of H, in particular we select [39]

$$Q = -a\log H + (\log H)^2 + b\log(1-H) \tag{7.3}$$

If a, b>0, then dQ/dH<0 for 0<H<1 and the required monotonicity condition is satisfied. Equating (7.2) and (7.3), we have

$$-a\log H + (\log H)^2 + b\log(1-H) = \alpha_0 + \alpha_1 Y_i + \alpha_2 U_i + \sum_{j=1}^{n} b_{ij} L_{ij} + \sum_{k=1}^{n} \gamma_{ik} P_{ik} + \sum_{l=1}^{n} \xi_{il} D_{il} + \varepsilon_i \tag{7.4}$$

The parameters of (7.4) can be estimated using maximum likelihood estimation. For example, see Greene (1991). For normally distributed disturbances, the probability density of H_i for given parameters is

$$f(H_i \mid \cdot) = \left|\frac{\partial \varepsilon_i}{\partial H_i}\right| (2\pi\sigma^2)^{-1/2} \exp\Big[-\frac{1}{2\sigma^2}\{-a\log H + (\log H)^2 + b\log(1-H) - (\alpha_0 + \alpha_1 Y_i + \alpha_2 U_i + \sum_{j=1}^{n} b_{ij} L_{ij} + \sum_{k=1}^{n} \gamma_{ik} P_{ik} + \sum_{l=1}^{n} \xi_{il} D_{il})\}^2\Big] \tag{7.5}$$

The Jacobian of the transformation is

$$J(H_i, a, b) = \left|\frac{\partial \varepsilon_i}{\partial H_i}\right| = \left|-\frac{a}{H} + \frac{2(\log H)}{H} - \frac{b}{1-H}\right| \tag{7.6}$$

The log likelihood function is

$$\log L = -\frac{T}{2}\log 2\pi - \frac{T}{2}\log\sigma^2 + \sum_{i=1}^{T}\log J(H_i, a, b) - \frac{1}{2\sigma^2}\sum_{i=1}^{T}[\varepsilon_i^2] \tag{7.7}$$

---

[39] Amemiya (1973) suggested using H=1/(1+exp Q) which can be rewritten as $Q=\log(1-H)-\log H$. To generalize this transformation, we can use $Q = a\log H + c(\log H)^2 + b\log(1-H)$. In particular, we choose c=1 equated with (2.2), the equality still holds even if all the coefficients of the LHS and the RHS were doubled. Therefore, we choose one coefficient, c, to be one.

Introducing the maximum likelihood estimator of σ^2 in (2.7), $\hat{\sigma}^2=(1/T)\sum_{i=1}^{T}\varepsilon_i^2$, we obtain the concentrated log likelihood,

$$\log L_c = \sum_{i=1}^{T} \log J(H_i, a, b) - \frac{T}{2}(1+\log(2\pi)) - \frac{T}{2}\log\left[\frac{1}{T}\sum_{i=1}^{T}\varepsilon_i^2\right] \quad (7.8)$$

In estimating the parameters by maximizing the concentrated likelihood function, conditional maximization and unconditional maximization will produce the same result. Unconditional maximization is well known with no need of explanation, but it takes a considerable computation time, so that we apply a conditional maximization method. See Zellner and Revankar (1969) for more explanation of this technique. We fix the values of a and b, and then estimate the remaining parameters, α_0, α_1, α_2, b_{ij}, y_{ik}, γ_{ik}, ξ_{ij} by maximizing the likelihood function, which is equivalent to the least squares method in (7.4). We repeat this procedure for various values of a and b.

7.3 Posterior Odds Ratios to Compare Alternative Regression Hypotheses

We have presented a regression model (7.4) and a parameter estimation method, but it is not clear why we should include all the variables considered in (7.4) in our regression analysis. The motivation for introducing a posterior odds ratio for our analysis is to provide some justification for excluding certain variables. As an example, in the following section, we find that those states with higher unemployment rates have lower perceived hunger measures. This might seem to be counter intuitive to some. There are studies, however, that have found that states with high wages tend to pay these high wages because workers require them. Since they are subject to longer layoff periods, high unemployment and low poverty might be observed in these states. In the following, we compare two alternative hypotheses, H_A which does not include the unemployment rate and H_B which includes the unemployment rate. We have chosen a posterior odds ratio for our model selection criteria. The posterior probabilities represent the weight of prior belief and sample evidence for the particular hypotheses.

The ratio of the posterior probabilities associated with two hypotheses given by, $f(H_A|D)$ and $f(H_B|D)$ is the posterior odds, denoted by H_{AB} and

$$H_{AB}=\frac{f(H_A|D)}{f(H_B|D)}=\frac{P_r(H_A)}{P_r(H_B)}\cdot\frac{f(D|H_A)}{f(D|H_B)}$$

$$=\frac{P_r(H_A)}{P_r(H_B)}\cdot\frac{\int f(\theta)f(D|\theta)d\theta}{\int f(\phi)f(D|\phi)d\phi} \tag{7.9}$$

where D stands for data. Therefore the posterior odds ratio is the product of the prior odds $Pr(H_A)/Pr(H_B)$ and Bayes factor $f(D \mid H_A)/f(D \mid H_B)$ which is the ratio of averaged likelihood functions with the prior pdf's $f(\theta)$ and $f(\phi)$ serving as the weighting functions. We do not require that $Pr(H_A)+Pr(H_B)=1$. The posterior odds ratio is designed to evaluate the relative merits of two models without assuming that these models are necessarily the only appropriate models.

Zellner and Siow (1980) and Zellner (1984) considered the following regression,

$$Q=\alpha\iota+X_1\beta_1+X_2\beta_2+u \tag{7.10}$$

where Q is a T x 1 vector, ι is an T x 1 vector with all elements equal to one, X_1 and X_2 are T x k_1 and T x k_2 matrices, β_1 and β_2 are k_1 x 1 and k_2 x 1 vectors, and u is a T x 1 vector with mean zero and variance σ^2. For convenience, they reparametrized (3.2) as follows :

$$Q=\alpha\iota+X_1\eta+V\beta_2+u \tag{7.11}$$

where $V=[I-X_1(X_1'X_1)^{-1}X_1']X_2$ and $\eta=\beta_1+(X_1'X_1)^{-1}X_1'X_2\beta_2$. Note that $X_1'V=0$. A posterior odds ratio relating to the following two hypotheses were derived :

$$H_A : \beta_2=0 \qquad \text{and} \qquad H_B : \beta_2\neq 0 \tag{7.12}$$

Under certain assumptions, they derived a simple expression for H_{AB},[40]

[40] Under H_A, we employ the following diffuse prior pdf for the parame-

$$H_{AB} \doteq b(\nu_B|2)^{k_2/2}(\nu_B s_B^2/\nu_A s_A^2)^{(\nu_B-1)/2} \tag{7.13}$$

where $\doteq$ means approximately equal to and $b=\sqrt{\pi}/\Gamma[(k_2+1)/2]$, $\nu_A = T-k_1-1$, $\nu_B = T-k_1-k_2-1$, and

$$\overline{Q}=\sum_{i=1}^{T} Q_i/T, \quad \hat{\eta}=(X_1'X_1)^{-1}X_1'Q, \tag{7.14}$$

$$\nu_A s_A^2=(Q-\overline{Q}\iota-X_1\hat{\eta})'(Q-\overline{Q}\iota-X_1\hat{\eta}),\ \hat{\beta}_2=(V'V)^{-1}V'Q,$$

$$\nu_B s_B^2=(Q-\overline{Q}\iota-X_1\hat{\eta}-V\hat{\beta}_2)'(Q-\overline{Q}\iota-X_1\hat{\eta}-V\hat{\beta}_2)$$

The likelihood functions under the two hypotheses are given by

$$f(Q|\alpha,\sigma,\eta,H_A)\propto\sigma^{-T}\exp\{-[\nu_A s_A^2+T(\alpha-\overline{Q})^2 \\ +(\eta-\hat{\eta})'X_1'X_1(\eta-\hat{\eta})]/2\sigma^2\} \tag{7.15}$$

and

$$f(Q|\alpha,\sigma,\eta,\beta_2,H_B)\propto\sigma^{-T}\exp\{-[\nu_B s_B^2+T(\alpha-\overline{Q})^2 \\ +(\eta-\hat{\eta})'X_1'X_1(\eta-\hat{\eta})+(\beta_2-\hat{\beta}_2)'\nu_1'\nu_1(\beta_2-\hat{\beta}_2)]/2\sigma^2\} \tag{7.16}$$

-ters :

$$f_A(\alpha,\sigma,\eta|H_A)\propto|X_1'X_1|^{1/2}/\sigma$$
$$-\infty<\alpha,\eta_i<\infty \qquad i=1,2,\cdots,k_1$$
$$0<\sigma<\infty$$

While under H_B, the prior pdf is :

$$f_B(\alpha,\sigma,\eta,\beta_2|H_B)\propto|X_1'X_1|^{1/2}h(\beta_2)/\sigma$$
$$-\infty<\alpha,\eta_i<\infty \qquad i=1,2,\cdots,k_1$$
$$0<\sigma<\infty$$

with

$$h(\beta_2|\sigma)=b|V'V/T\sigma^2|^{1/2}(1+\beta_2'V'V\beta_2/T\sigma^2)^{(k_2+1/2)}$$
$$-\infty<\beta_{2i}<\infty \qquad i=1,2,\cdots,k_2$$

The prior pdf for β_2 given σ is the form of a k_2 dimensional multivariate Cauchy pdf with zero location vector and matrix $V'V/T$, a matrix suggested by the form of the information matrix.

Introducing (7.15) and (7.16) into (7.9), the posterior odds ratio is represented as a ratio of averaged likelihoods based on observations of Q, X_1 and X_2 with the prior pdf's serving as the weighting functions. Zellner and Siow (1980) approximated the posterior odds ratio and derived a simple expression given in (7.13). However, since Q is a latent variable, we wish to find a ratio of averaged likelihoods using only observed values of H, X_1 and X_2. We have seen that the likelihood function for H is a product of a Jacobian factor J and a likelihood function of Q, as given in (7.9). The posterior odds ratio based on the posterior pdf of H is

$$K_{AB} = \frac{\prod_{i=1}^{T} J_A(H_i, a, b)}{\prod_{i=1}^{T} J_B(H_i, a, b)} \cdot H_{AB} \tag{7.17}$$

Fortunately, the Jacobian in (7.6) does not include the parameters α, σ, η, and β_2, thus the averaging integration of the likelihood function in (7.9) is not affected by the presence of the Jacobian.

7.4 The Empirical Results

We utilize the data described above to examine how the macroeconomic, legislation, policy, and demographic variables affect the perceived Hunger measure. In Table 7.1, the number and percent of hungry children in each state reported in 1991 are listed. The state of Wyoming reported the lowest rate at 8% and the state of Mississippi reported the highest rate at 19.4%. Those states with smaller populations showed a significant variation in the perceived Hunger measure. Alaska, Connecticut, Minnesota, Wisconsin, and Wyoming are doing relatively well, but Louisiana, New Mexico, and Mississippi are not doing well. In comparison, those states with larger populations showed a smaller variance in the perceived hunger measure as can be seen in the states of California, Florida, Illinois, Michigan, New York, Ohio, Pennsylvania, and Texas. As the size of the state becomes larger, many state specific factors appear to be averaged out and the large states tend to converge to the U.S. average rate.

One main objective in this chapter is to explore possible reasons for the difference in the perceived hunger rate. As a first step, we included all of the variables listed above and estimated the parameters by the conditional maximization method previously described. Rewriting (7.4), the level of child concern is

$$\begin{aligned} Q &= -a \log H + (\log H)2 + b \log (1-H) \\ &= \beta_0 + \beta_1 \text{ UNEMP} + \beta_2 \text{PERSINC} + \beta_3 \text{GSPROD} + \beta_4 \text{AFDC} \\ &+ \beta_5 \text{EDCOL} + \beta_6 \text{EDHS} + \alpha_7 \text{BLACK} + \beta_8 \text{FOODSTP} + \beta_9 \text{LEGREP} \\ &+ \beta_{10} \text{LEGDEM} + \beta_{11} \text{REPREP} + \beta_{12} \text{REPDEM} + \beta_{13} \text{SFSCORE} + \varepsilon \end{aligned} \tag{7.18}$$

To apply a grid search method, we have taken the ranges of $0 \leqq a \leqq 0$ and $0 \leqq b \leqq 40$. For each point of a and b, the concentrated likelihood function is computed by (7.8). At $\hat{a}=0.002$ and $\hat{b}=6.8$, the computed likelihood function marked the global peak. In Table 7.3, we listed these parameter estimates under the Full Model. Since the unit of measurement of the RHS variables is arbitrary, a variable with a larger coefficient does not necessarily mean that it is an important variable in our analysis. Among the macroeconomic variables, the coefficients on the unemployment rate and the goods produced within the states have opposite signs. When the unemployment rate increases, the level of child concern is shown to be associated with a positive coefficient while that on the hunger rate decreases. A similar effect can be observed for the gross state production variable.

In the following, we consider model selection problems where we compare various regression functions made of various RHS variables. To compare nested regression functions, we can apply cross validation, Mallow's Cp, posterior odds ratio, etc. In particular, we apply R^2 and posterior odds ratio. We note R^2 criterion is easy to compute but its value becomes larger as we increase the number of parameters so that there should be some penalty for adding extra parameters inside the regression. For this purpose we have chosen posterior odds ratio to compare relative merits of two regression functions made of different RHS variables.

For the 13 RHS variables listed above, many of those variables will have a negligible effect in our regression analysis. To evaluate the importance of each variable, we exclude one variable at a time and see how the estimated parameters and R^2 are affected by exclusion of this variable. If UNEMP is excluded, we have the regression model

Table 7.3 Model Selection by Comparing Parameter Estimates, R^2, and Posterior Odds Ratio

Variables	Full Model (Parameter Estimates)	Omit One Variable (R^2)	With One Variable (R^2)	EDHS Only (Parameter Estimates)	EDHS and Black Only (Par. Est.)	Posterior Odds $H_{AB}(K_{AB})$
	$\hat{a}=0.02$ $\hat{b}=6.8$			$\hat{a}=0.02$ $\hat{b}=6.0$	$\hat{a}=0.02$ $\hat{b}=14.4$	
UNEMP	0.129	0.6739	0.0074	—	—	8.521(169.220)
PERSINC	0.0000236	0.6844	0.0014	—	—	7.254(2,782)
GSPROD	−0.00000697	0.6777	0.0002	—	—	8.635(22.935)
AFDC	0.000888	0.6807	0.0056	—	—	8,598(22.837)
EDCOL	−0.00382	0.6856	0.0746	—	—	8.710(0.518)
EDHS	0.134	0.5114	0.6099	0.132	0.1450	1.0
BLACK	−0.00968	0.6800	0.2953	—	−0.0178	$1.983(2.09\times10^{-13})$
FOODSTP	0.00865	0.6855	0.0070	—	—	8.104(0.0797)
LEGREP	0.000216	0.6857	0.0500	—	—	8.271(0.0339)
LEGDEM	0.00349	0.6791	0.0333	—	—	7.794(0.463)
REPREP	0.106	0.6702	0.0001	—	—	8.666(0.515)
REPDEM	0.0420	0.6841	0.0001	—	—	8.659(8.659)
SFSCORE	1.485	0.6786	0.0006	—	—	6.788(95387)
CONST	−9.566	—	—	−6.514	−8.446	—
R^2	0.6858	—	—	0.0699	0.6332	—

$$\begin{aligned} Q &= -a\log H + (\log H)^2 + b\log(1-H) \\ &= \beta_0 + \beta_2\text{PERSINC} + \beta_3\text{GSPROD} + \beta_4\text{AFDC} + \beta_5\text{EDCOL} \\ &+ \beta_6\text{EDHS} + \beta_7\text{BLACK} + \beta_8\text{FOODSTP} + \beta_9\text{LEGREP} \\ &+ \beta_{10}\text{LEGDEM} + \beta_{11}\text{REPREP} + \beta_{12}\text{REPDEM} + \beta_{13}\text{SFSCORE} + \varepsilon \quad (7.19) \end{aligned}$$

For simplicity of estimation, we introduced those values of a and b estimated in (7.18). The least squares method obviously will result in different parameter estimates and R^2 values. We do not report the parameter estimates but R^2 values are listed in the third column of Table 7.3. When UNEMP is excluded we have $R^2=0.6739$ and when PERSINC is excluded we have $R^2=0.6844$. If EDHS is excluded a low value of $R^2=0.5114$ is produced. Though not listed in Table 7.3, if EDHS and BLACK are excluded, we have a very low value of $R^2=0.3327$, and thus variation in the perceived hunger measure can not be explained well using other exogenous variables if both EDHS and BLACK were excluded in the regression.

In approaching the model selection problem, we may begin from the largest model and move toward a smaller model, or alternatively, we may begin from the smallest model and move to a larger model. Consider the following simple model,

$$Q = -a\log H + (\log H)^2 + b\log(1-H) = \beta_0 + \beta X + \varepsilon \qquad (7.20)$$

When X=UNEMP estimated R^2 is 0.0074 and when X=PERSINC estimated R^2 is 0.0014. These values are listed in the fourth column, and X =EDHS produced the highest R^2 value and its estimated parameter values are listed in the fifth column. To consider influence of BLACK in explaining the perceived hunger measure, we may include both EDHS and BLACK in X. The estimated parameter values and R^2 value are affected not much as can be seen in the sixth column of Table 7.3.

We have seen that differences in the EDHS variable is the most important in explaining variation in the perceived hunger measure based on R^2 criteria. To emphasize the role of EDHS, we consider the following model which we refer to as [41]

---

[41] For simplicity of exposition, we begin from Hypothesis A and will

Hypothesis A :

$$Q = -a \log H + (\log H)^2 + b \log(1-H) = \beta_0 + \beta_6 \text{EDHS} + \varepsilon \tag{7.21}$$

From the estimated parameter values ($\hat{a}=0.02$, $\hat{b}=6.0$, and $\hat{\beta}_6=0.132$), the high school graduation rate (EDHS) is inversely related with the perceived hunger measure. In Figure 7.3, we plotted the relationship proposed by Hypothesis A. The slope becomes flatter as we increase the high school graduation rate. To decrease the perceived hunger rate by one percent in the states with higher perceived hunger rate, the high school graduation rate needs to be increased by two percent. However, to get a similar effect in the states with lower perceived hunger measure, we would require a five percent increase in the high school graduation rate.

To extend the above simple model, we may add the unemployment rate in the RHS of (7.21) which we refer to as

Hypothesis B :

$$\begin{aligned} Q &= -a \log H + (\log H)^2 + b \log(1-H) \\ &= \beta_0 + \beta_1 \text{UNEMP} + \beta_6 \text{EDHS} + \varepsilon \end{aligned} \tag{7.22}$$

To compare two alternative hypotheses H_A and H_B, we computed the posterior odds ratio using (7.21) and (7.22). In the last column of Table 2, H_{AB} is 8.521 while $K_{AB}=169.220$. This means that the relatively simple Model A is supported by the data more than the extended model B. We repeat the above procedure using various RHS variables. We may introduce PERSINC, or GSPROD, or any other variable in place of UNEMP in

---

consider relative merits of adding extra variables. However, if we want to be very general, we can begin from the following assumptions and move toward the larger models. Consider the following two hypotheses.

$$H_A^0 : Q = \beta_0 + \varepsilon \qquad \text{and} \qquad H_B^0 : Q = \beta_0 + \beta X + \varepsilon$$

By introducing UNEMP, or PERSINC, or other variables for X, and by computing $H_{A^0 B^0}$, we can choose the most important variable to explain the difference in Q. Using this variable in place of EDHS in Hypothesis A, we can continue to increase the regression span

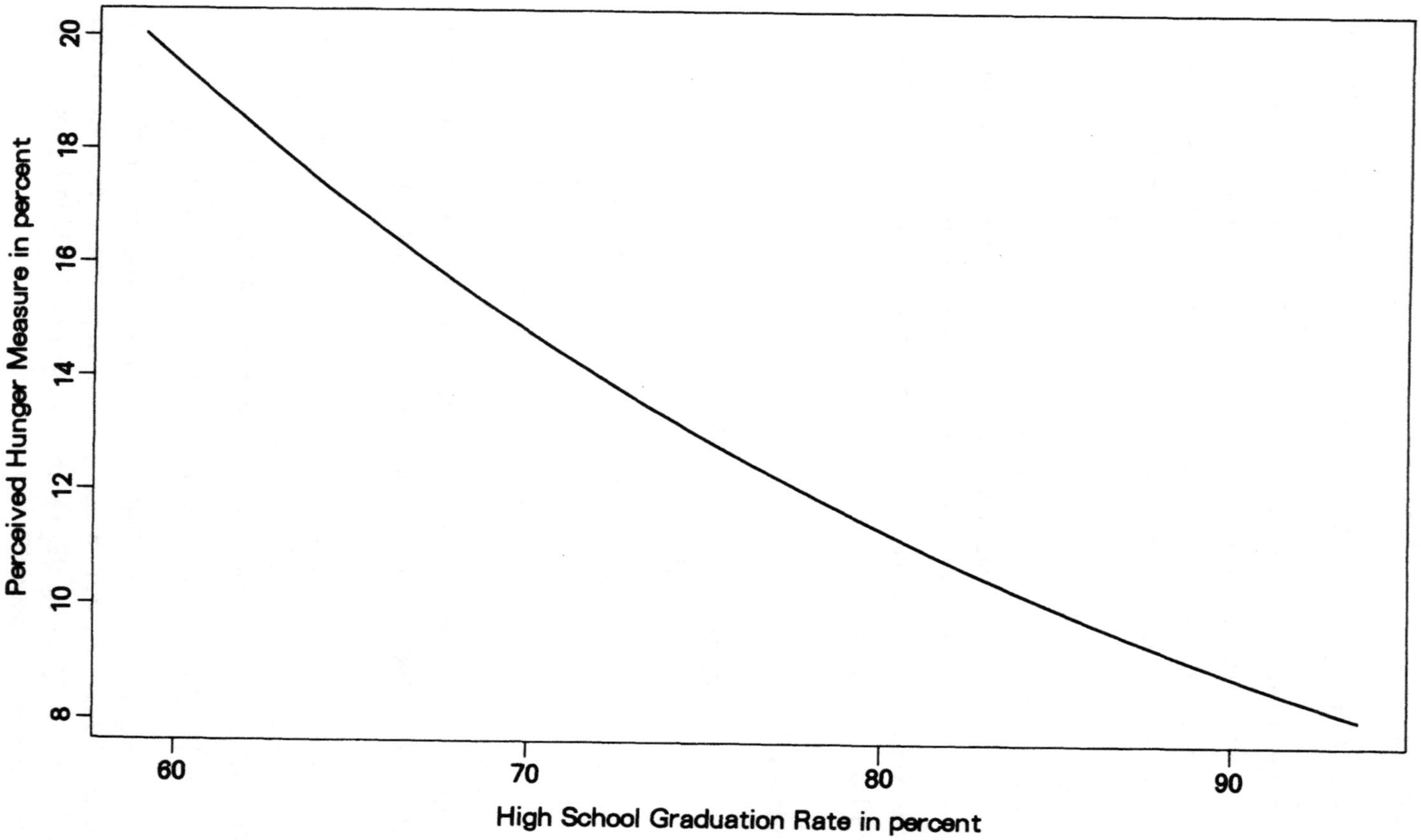

Fig. 7.3. Relationship of High School Graduation Rate and Perceived Hunger Measure.

Hypothesis B. From the posterior odds ratios listed in the last column of Table 7.3, when we use H_{AB} as a model selection criteria, differences in all the other variables except the high school graduation rate are not important to explain the variations in the perceived hunger measure. If K_{AB} is used as a model selection criteria, EDCOL, BLACK, FOODSTP, LEGREP, LEGDEM, and REPREP can be used as explanatory variables to analyze the differences of the perceived hunger measure, but UNEMP, PERSINC, GSPROD, REPDEM, and AFDC need not be included in the regression. This suggests that the political structure is important as are educational impacts, but that macroactivity appears to "wash out" across the states.

7.5 Summary and Concluding Remarks

There are several conclusions which can be drawn from this chapter. To explain the causes of perceived hunger among children under 12, we introduced a regression model where macroeconomic, legislation, and demographic variables are included as explanatory variables. Under the particularly chosen model selection criteria, the posterior odds ratio, the high school graduation rate appears to be the most important variable in explaining the causes of variation in the perceived hunger measure. Once the high school graduation rate is included, the perceived hunger rate is not affected much by the presence of the other macroeconomic, legislation, and demographic variables. To justify inclusion or exclusion of other variables as explanatory variables, we applied the posterior odds ratio, but any other model selection criterion can be used such as cross validation, Mallow C_p, and the Schwarz method to compare the two nested models.

We found the slope of the relationship between perceived hunger and the high school graduation rate becomes flatter as the high school graduation rate increases. In Mississippi and the District of Columbia, the perceived hunger measure can be lowered by one percent when we increase the high school graduation rate by two percent, but in Wyoming and Minnesota, the high school graduation rate would have to increase by five percent to get the same effect. However, it is important to note that our suggested model is in no way complete. There may be other variables which are crucial in explaining the perceived hunger measure particularly at low levels of the perceived hunger measure. In Wyoming, the perceived hunger measure is eight percent, and here we can not decrease the hunger measure simply by increasing the high school graduation rate because the rate is already a robust 86 percent.

The full model in Table 7.3 means $-a \log H+(\log H)^2+b \log(1-H)=\beta_0+X\beta$ where the RHS variable X includes UNEMP, PERSINC, ⋯, SFSCORE. The parameters were estimated by maximum likelihood estimation method and are listed in the second column. To consider the influence of each variable, we may omit one variable in the RHS at a time and check how R^2 values are affected by omission of this variable. When UNEMP is omitted estimated R^2 is 0.6739 and reported in the third column. Alternatively, we may include only one variable inside the regression to compare the influence of each variable. When X=UNEMP estimated R^2 is 0.0074 and listed in the fourth column. From R^2 values of the third and fourth columns, we found EDHS affect the perceived hunger measure most significantly. For the model with x=EDHS, parameters are estimated and listed in the fifth column. If X includes both EDHS and BLACK, then the estimated parameters are listed in the sixth column. To compare the relative merits of using two alternative models, we calculated the posterior odds ratio. The model A is the most parsimonious model with X=EDHS, but the model B is an extended model. If UNEMP is added in X, the posterior odds is $H_{AB}=8.521$ ($K_{AB}=169.220$) so that model A is supported by the data.

Bibliography

Arnold, B., 1983, *Pareto Distributions, International*, Cooperative Publishing House, Fairfield, Maryland.

___________, 1986, A Class of Hyperbolic Lorenz Curves, *Sankhya* 48B, 427–436.

___________, 1987, Majorization and the Lorenz Curve: A Brief Introduction, *Lecture Notes in Statistics* 143, Berlin: Springer–Verlag.

Arnold, B., P. Brockett, C. Robertson and B. Shu, 1987, Generating Ordered Families of Lorenz Curves by Strongly Unimodal Distributions, *Journal of Business and Economic Statistics* 5, 305–308.

Atkinson, A. B. 1970, On the measurement of Inequality *Journal of Economic Theory* 2, 244–263.

Amemiya, To, 1973, Regression Analysis When the Dependent Variable is Truncated Normal, *Econometrica* 41, 997–1016.

Balke, N. and D. Slottje, 1993, A Macroeconometric Model of Income Inequality in the U.S., in *The Changing Distribution of Income in an Open U.S. Economy,* J. Bergstrand, T. Cosimano and R. Sheehan (eds.), Amsterdam, Holland: North Holland publishing company.

Basmann, R., K. Hayes, J. Johnson, and D. Slottje, 1990, A General Functional Form for Approximating the Lorenz Curve, *Journal of Econometrics*, 43, 77–90.

Beach, C., 1976, Cyclical Impacts on the Personal Distribution of Income, *Annals of Economic and Social Measurement*, 5, 29–52.

Beach, C., 1977, Cyclical Sensitivity of Aggregate Income, *Review of Economics and Statistics* 58, 56–66.

Beach, C. and R. Davidson, 1983, Distribution–Free Statistical Inference with Lorenz Curves and Income Shares, *Review of Economic Studies*, 723–535.

Beach, C. and J. Richmond, 1985, Joint Confidence Intervals for Income Shares and Lorenz Curves, *International Economic Review* 26, No. 2, 439–450.

Bera, A. and C. Jarque, 1981, An Efficient Large–Sample Test for Normality of observations and Regression Residuals. Working Papers in

Econometrics No.40. Canberra: Australian National University.

Becker, G., 1975, *Human Capital*, Second Edition, Chicago: The University of Chicago Press.

Bishop, J., A. Chakraborti, and P. Thistle, 1989, Asymptotically Distribution—Free Statistical Inference for Generalized Lorenz Curves, *Review of Economics and Statistics* 71, 725—727.

Bishop, J., J. Formby, and J. Smith, 1991, Lorenz Dominance and Welfare: Changes in the U.S. Distribution of Income, 1967—1986, *Review of Economics and Statistics* 73, 134—139.

Blackburn, M. and D. Bloom, 1987, Earnings and Income Inequality in the United States, *Population and Development Review* 13, 569—575.

Blank, R., 1989, Disaggregating the Effect of the Business Cycle on the Distribution of Income, *Economica* 56, 14—63.

Blank, R. and A. Blinder, 1986, Macroeconomics, Income Distribution and Poverty, S. Danzinger and D. Weinberg (eds.), *Fighting Poverty*, Cambridge, MA: Harvard University Press.

Blank, R. and D. Card, 1993, Poverty, Income Distribution, and Growth: Are They Still Connected? *Brookings papers on Economic Activity* 2, 285—339.

Blinder, A. and H. Esaki, 1978, Macroeconomic Activity and Income Distribution in the Postwar United States, *The Review of Economics and Statistics*, 59, 04—609.

Boos, D. and J. Monahan, 1986, Bootstrap Methods Using Prior Information, *Biometrika* 73, 77—83.

Bound, J. and R. Freeman, 1992, What Went Wrong? The Erosion of Relative Earnings and Employment Among Young Black Men in the 1980s, *Quarterly Journal of Economics* 107, 201—232.

Cancian, M., S. Danziger and P. Gottschalk, 1993a, The Changing Contributions of Men and Women to the Level and Distribution of Family Income, 1968—1988, in D. B. Papdimitriou and E. Wolff (eds.), *Poverty and Prosperity at the Close of the Twentieth Century*, New York: St. Martins Press.

__________ 1993b, Working Wives and the Distribution of Family Income, 1968—1988 in S. Danziger and P. Gottschalk (eds), *Rising Tides*:

Rising Inequality in America, New York, Russell Sage Foundation.

Card, D. and A. Krueger, 1992a, School Quality and Black—White Relative Earnings: A Direct Assessment, *Quarterly Journal of Economics* 107, 151—200.

__________, 1992b, Does School quality Matter? Returns to Education and the Characteristics of Public Schools in the United States, *Journal of Political Economy* 100, 1—40.

Chakravarty, S., 1990, *Ethical Social Index Numbers*, Berlin: Springer—Verlag.

Chamberlain, G., 1987, Asymptotic Efficiency in Estimation with Conditional Moment Restrictions, *Journal of Econometrics* 34, 305—334.

Chambers, J. W. Cleveland, B. Kleiner, and P. Tukey, 1983, *Graphical Methods for Data Analysis* Wadsworth and Brooks/Cole, Pacific Grove, California.

Champernowne, D., 1953, A Model of Income Distribution, *Economic Journal* 63, 318—351.

Chiang, C., 1952, On Regular Best Asymptotically Normal Estimates with an Application to a Stochastic Process, *Doctoral Dissertation*, University of California.

Cowell, F., 1977, *Measuring Inequality*, London: Phillip Allan.

Creedy, J., 1985, *Dynamics of Income Distribution*, Oxford: Basil Blackwell.

__________, 1992, Rising Inequality? Changes in the Distribution of Income and Consumption in the 1980s, *American Economic Review* 82, 546—551.

__________, 1994, *Taxation, Poverty and Income Distribution*, Edward Elgar Publishing Company, Vermont.

Dagum, C. 1980, The Generation and Distribution of Income, the Lorenz Curve and the Gini Ratio, *Economie Appliquee* 33, 327—367.

Department of Health and Human Services, 1991, Child Support Enforcement: A Framework for Evaluating Cost, Benefits, and Effects, United States General Accounting Office, Washington, D.C.

Eichhorn, W., 1994, *Models and Measures of Welfare and Inequality*, Berlin: Springer—Verlag.

Esteban, J., 1986, Income Share Elasticity and the Size Distribution of Income, *International Economic Review* 27, 439—444.

Ferguson, T., 1958, A Method of Generating Best Asymptotically Normal Estimates with an Application to the Estimation of Bacterial Densities, *Annals of Mathematical Statistics* 29, 1046—1062.

Gale, D. and H. Nikaido, 1965, The Jacobian Matrix and Global Univalence of Mappings, *Mathematische Annalen* 159, 8593.

Gallant, A., 1981, On the Bias in Flexible functional Forms and an Essentially Unbiased Form: the Fourier Flexible Form, *Journal of Econometrics* 15,211—246.

Gastwirth, J., 1971, A General Definition of the Lorenz Curve, *Econometrica* 39, 1037—1039.

Gastwirth, J. and M. Gail, 1985, Simple Asymptotically Distribution—Free Methods for Comparing Lorenz Curves and Gini Indices Obtained from Complete Data, in R.L. Basmann, and G.F. Rhodes, Jr. (eds.), *Advances in Econometrics*, Vol. 4, JAI Press, Greenwich, CT.

Georgescu-Doegen, N., 1971, The Entropy Law and Economic Process, Cambridge: Harvard University Press.

Geweke, J., 1986, Exact Inference in the Inequality Constrained Normal Linear Model, *Journal of Applied Econometrics* 1, 127—142.

Gibrat, R., 1931, *Les Inegalites Economiques*, Paris: Sirey.

Gini, C., 1912, Variablilita e Mutabilita, Bologna.

Good, D. and M. Pirog—Good, 1990, The Efficiency of State Child Support Enforcement Programs, *Public Budgeting and Finance Fall*, 24—37.

Greene, W., 1991, *Econometric Analysis*, MacMillan Publishing Company, New York, NY.

Hansen, L., 1982, Large Sample Properties of Generalized Method of Moments Estimators, *Econometrica* 50, 1029—1054.

Haslag, J. W. Russell, and D. Slottje, 1989, *Macroeconomic Activity and Income Inequality in the United States*, Greenwich, Connecticut: JAI Press Inc.

Haslag, J. and D. Slottje, 1994, Cyclical Fluctuations, Macroeconomic Policy and the Size Distribution of Income: Some Preliminary Evidence, *Journal of Income Distribution*, 4, 3—23

Jaynes, E., 1979, Concentration of Distributions, R. Rosenkrantz (ed.) E. *Jaynes: Papers on Probability, Statistics and Statistical Physics*, Dordrecht, Reidel, Holland.

Jeffreys. H., 1967, *Theory of Probability*, Oxford: Oxford University Press.

Johnson, D. and S. Shipp, 1995, Changing Inequality in the U.S. from 1980 – 1994: A Consumption Viewpoint, *unpublished mimeo*, Washington, D. C.: Bureau of Labor Statistics.

Jorgenson, D., 1990, Aggregate Consumer Behavior and the Measurement of Social Welfare, *Econometrica* 58, 1007 – 1040.

Jorgenson, D. and D. Slesnick, 1984, Inequality in the Distribution on Individual Welfare, *Advances in Econometrics* 3, 67 – 130.

__________, 1990, Inequality and the Standard of Living, *Journal of Econometrics* 43, 103 – 120.

Judge, G., W. Griffiths, R. Hill, H. Lütkepohl, and T. Lee, *The Theory and Practice of Econometrics*, Wiley, New York, N.Y.

Judge, G., R. Hill, W. Griffiths, H. Lütkepohl, and T. Lee, 1988, *Introduction to the Theory and Practice of Econometrics*, second edition, New York: Wiley.

Juhn, C., K. Murphy and B. Pierce, 1993, Wage Inequality and the Rise in the Return to Skill, *Journal of Political Economy* 101, 410 – 442.

Kakwani, N., 1980, *Income Inequality and Proverty: Methods of Estimation and Policy Application*, New York: Oxford University Press.

Kakwani, N. and N. Podder, 1973, On the Estimation of Lorenz Curve from Grouped Observation, *International Economic Review* 14, 278 – 292.

__________, 1976, Efficient Estimation of the Lorenz Curve and Associated Inequality Measures from Grouped Observations, *Econometrica* 44, 137 – 148.

Karoly, L., 1994, Trend in Income Inequality: The Impact of, and Implications for, Tax Policy, in J. Slemrod (ed.), *Tax Progressivity and Income Inequality*, Cambridge: Cambridge University Press, 95 – 129.

__________, 1995, Anatomy of the U.S. Income Distribution: Two Decades of Change, unpublished mimeo, RAND Corporation.

Katz, L. and M. Murphy, 1992, Changes in Relative Wages, 1963 – 1987: Supply and Demand Factors, *Quarterly Journal of Economics* 107, 35 – 78.

Kolmogorov, A., 1933, Sulla determinazione empririca di una legge di distribuzione, G. Ist. Ital. Attuari 4, 83.

Kuznet, S., 1976, Demographic Aspects of the Size Distribution of Income: An Exploratory Essay, *Economic Development and Cultural Change* 25, 1—94.

Lambert, P., 1993, *The Distribution and Redistribution of Income*, Manchester: University Press.

Levy, F., 1987, *Dollars and Dreams: The Changing American Income Distribution*, New York: Russell sage.

Levy, F., and R. Murnane, 1992, Earnings Levels and Earnings Inequality: A Review of Recent Trends and Proposed Explanations, *Journal of Economic Literature* 30, 1331—1368.

Lorenz, G., 1986, *Bernstein Polynomials*, second edition, Chelsea Publishing Company, New York, N.Y.

Luenberger, D., 1969, *Optimization by Vector Space Methods*, New York: Wiley.

Mandelbrot, V., 1960, The Pareto—Levy Law and the Distribution of Income, *Review* 1, 79—106.

McDonald, D., 1984, Some Generalized Functions for the Size Distribution of Income, *Econometrica* 52, 647—665.

Mead, L. and N. Papanicolaou, 1984, Maximum Entropy in the Problem of Moments, *Journal of Math. Phys.* 25(8), August 1984.

Milne, W., 1973, *Numerical Calculus*, Princeton University Press, Princeton, N.J.

Mood, A., F. Graybill, and D. Boes, 1974, *Introduction to the Theory of Statistics*. N.Y, McGraw-Hill.

Murphy, K. and F. Welch, 1992, The Structure of Wages, *Quarterly Journal of Economics* 107, 285—326.

Nolan, B., 1987, *Income Distribution and the Macroeconomy*, Cambridge, U.K.: Cambridge University Press.

Pareto, V., 1896, La Courbe de la Repartition de la Richesse, Universite Lausanne.

Rao, C. 1973, *Linear Statistical Inference and Its Applications*, Second Edition, New York: Wiley.

Raj, B. and D. Slottje, 1994, The Trend Behavior of Alternative Inequality Measures, *Journal of Business and Economic Statistics* 12, 479—488.

Robins, P., 1992, Why Did Child Support Awards Levels Decline for 1978 to 1985?, *Journal of Human Resources* 27, 366 — 379.

Rossi, P., 1984, Comparison of Alternative Functional Forms in Production, *Journal of Econometrics* 30, 345 — 361.

Roy, A., 1950, The Distribution of Earnings and of Individual Output, *Economic Journal*, vol.60, 489 — 505.

Ruggles, P. and C. Stone, 1992, Income Distribution Over the Business Cycle : The 1980s were Different, *Journal of Policy Analysis and Management* 11, 709 — 715.

Ryscavage, P., 1993, Has Growing Inequality Come to an End?, presented at the 68th Annual Conference of the Western in Econometrics, New York : Wiley.

Ryscavage, P., G. Green and E. Welniak, 1992, The Impact of Demographic, Social, an Economic Change on the Distribution of Income, *Studies in the Distribution of Income*, 60 — 183, U.S. Department of Commerce, Bureau of the Census, October.

Ryu, H., 1990, Orthonormal Basis and Maximum Entropy Estimation of Probability Density and Regression Functions, unpublished Ph.D. dissertation, University of Chicago, Chicago, Illinois.

__________, 1993, Maximum Entropy Estimation of Density and Regression Functions, *Journal of Econometrics* 56, 397 — 440.

Ryu, H. and D. Slottje, 1994a, Coordinate Space vs. Index Space Representations as Estimation Methods : An Application to How Macro Activity Affects the U.S. Income Distribution, *Journal of Business and Economic Statistics* 12, 243 — 251.

__________, 1994b, Estimating the Impact of Capabilities on the Distribution of Earnings, in *Taxation, Poverty and Income Distribution*, J. Creedy (ed.), Edward Elgar Publishing Company, Vermont.

__________, 1996a, Two Flexible Functional Form Approaches for Approximating the Lorenz Curve, *Journal of Econometrics* 72, 251 — 274.

__________, 1996b, Parametric Approximation to the Lorenz Curve, in *Inequality Measurement : From Theory to Practice*, J.Silber(ed.), Amsterdam : Kluwer(forthcoming).

__________, 1997, Another Perspective on Recent Changes in the U.S. Income Distribution : An Index Space Representation, *Advances in Econo-*

metrics, vol. 12. 319—340.

Sahota, G., 1978, Theories of Personal Income Distribution: A Survey, *Journal of Economic Literature 16(1)*, 1—55.

Sargan, J., 1958, The Estimation of Economic Relationships using Instrumental Variables, *Econometrica* 26, 393—415.

Sen, A., 1985, *Commodities and Capabilities*, Amsterdam: North-Holland.

Shannon, C., 1948, The Mathematical Theory of Communication, *Bell System Technical Journal* July-Oct. reprinted in C. Shannon and W. Weaver, *The Mathematical Theory of Communication*, 3—91, Urbana, IL: University of Illinois Press.

Shorrocks, A., 1980, The Class of Additively Decomposable Inequality Measures, *Econometrica*, 48, 613—625.

Silber, J., 1997, *Income Inequality Measurement: From Theory to Practice*, Amsterdam: Kluwer.

Slottje, D., 1987, Relative Price Changes and Inequality in the Size Distribution of Various Components of Income: A Multidimensional Approach, *Journal of Business and Economic Statistics*, 5, 19—26.

Slottje, D. 1989, *The Structure of Earnings and the Measurement of Income Inequality in the U.S.* Amsterdam: North—Holland.

Slottje, D., K. Hayes and J. Shackett, 1992, Labor Force Participation and Human Capital: Influence on Earnings Distributions Across States, *Review of Income and Wealth* 38, 27—37.

Slottje, D., S. Yitzhaki and S. Zandvakili, 1995, Educational Impacts and Rising Inequality in the U.S. unpublished mimeo, Southern Methodist University, Dallas, TX.

Theil, H., 1967, *Economics and Information Theory*, Amsterdam, Holland: North-Holland.

Thurow, L., 1970, Analyzing the American Income Distribution, *American Economic Review* 60, 261—269.

Villasenor, J. and B. Arnold, 1989, Elliptical Lorenz Curves, *Journal of Econometrics* 40, 327—338.

White, H., 1984, *Asymptotic Theory for Econometricians*, Orlando: Academic Press.

World Development Report, 1990, Oxford University Press, New York, N.Y.

Zellner, A., 1962, An Efficient Method of Estimating Seemingly Unrelated Regressions and Tests for Aggregation Bias, *Journal of the American Statistical Association*, 57, 348−368.

__________, 1971, *An Introduction to Bayesian Inference in Econometrics*, New York : Wiley.

__________, 1984, Posterior Odds Ratios for Regression Hypotheses : General Considerations and Some Specific Results, reprinted in Arnold Zellner, *Basic Issue in Econometrics*, (the University of Chicago Press, Chicago, IL).

Zellner, A. and N. Revankar, 1969, Generalized Production Functions, *Review of Economic Studies* 36, 241−250.

Zellner, Arnold and A. Siow, 1980, Posterior Odds Ratios for Selected Regression Hypotheses, Paper presented at the International Meeting on Bayesian Statistics, Valencia, Spain, May 28−June 2, 1979. In J. M. Bernardo, M. H. DeGroot, D. V. Lindley, and A.F.M. Smith, eds. *Bayesian Statistics : Proceedings of the First International Meeting Held in Valencia* (Spain), May 28 to June 2, 1979, 585−603, University Press, Valencia, Spain.

Zellner, A. and R. Highfield, 1988, Calculation of Maximum Entropy Distributions and Approximation of Marginal Posterior Distributions, *Journal of Econometrics* 37, 195−209.

Author Index

Printing: Weihert-Druck GmbH, Darmstadt
Binding: Buchbinderei Schäffer, Grünstadt

GPSR Compliance

The European Union's (EU) General Product Safety Regulation (GPSR) is a set of rules that requires consumer products to be safe and our obligations to ensure this.

If you have any concerns about our products, you can contact us on ProductSafety@springernature.com

In case Publisher is established outside the EU, the EU authorized representative is:

Springer Nature Customer Service Center GmbH
Europaplatz 3
69115 Heidelberg, Germany

Batch number: 10844675

Printed by Printforce, the Netherlands